"Pam Douglas takes on the complicated business of episodic television and makes great, grand sense of it. For years she's been a star of USC's School of Cinematic Arts, imparting these secrets to her students. Now these secrets have been written down. A textbook, a how-to, a resource, an inspiration, this book has knowledge, has wisdom, is a joy to read."

Howard A. Rodman, Artistic Director, Sundance Screenwriting Labs

"Solid career advice and industry insights. Provides crucial foundational guidance for the aspiring television drama writer."

David Trueman, reviewer, *Script Magazine*

"*Writing the TV Drama Series* sheds much-needed light onto the befuddled, and oft overlooked subject of television programming development—invaluable to teachers, students, or anyone else interested in the world of television."

Brian Johns, Eastman Kodak Scholarship Program Director

"Written by a television insider, this well-written text takes one, step by step, through the maze on why and how television programs make it from pitch to script to pilot to series. Pam Douglas' style is fun to read; she packs in information and the definite how-to's of making it as a series television writer."

Jule Selbo has been a series writer/producer on *Life Goes On, Young Indiana Jones Chronicles, Melrose Place, Undressed, Maya and Miguel* and many others

"Remarkably comprehensive and up-to-date, *Writing the TV Drama Series* is a candid, enthusiastic introduction to the craft and culture of dramatic television."

Jeff Melvoin, Executive Producer, *Alias, Northern Exposure*

"Pamela Douglas provides valuable insights and insider tips in this essential guide to writing the television drama. Her step-by-step instruction to jumpstarting and surviving a career in the television business is packed with current industry information and practical advice from renowned industry pros. Chapter Five, which highlights working on staff, is dead-on. It took me years to learn what Pam has so artfully and honestly laid out. A must-read for any aspiring television writer."

Toni Graphia, Writer-Producer, *Roswell, Carnivale, Battlestar Galactica*

"This book covers the waterfront in writing for dramatic television."

Peter Lefcourt, Writer-Producer, *Beggars & Choosers, Karen Sisco, Cagney & Lacey*

"A knowledgeable insight to writing TV drama. A book that is a delight to read."

Amy Taylor, Cedar Grove Entertainment

"Right now is the golden age of TV drama, and this book is far and away the best resource I know of for any writer wishing to work in this tremendously challenging and rewarding field."

Daniel Petrie, Jr., President, Writers Guild of America, West; *The Big Easy, Beverly Hills Cop*

"Pamela Douglas demystifies the entire process of writing one of the most intimidating and challenging formats — the television drama series. This comprehensive book takes the reader on a step-by-step journey from the birth of a series concept to what happens long after the final scene has been shot. Suddenly, the impossible seems possible, thanks to *Writing the TV Drama Series*."

Marie Jones, book reviewer, www.absolutewrite.com

"The breadth and depth of practical advice on real-world writing should enlighten and inspire any aspiring TV drama writer. It should enlighten because it is clear, free of jargon, and explains the business and the design of television dramas. It should inspire because it cuts to the chase — a writer get an outline of the drama life cycle and knows what is required from pitch to pilot to longevity of a series. The interviews with successful writers makes this book valuable all by themselves, but there's so much more."

Diane Carson, Ph.D., Editorial Vice President, University Film & Video Association

"*Writing the TV Drama Series* is an invaluable resource for anyone aspiring to be a television writer. Having worked with beginning writers for years, the information in Pamela's book is exactly what they need to know: how to write excellent scripts and how to become savvy enough about the business to break in and get their first job writing for television. I recommend it to every new writer I work with."

Carole Kirschner, Head of the CBS Diversity Institute Writers Mentoring Program; Program Director, WGA Showrunner Training Program

"Pam Douglas has just rewritten 'the book' on writing for television! Hard to believe she could best herself, but the second edition of *Writing the TV Drama Series* is cutting edge and covers everything from series to pilots to the new evolving relationship between television and the Internet. It doesn't matter if you're a novice or a seasoned professional, this book is a thorough education in the world of television today. A must have for the serious television writer."

Jack Epps, Jr., Chair of the Writing Division, School of Cinematic Arts, University of Southern California; Screenwriter of *Top Gun*, *Dick Tracy*, *The Secret of My Success*

"Pamela Douglas has written 'the' book on writing hour episodic drama. She breaks the process down into simple-to-understand steps, while carefully weaving the inseparable elements of craft and business. This is a must read for any screenwriter who wants to get in — and stay in — the television series loop. In the rapidly changing landscape of hour episodic television, Pamela Douglas is on top of the trends and thinking one step ahead of them. Essentially, she has created the gold standard for any book on this topic."

Catherine Clinch, Contributing Editor, *Creative Screenwriting Magazine*; Publisher, *www.MomsMediaWorld.com*

"*Writing the TV Drama Series* is both practical and enjoyable; I repeatedly recommend this guide to series writing to aspiring television writers. Douglas keeps it easy to follow, and every page is loaded with valuable information that will help writers navigate those challenging first years."

Erika Kennair, Entertainment Diversity Representative, NBC Entertainment Strategy Dept.

WRITING THE TV DRAMA SERIES

HOW TO SUCCEED AS A PROFESSIONAL WRITER IN TV

2ND EDITION

BY
PAMELA DOUGLAS

MICHAEL WIESE PRODUCTIONS

Published by Michael Wiese Productions
12400 Ventura Blvd #1111
Studio City, CA 91604
(818) 379-8799, (818) 986-3408 (FAX).
mw@mwp.com
www.mwp.com

Cover design by
Interior design by William Morosi
Copyedited by Paul Norlen
Printed by McNaughton & Gunn

Manufactured in the United States of America

Library of Congress Cataloging-in-Publication Data

Douglas, Pamela.
  Writing the TV drama series : how to succeed as a professional writer in TV /
Pam Douglas.
     p. cm.
  ISBN 978-1-932907-34-6
  1. Television authorship. 2. Television serials--Authorship. I. Title.
  PN1992.7.D68 2007
  808.2'25--dc22
                                        2007019737

Mixed Sources

Product group from well-managed
forests and other controlled sources
www.fsc.org Cert no. SW-COC-002283
© 1996 Forest Stewardship Council

FSC

To Raya Yarbrough and John Spencer
with love

Table Of Contents

After Class #1 THIS TO PAGE 62

Chapter One

Chapter Two

Afte Chap #2 to Page 156

Chapter Three

Guest Speakers: Ann Donahue, Executive Producer, *CSI:Miami*
and **Melissa Rosenberg**, Co-Executive Producer, *Dexter*

CHAPTER FOUR

Guest Speaker: Georgia Jeffries
Supervising Producer, *China Beach*, *Cagney & Lacey* and many pilots

CHAPTER FIVE

CHAPTER SIX

CLASS # 4

CHAPTER SEVEN

Preface to the Second Edition

In 2005 when *Writing the TV Drama Series* first came out, it was greeted with wonderful reviews and welcomed by professionals in the television industry — the kinds of responses any author would hope to receive. I'm grateful for all that support. Soon the book was adopted by writing classes at film schools and by some mentoring programs at TV networks, and had begun to sell around the world.

So if it ain't broke, why fix it?

Because we're in the heart of a dynamically evolving art and business, and like Alice in Wonderland, we have to run very fast just to stay in the same place.

This volatility is not only about new shows, though I will discuss some interesting series that weren't in the first edition including *Lost, Grey's Anatomy, Battlestar Galactica, CSI: Miami, House*, and others. But so-called "hot" shows come and go (sometimes very quickly!), and learning to be an effective television writer isn't about chasing each season's hits.

In the last two years, new industry-wide patterns and opportunities have appeared which have an impact on writers who are coming into the business. For example, original pilots by novices are being sought by agents and producers, so I've added a section on writing your own pilot.

Mobisodes and webisodes not only interface with current series, but also open fresh creative prospects for writers. So I've added material on "eTV" (enhanced TV) and other emerging outlets to a final chapter, "In the Future."

Kinds of storytelling are in flux too. At the same time as venues open, networks are scrambling to adjust, some changing from the traditional four-act structure to five or even six acts. Strongly serialized dramas, like *24, Lost,* and the great shows on HBO proved that "long narratives" would draw and hold devoted viewers. But they also spawned a number of network serials that didn't succeed, while procedurals like *CSI* (in all its incarnations) have continued to top the ratings. So in this edition I've added a section on writing procedurals.

Meanwhile, increasing fragmentation of the audience on specialized cable channels has enabled niche programming that would never have made the cut in the era of three networks. That narrow-casting is producing adventurous, high-quality products like *Battlestar Galactica* (on the SciFi Channel), *The Shield* (on FX), and *Dexter* (on Showtime).

If opportunities seemed promising when the first edition was published, they're blossoming now. It's a great time to write for television.

INTRODUCTION

More than a thousand students have come through my classes in the two decades I've taught at the U.S.C. School of Cinema-Television (now re-named the USC School of Cinematic Arts). At the same time, my professional career was growing to include story editor and producer credits on television dramas, the Humanitas Prize, and awards and nominations including Emmys, Writers Guild, and American Women in Radio and Television, and a position on the Board of Directors of the Writers Guild. Always, my screenwriting and teaching have complemented each other.

I bring my working life into the classroom: What is it like to be actively breaking stories, writing, rewriting, giving and getting notes, seeing how your scripts translate to screen? I clearly recall freelancing television episodes, but I also know how the other side of the desk reacts to pitches because I've been in both chairs. I've written for networks, cable, syndication, public TV, primetime and off-prime, and for virtually every dramatic genre. In my class, students learn from someone who has been there.

Imagine you've stopped by a typical episodic drama class in the middle of a term. Ten students sit at a table, scripts and DVDs from our in-class library — *House, Big Love, Lost, Battlestar Galactica, Grey's Anatomy, The Sopranos, Nip/Tuck, C.S.I.* — among others in the middle. The class has not begun, but people are returning scripts and videos reaching for one they want next. Then we start. *on reserve?*

Someone asks why a story was left hanging at the end of an episode she saw, and I discuss the 22-hour "long narrative" of a season, or how character arcs cross multiple episodes, or stories that are closed on one level but not another.

Now we're warmed up. The class operates like the writing staff of a TV series in which writers suggest improvements on each other's work, while I function as "show-runner," or final authority on revisions. The standard is professional quality, and our models are the most brilliant, incisive, daring scripts on networks or cable. Since I hold the bar so high, no one brings in trivial subjects. Because television drama frequently reflects complex and wrenching problems in contemporary society — such as racism, sexism, violence, spirituality, and sexual identity — the writers must confront these issues with honesty at the same time as they learn their craft.

On other occasions, I come to class in the midst of my writing, full of some creative problem, and let the class in on my process. Or I might screen a clip and deconstruct its elements and discuss how it fits within the total structure of a show. All this leads to finished scripts that aim to be competitive with the best drama written for screen.

That's my goal for you too as you work with this book. My students are sophisticated, smart, dedicated, and some are wonderfully talented. Still, I was initially surprised at what they didn't know. When I add my summer seminars which are open to the public, I discovered strange misconceptions about television, the art and craft of TV drama, and the life of a working writer. That's one of my reasons for creating this book, since I'm uniquely aware of what beginning writers want and need to learn.

My approach is practical: The better you write the more work you'll get. Give 'em better than they deserve because *you* deserve the best, even if your first assignment is on something you leave off your resume years later.

As you go through this book, imagine you're in my classroom. I'll be talking to you, even asking you questions. Though I can't hear your answers, I suggest you treat the chapters interactively anyway so you'll be applying the principles.

Between chapters and in "Spotlights" I've invited illustrious "guest speakers" to address you. We're proud to host: John Wells (*ER, The West Wing*), David Milch (*Deadwood, NYPD Blue*), Steven Bochco (*Hill Street Blues, NYPD Blue*), Ann Donahue (*CSI*), Melissa Rosenberg (*Dexter*), Georgia Jeffries (*China Beach* and pilots), Damon Lindelof (*Lost*), Ron Moore (*Battlestar Galactica*) and other insightful television writer-producers.

Towards the end, we follow a group of former students from graduation through breaking into the business and launching careers as television writers. It's an opportunity to learn from writers in the trenches.

And the final chapter takes you into the future with a discussion of emerging venues and possibilities that await new writers.

Throughout this book, you'll find useful tools, a complete map of the TV series terrain, and lessons from those who have traveled it before. But, ultimately, the way to write better is to be true to what's real in your stories and to write more. You're not alone — I'll show you how.

FROM
JOHN WELLS

John Wells is Executive Producer of *ER*, *The West Wing*, *Third Watch*, and past president of the Writers Guild of America, West.

PD: If you could go back in time and talk to your own young self when you were a student in film school or college, what do you know now that you wish you'd known then about writing and producing television series?

JW: I wish I'd known how long it was going to take. You come out and you sort of assume it's going to be a couple-of-years process and you don't really start making any headway until you've written about a foot and a half of material, measured up off the floor. That's when you really start to think of yourself as a writer in the way you look at the world. It's a craft that takes a tremendous amount of time.

I wish I had more of a sense that it was much more like learning to play a musical instrument. After four or five years you start to not embarrass yourself. It takes 10 years before you can even begin to call yourself proficient. And that's very difficult for students because they've been through 12 years of primary school, four years of college, and often a couple of years of graduate school and they think they've already done 16, 18 years of education, so they want to go do it right now, though they've actually just started.

It looks deceptively easy from the outside. If you look at the lowest common denominator you think "I can do that." The craft that's necessary — the time it takes to have enough trial and error and to keep going with it — that takes a very long time to develop. I'm very suspicious of writers who haven't been writing for 10 years. I will often ask people for three or four or five pieces of material if I've read one thing of theirs that I like. I know they've given me the thing they're proudest of, and I'm looking to see the growth, and how much they've done and how much they've committed themselves to the long-term process of writing.

I've supervised well over 600 scripts, and personally written well over 100, and I still finish each one disappointed in my work. It's a life-long endeavor, never something you succeed at. I've been working professionally for 20 years and I'm always learning something new every day about writing.

PD: You could have chosen to write in any medium. Why did you choose television?

JW: The feature world, which I remain involved in, is not a medium, generally, where you're able to write about character in the depth I like to write about character. There are characters now on *ER* whose growth I've been writing about for years. I don't mean to compare myself to Dickens, but I heard Steven Bochco talk about that years ago, when he explained that what he was trying to do on *Hill Street* was like the way Dickens published a chapter a week.

And subject matter is different in television. The kinds of things we can write about seriously are more appealing than most of what you're offered to do in features.

Beyond that, it's much easier to be involved creatively in your work in television than in feature films. It happens a lot faster, so there's not time for as many cooks in the kitchen. But also you get to see your work and see it quickly. I've done work on features that haven't been produced for years, and [when asked for another draft] it becomes hard to remember what you had in mind when you first wrote it three years ago. In television, you'll finish a script and see dailies on it 10 days later.

PD: People talk about how television is changing now with cable and the influence of TiVo. What does the future hold for the art of television drama?

JW: The technology makes for short-term changes, but we're still doing what Chaucer was doing a thousand years ago. We're still writing stories. I think we are structured in such a way that we're interested in people, and we're interested in hearing their stories and metaphors for our own lives and going through cathartic experiences. That hasn't changed.

I actually think it's a more exciting time for a writer because there are many more ways for your material to get made. You can write something and make it on a digital videocam that you buy at a store. You have an opportunity to work on shows on cable which have content you can't do on broadcast television. The opportunities are limitless. There isn't as much money to be made doing it, but you have thoughts and impressions about the human experience you want to share with others. This is the way to share it, and now there are more opportunities than ever.

PD: Any final words of wisdom for a beginning writer?

JW: It's going to take a lot longer than you think, and don't give up. Just keep writing.

There was a guy I went to USC with whom I used to see every year at a New Year's party. And every year I'd ask him what he was doing. He told me what he was working on, and I realized it was the same thing he was working on last year. That went on for three or four years. You need to be writing, at the minimum three or four specs a year, different shows. And you need to do that while you've got whatever day job you have to keep you alive. That's the sort of commitment you need to really succeed.

Even my friends who came out of school and immediately got jobs or sold screenplays — within three or four years they ended up having to do their period of four or five or six years slogging. I really don't know any talented writers who ended up being successful who haven't had a struggle. That's just what being an artist is all about.

The West Wing

CHAPTER 1

WHAT'S SO SPECIAL ABOUT TV DRAMA SERIES?

Imagine the power.

Picture the whole world dotted with hundreds of millions of homes glowing with the blue light of TV sets. Inside each home — your own home, for example — visitors tell stories about their dreams and problems, loves and rages, their thrills and their losses. You care about them, probably more than you admit; you even talk about them when they're not around — after all, they come every week. Sometimes they're broiling over issues in the news. Or sick and scared about that, or lying, or brave. At one time they were attacked and fought back and barely survived. But no matter what, they'll be back next week, your same friends, there with you in your most vulnerable place, at home when you're tired after work. Intimate.

Maybe one of them is Tony Soprano, the mob boss, asking Uncle Junior, "I thought you loved me," and watching Junior's lip quiver, unable to answer. Or Detective Andy Sipowicz of *NYPD Blue*, just reconciled with his adult son, lifting the sheet off a corpse, to discover his son. On *West Wing*, you were surprised by a swell of pride when reason triumphed in a hard-won Supreme Court appointment. You were drawn into the D.A.'s moral quandary when an old man can't be stopped from confessing revenge against a swindler who took his house, on *Law and Order*. And you couldn't resist rooting for the nurses on *ER* in the midst of tragedies as they dealt with an irascible patient by pushing his gurney in the hall and "taking his temperature" with a plastic flower in his rear. Joy and tears up close and personal.

Think about the impact. Once you understand the way viewers relate to their favorite shows, you'll get a feel for the kinds of stories that work and how to wield this awesome power.

THREE QUALITIES OF EPISODIC TV SERIES

Among the traits that distinguish primetime series (both dramas and comedies) from other kinds of screenwriting, three are especially significant for writers: endless character arcs, the "long narrative" for serials, and the collaborative process.

EPISODIC CHARACTERIZATION

In feature writing you were probably told to create an arc for your protagonist that takes him from one state to its opposite; the character struggles towards a goal and once that is attained, your story ends. Someone who is unable to love is changed when a mate/child/friend appears and, through fighting the relationship, the character is finally able to love. Or someone who has been wronged seeks revenge and either achieves it or dies for the cause. All fine for movies that end. But series don't.

So how do you progress a narrative without an arc? Well, you create a different kind of arc. Remember what I said about series characters being more like people you know than figures in a plot. If your friend has an extreme experience, you continue knowing him after the event. You're invested in the process, not just the outcome.

But watch out — this does not mean the characters are flat. Your continuing cast should never be mere witnesses to the challenge of the week. On the contrary, characters who are not transformed by the plot need something instead: dimension. Think of it like this: instead of developing horizontally towards a goal, the character develops vertically, exploring internal conflicts that create tension. The character may be revealed incrementally within each episode and throughout the series, but viewers need to depend that Meredith Grey or Tim Riggins are the same people they knew last week. Does that mean those characters are without range or variation? Of course not, and neither are your friends.

THE "LONG NARRATIVE"

Episodic drama comes in three forms: anthologies, series with "closure," and "serials."

The Sopranos

Anthologies are free-standing stories, like short movies, unconnected to other installments except by a frame. *Twilight Zone* had a continuing host, style and franchise, but the casts were different each week. As the precursor of today's episodic television, anthologies flourished in the 1950s when showcases like *Playhouse 90* presented literature more like stage plays. But anthologies are rare today, and we're not focusing on writing them.

Series with closure — or "modular" episodes — have continuing main casts but new situations which conclude at the end of each episode: They close. Most series have some closure, even if they continue other story lines. Any *Law and Order* and any *CSI* close each episode. Syndicators prefer this kind of show because they buy large packages (the first four seasons, or 88 episodes is typical) and sell them to local and overseas stations who may re-run them in any order. If the episodes have no "memory," that is, no significant development of ongoing relationships, the order of the episodes isn't supposed to matter. Or so the thinking goes.

Not as easy as it sounds. When a series is well developed, the writers and fans follow the characters and find it hard to resist their history as it inevitably builds over time. In its early seasons, *The X-Files* had a new alien or paranormal event each week, and though the romantic tension between Mulder and Scully simmered, it didn't escalate. Then interest from viewers pushed more and more of a relationship and turned the partners into lovers by the end of the series. Most *X-Files* episodes can still be enjoyed in any order, but serial storytelling is beguiling.

Serials: Now, there's a dirty word in some minds because it also describes soap operas. Daytime soaps like *The Young and the Restless* and *General Hospital* have had loyal viewers and succeed according to their own aims. But primetime writers and producers don't like to be identified with them because the heightened melodrama (which is needed to drive the story enough to run five days a week), and the speed with which episodes are produced too often result in stereotypical characters, dialogue that lacks subtlety, and unbelievable situations.

Can the same be said about primetime serials? Decades ago, shows like *Dallas* and *Knots Landing* were described as nighttime soaps, and did have the overblown romanticism and hyperbole typical of their daytime cousins. But most primetime series aren't like that anymore. Today's serials include award-winning dramas on HBO: *Big Love, The Sopranos, Rome, The Wire*. And most of the acclaimed series on networks and other cable outlets including *24, Lost,* and *Grey's Anatomy* use serialized storytelling along with closed stories.

A serial is any drama whose stories continue across many episodes in which the main cast develops over time. It's called the "long narrative," the epitome of what episodic television can offer: not one tale that ties up in an hour or two but lives that play out over hundreds of hours. Think about it — as a writer you have the opportunity to tell a story that is so rich that it expands for years. At the conclusion of *NYPD Blue*'s 12-year run, the series produced around 250 hours. That's not 250 police cases (actually two or three times that many because each episode includes several cases); the significance is 250 hours of living with Detective Sipowicz and the rest of the cast, 250 hours dealing with the consequences of 12 years of experiences.

As you watch television, look for the way closed stories mingle with the long narrative. Not only will that give you insight into the show's construction, but also a larger sense of what a story can be.

COLLABORATION

If you go on to write for television, you'll never work alone. Series are like families, and even though each episode is written by one writer, the process is collaborative at every step. Writers sit around a table to "break" each story, then review the outline and all the drafts together. Sometimes a writer may be placing a long arc in many episodes rather than writing a single episode. On *ER*, medical consultants, some of whom are also writers, supply emergency room scenes. And sometimes one writer may do a revision or dialogue polish on another's script. The image of the isolated artist creating his precious screenplay secretly in the night isn't the reality of life on a series. (Though that's not to say staff members don't write their drafts privately, or that they aren't artists — some are brilliant!)

You may have heard the comment that happy families are all alike but each unhappy family is unhappy in its own way. Television staffs are full of writers, so how normal can they be? Dysfunctional staff families abound, but so do creative mixes that are encouraging and inspiring. As a beginner, you'll learn tremendously on a staff. Read Chapter Six for how staffs function and tips for getting along and getting ahead.

But first, if you're going to write for TV, you need to dump some misconceptions.

FIVE MYTHS ABOUT TELEVISION

MYTH 1: TV IS SMALL MOVIES

Not really, though that does seem to make sense on the surface. Both TV dramas and movies deliver stories played by actors who are filmed and shown on screens. And many filmmakers — writers, directors, actors, cinematographers, editors and so forth — work in both theatricals and television. In fact, Michael Crichton and Steven Spielberg were involved with TV veteran John Wells at the inception of *ER*. Action movie producer Jerry Bruckheimer does *C.S.I.* Alan Ball, who wrote the movie *American Beauty*, became executive producer of *Six Feet Under*. *West Wing* creator Aaron Sorkin wrote the Academy Award–nominated movie *A Few Good Men* (which, in turn, was an adaptation of his play).

A funny experience on a series brought home how connected film and TV writing can be. My agent told me that several writers had quit the staff of a show I admired. I couldn't figure out why — the series was winning awards, it was renewed, and the characters had plenty of potential. Not to mention the writers were making a bundle. Maybe the show-runner was a monster. But I met him, a bright guy, no crazier than anyone else in town. So I went to work.

First day in my new cubicle, I waited to be called to a story meeting, or given an assignment, or a script to re-write. Nothing. I read the newspaper. Second day, I observed everyone else writing furiously on their office computers. Why was I left out? Had I offended someone? My mind fell to dark ruminations.

Finally, I popped into the cubicle next to me — "What are you writing?" The writer looked up, wide-eyed, didn't I know? Everyone was working on their features. "He wants to do it all himself," my fellow staffer said about the executive producer. "He keeps us around to bounce ideas and read his drafts. But he thinks it's quicker if he just writes the show." There I was on a TV staff and everyone was writing a movie. Pretty soon the studio pulled the plug on our feature scholarships, and that was the end of that job. But that illustrates an axiom: a writer is a writer, whether television or feature or for any new media.

Still, the more you know about features and television, the more unique each is. People go to movies to escape into a fantasy larger than life with spectacular stunts, effects and locations. At upwards of ten dollars per ticket, audiences demand lots of bang for their bucks. And teenage boys — a prime target for features — relish the vicarious action that big screens do so well. If you saw *Lord of the Rings* re-run on television, or rented a summer blockbuster, the armies of thousands were reduced to ants. Some bubbles are not meant to be burst.

From the beginning, theatrical features grew out of shared entertainment — think of crowds watching vaudeville. Television didn't intend that kind of experience. In fact, the parent of TV is more likely radio. A generation before television, families gathered around their radios for vital information, whether the farm report or the war. And radio dramas were character-driven; beloved familiar personalities scrapping and coping with each other, bringing someone (often women, hardly ever teen boys) to tears or laughter every day. Close, personal, at home.

And real. Before radio, people got their information about the world from newspapers. That lineage continues in what we expect of television. Partly because (as they say on one of the networks) "more people get their news from us than any other source," television becomes fused with what people need to know and what they believe is fact. So it's not an escape, not fantasy, but the fabric of daily life.

Oh, you're saying what about *Star Trek* or *Smallville*, for just two examples — they're hardly real. Well, I did a brief turn on *Star Trek: The Next Generation*, and I can tell you the producers were interested in stories about people — people who lived in a distant environment with futuristic gadgets, yes, but the core was relationships among the crew, testing personal limits; and, at its best, the exploration wasn't distant galaxies but what it means to be human. As for *Smallville*, the young Clark Kent is a metaphor for every teenager who struggles with being different, figuring out who he is and how to be with his friends. This is heart stuff, not spectacle.

Which is not to say you should write without cinematic qualities. *The X-Files* used to open with visually tantalizing images that drew the viewer into the mood and quest of the episode. But even there, the focus was personal jeopardy — a foot sinking into the ground, someone blinded by a light or lost amidst eerily rustling branches. Immediate, direct, close.

Screenwriting students are taught to write visually and minimize talk — "play it don't say it." Generally, that's good advice, so I was writing that way when I started in television. Then a producer pointed to a chunk of description (which I'd thought was a clever way of replacing exposition) and said, "Give me a line for this — they may not be watching." Not watching? That's my brilliant image up there!

But come back to the reality of the medium. It's at home, not a darkened theatre. No one is captured, and the viewers might be eating, painting toenails, doing homework — you know how it goes. As the creator, of course you want to make the screen so beguiling they won't turn their eyes away, but if the "viewers" have to get a point, put it in dialogue. People may be listening to the TV more than watching it. That's not such a bad thing. Whereas viewers are distanced from the screen in theatrical films, voyeurs to other people's stories, television drama has the effect of people talking to you, or at least talking to each other in your home. It's compelling in a different way.

When students ask whether I advise them to write for features or television, after I tell them to try both, I ask about their talent. Do they have an ear for the way people speak naturally? Are they able to convey the illusion of today's speech while actually writing tight, withheld lines? Can they write distinct voices for dissimilar characters? If they don't have the talent for effective dialogue, I nudge them away from TV because action would be easier for them.

No, television is not a small version of movies; it's a different medium; and it's bigger. Yes, bigger. The most successful features are seen by millions of people in theatres, and more when the movies rent as videos and re-run on TV. But even a moderately successful series, if it continues for enough years to go into syndication, is seen by hundreds of millions — all those blue lights glowing from windows around the world.

MYTH 2: TV IS CHEAP

Well, I don't think $2 to $10 million to produce a single hour is all that cheap, or around $100 million for a full season. Sure, when you compare that television hour to a two-hour feature whose budget is more than the GNP of several small countries, maybe it doesn't seem so much. But at the high-end no one's hurting in TV, and for writers, being on a series is a way to get rich (more about staff work in Chapter Six). Of course, not all series are on the high end, and the business side of television is more like a manufacturing company than an entrepreneurial venture. Pay scales (at least the floors) are set by guilds and unions and a budget for the year is managed by the show's executives. It's a lot of money but it's all allocated.

So towards the end of a season, some shows do tighten their belts. One show-runner gave me a single instruction as I joined his series: "It doesn't rain in this town." After he had sprung for high-profile guest stars, overtime shooting, and sweeps week specials, he couldn't afford to make rain on the set for the rest of the year. You may have noticed another sign of overrun: the "wrap-around" episode — the one where the main character relives his previous episodes. Chances are, those memories were triggered not by nostalgia but by the need to use clips instead of spending on production.

That said, series budgets are ample for what you want dramatically within the world of the show. As a writer, your investment needs to be in the quality of the story and depth of feelings you can elicit rather than production dazzle, so avoid: distant or difficult locations, special effects, extreme stunts, large guest casts, crowd scenes, and CGI (computer-generated images) unless those are part of your series. If you write them, they'll probably be cut, and by tightening you gain focus on the main characters, which are the strength of television drama.

MYTH 3: YOU CAN'T DO THAT ON TV

Come on, you can do anything on cable television — language, nudity, controversial subjects or lifestyles, experiments in ways of telling stories. However, broadcast stations are licensed by the FCC (Federal Communications Commission) which obligates them to operate in the public interest. So local stations are susceptible to pressure from groups which might threaten their licenses when they're up for renewal; and the networks, which also own stations, are sensitive to public mores — though those cultural standards change with time. Certainly, public norms have come a long way since the 1950s when married couples had to be shown fully dressed and sleeping in separate beds. Now even the least adventurous television is closer to real life. And none of this applies to HBO, Showtime, or the other cable outlets.

The old days of censorship are past... but not entirely. In 2004, network censors stunned the creators of *ER*. It involved one episode where an 81-year-old woman is having a medical exam — an emotional moment in which the elderly woman learns about cancer, and some of her aged breast is visible. Essential for the dramatic impact of the scene, the show's producers argued, but the network pressured them to re-edit the scene so the breast could not be glimpsed.

A new level of accommodation was reached when HBO's bold drama *The Sopranos* was sold into syndication on A&E. Having planned ahead, HBO filmed alternate scenes and lines during the original production. While most of the "sanitized" episodes retain their power, some bizarre moments result like Paulie (a tough gangster) cursing about the "freakin'" snow while they go off to kill someone. That sort of thing drives some serious writers to cable where they can practice their art without interference, although even there, Sci-Fi Channel's *Battlestar Galactica* makes do with "frack."

So, yes, on broadcast television some limits still exist. But here's my advice: Don't censor yourself as you write your first draft. Have your characters talk and behave the way people actually do today. Stay real. If a word or image has to be edited, fix it later, but keep the pipeline open to how people truly are because that's the source of powerful writing.

MYTH 4: ALL TV SERIES ARE THE SAME

I once heard that statement from a producer who'd been successful in the era before audiences had 400 channels to surf. Now, with competition for fresh programming, a show that rests on formulas and conventional prototypes risks going unnoticed, cancelled after four episodes.

But television series do follow rules, and you'll find a list of them at the end of this chapter.

MYTH 5: TELEVISION IS A WASTELAND

In 1961, Newton Minnow, an FCC commissioner, declared television a "vast wasteland," and the epithet stuck. Minnow was referring to shows such as *Bonanza*, *The Flintstones*, and *Mr. Ed* in an era when three networks, each smaller than now, shared airwaves that were considered a scarce commodity dedicated to informing or elevating the public. The talking horse just didn't do it for him.

Well, half a century later, part of the wasteland has become a garbage dump strewn with fake jilted lovers beating up on each other on certain daytime shows. The rest ranges from televangelists to pornography, sports to scientific discoveries, wannabe singers to singing animals, and includes fiction of all kinds that may be funny, freaky, fascinating or familiar. And some is brilliant literature, on a par with the greatest writing and filmmaking created anywhere. Those are the shows I focus on when teaching hour drama because I believe you learn best if you learn from the best. As to the wasteland — with more than 400 channels, and access to programming from all over the world, television is whatever you choose to watch.

Nor is television monolithic even within American primetime. I've heard people disparage TV as aimed at 12-year-olds. I answer, yes, TV shows are aimed at 12-year-olds if you watch at eight o'clock. Traditionally, the prime-time evening, from 8:00 to 11:00 PM, was divided into components:

8:00 — family sitcoms featuring children and cartoon-like action hours; some family-oriented variety shows;

8:30 — more sitcoms though not necessarily with children; variety shows continue;

9:00 — sophisticated comedies; hour dramas that are thoughtful, romantic, inspirational or teen; demographic favors women (TV movies air from 9 to 11);

10:00 — the most sophisticated hour dramas for adults; serious news magazines.

At least that's how it used to line up. Now with TiVo and recording, you can view anything at any time, and cable re-runs its programming throughout the week. Still, the schedule hints at the range of primetime. Most talented writers want to work on the 9:00 or 10:00 PM shows, and in fact those are the ones I recommend learning. When you're out in the business, though, you may find more openings at 8:00 o'clock and in less lofty outlets at first. That's okay, you have to start somewhere, and in Chapter Six you'll read about breaking in.

THE RULES OF SERIES TV

• AN HOUR SHOW HAS TO FIT IN AN HOUR.

Actually, a network hour is less than 50 minutes, with commercial breaks, though pay cable may be longer, and syndicated hours are shorter. Usually, scripts for drama series are around 55 to 60 pages, though a fast-talking show like *The West Wing* sometimes went to 70 pages. On networks that break shows into five acts plus a teaser, writers are stuck with reduced screen time, and find themselves with eight-page acts and scripts coming in around 48 pages; and some six-act scripts may be only 42 to 45 pages. Each script is timed before production, and if it runs long (despite the page count), the writer needs to know what to trim in dialogue or which action to ellipse; if it runs short, where a new beat could add depth or a twist, not padding. And you need the craft to get it revised overnight, which leads to the next rule:

• SERIES DEADLINES ARE FOR REAL.

Your show is on every week, and that means there's no waiting for your muse, no honing the fine art of writing-avoidance, no allowing angst to delay handing in your draft. If you can't make the deadline, the show-runner has to turn over your work to another writer.

From the time your episode is assigned, you'll probably have one week to come in with an outline, a few days to revise it, two weeks to deliver the first draft teleplay, a gap of a couple of days for notes, then one week to write your second draft — a total of around six weeks from pitch to second draft (though polishes and production revisions will add another couple of weeks or so). Maybe that sounds daunting, but once you're on a staff you're living the series, and the pace can be exhilarating. You'll hear your words spoken by the actors, watch the show put together, and see it on screen quickly too.

It's fun until the nightmare strikes. On a series, the nightmare is a script that "falls out" at the last minute. It may happen like this: the story seems to make sense when it's pitched. The outline comes in with holes, but the staff thinks it can be made to work. Then they read the first draft and see the problems aren't solved. It's given to another writer to fix. Meanwhile the clock is ticking. Pre-production, including sets, locations, casting have to go ahead if the script is going to shoot next week. Tick tock. Another draft, and the flaw — maybe an action the lead character really wouldn't do, or a plot element that contradicts the episode just before or after, or a forced resolution that's not credible — now glares out at everyone around the table. Yet another draft, this time by the supervising producer. Tick tock. Or maybe it's not the writer's fault: the exact fictional crisis about a hostage has suddenly occurred in real life so the episode can not be aired. The script has to be abandoned — it "falls out." Meanwhile, the production manager is waiting to prep, and publicity has gone out.

I once heard a panel discussion where a respected show-runner told this very nightmare. The cast and crew were literally on the set and absolutely had to start shooting that day for the episode to make the air date. But they had no script. In desperation, the show-runner, renowned as a great writer, commenced dictating as a secretary transcribed and runners dashed to the set bringing one page at a time. A hand shot up from an admirer in the panel audience, "Was it the best thing you ever wrote?" "No," he laughed, "it didn't make sense."

• DRAMA SERIES HAVE A FOUR (OR FIVE OR SIX) ACT STRUCTURE.

Put away your books on three-act structure. Television dramas on networks have for decades been written in four acts, though many network shows now use five acts, and in 2006, ABC began mandating six acts for their hour dramas. Even a rare seven-act structure has surfaced. You'll learn more about all that in Chapter Four, where a teleplay is analyzed. For now, think about what happens every 13 to 15 minutes on a traditional network show. You know: a commercial break. These breaks aren't random; they provide a grid for constructing the episode in which action rises to a cliffhanger or twist ("plot point" may be a familiar term if you've studied feature structure). Each of the four segments are "acts" in the same sense as plays have real acts rather than the theoretical acts described in analyzing features. At a stage play, at the end of an act the curtain comes down, theatre lights come up, and the audience heads for refreshments or the restrooms. That's the kind of hard act break that occurs in television. Writers plan towards those breaks and use them to build tension.

Once you get the hang of it, you'll discover act breaks don't hamper your creativity; they free you to be inventive within a rhythmic grid. And once you work with that 15-minute block, you may want to use it off-network and in movies. In fact, next time you're in a movie theatre, notice the audience every 15 minutes. You may see them shifting in their seats. I don't know whether 15-minute chunks have been carved into contemporary consciousness by the media, or if they're aspects of human psychology which somehow evolved with us, but the 15-minute span existed before television. In the early 20th century motion pictures were distributed on reels that projectionists had to change every 15 minutes. Then, building on that historical pattern, some screenwriting theorists began interpreting features as eight 15-minute sequences. Whatever the origin, for decades four acts were the template for drama series on the networks.

But not off-network. Syndicated series, like the various *Star Trek* incarnations, had to leave time for local advertising on individual stations which buy the shows, and that means more commercial breaks. For a long time, syndicated series have been written in five acts, and may also have a teaser (explained in Chapter Three) which is sometimes almost as long as an act, giving an impression of six acts, each less than 10 pages long. Now, six act network shows have become more like syndicated series, with all the advertising minutes that implies. On the other side of the spectrum, cable series like those on HBO have no act breaks, and may be structured more like movies.

• EACH SERIES FITS A FRANCHISE.

Not Starbucks, though enough caffeine is downed on late rewrites to earn that franchise too. Some typical television franchises include detective, legal, medical, sci-fi, action-adventure, teen, and family. Each brings expectations from the audience that you should know, even if you challenge them. For series creators, franchises are both boundaries and opportunities. You'll find more about how shows are created in Chapters Two and Five, and in the Spotlight on Writing Your Pilot Script, but you can get a clue why franchises are useful if you ask how hundreds of stories can derive from a single premise.

The solution is to find "springboards" that propel dramatic conflicts or adventures each episode. Those catalysts occur naturally in most of the franchises: a crime sets the cop on a quest for the perp; someone in trouble beseeches lawyers who must mount a case; a patient is brought for a doctor to save. The hook for each episode is rooted in a specific world in which sympathetic main characters must take immediate action. In other franchises — family dramas especially — springboards are less obvious, relying on conflicts between characters rather than outside provocations. In these, a personal inciting incident (even if it's internal) sets each episode in motion.

Decades ago, audiences expected the franchises to deliver predictable storytelling where any problem could be resolved within the hour. Take Westerns, for example. The template was the frontier town threatened by bad guys (black hats). The good guy marshal (white hat) wrangles with weak or corrupt townspeople, gets a few on his side (room for one exceptional guest role), defends the town against the black hats, and rides off into the sunset.

With that old franchise in mind, think about *Deadwood* that ran on HBO (now available on DVD). Yup, there's the bad frontier town of rough nasties. And it has an ex-marshal, a lead character who left his badge in Montana to forge a future on the edge of the abyss. But similarities to the franchise are superficial. Everyone in Deadwood is surviving any way he

Deadwood

can in a world without an outside redeemer, struggling to make sense of life in a moral wilderness.

Clearly, *ER, House,* and *Grey's Anatomy* all use the medical franchise, where doctors must deal with new cases each week. But if you compare them to examples of the historic franchise such as *Marcus Welby, M.D.,* you'll see how far *ER* and the others had to stretch to reflect contemporary life. Welby, the kindly doctor, free of deep introspection, worked alone in his nice little office. But real doctors face ethical and legal issues as they treat both the victim of a gunshot and the man who shot him, and they cope with their own humanity — guilt, exhaustion, ambition, and the competing pulls of the job and the rest of life including romance on *Grey's* and a doctor's own physical limits on *House.* To express today's medical whirlwind, the form itself needed to change, so *ER* developed "vignette" techniques in which multiple short stories flit by, some on top of each other, and *Grey's* continues that layering.

From the moment ABC slotted *Grey's Anatomy* to follow *Desperate Housewives,* the network mandated the tone: "Sex and the Surgery." Executive Producer Shonda Rhimes responded in *Los Angeles Magazine,* "I don't think of it as a medical drama. It's a relationship show with some surgery thrown in. That's how I've always seen it."

For a different tweak on the doctor franchise, watch *Nip/Tuck* on FX about two plastic surgeons, where the real cutting edge is in the relationships and contemporary families.

Meanwhile, the family drama franchise is flourishing — like *Big Love* and *Weeds.* Some families. I suppose you could call Showtime's *The L Word* a family drama too because episodes emanate from relationships among the continuing cast (some of whom are related or living together) rather than external events. Not exactly *Leave It to Beaver*. On the networks more traditional family dramas do exist, of course, such as *Judging Amy* and *Gilmore Girls*. But take a closer look and see if you can identify the elements which update the franchise.

In the detective franchise, a light show like *Monk* on USA plays out the traditional form: one detective gets one new crime mystery each week and, after investigating red herrings that fall mostly at the act breaks, cleverly solves it by the end of the hour. Though *Monk's* obsessive-compulsive characterization is a fresh, entertaining element, structurally this is a basic "A" story series (more about A-B-C storytelling in Chapter Three).

But if you check out high-profile detective series now on the air, you'll see mostly ensemble casts and complex intertwining plots that are propelled by issues in the news or social concerns. Some use cutting-edge forensic technology, as in *CSI*, where the real star is science that engages the intellect. Detectives have always solved puzzles, of course, but the show's audience seems fascinated with futuristic tools that try the bounds of human capability.

Series that rely on stories that are solved by investigative procedures are called "procedurals" and include forensics (*CSI*), detective work (*Law and Order*), and medical diagnoses (*House*) that follow clues to wrap up a new case each week. Procedurals have always been attractive to syndicators because they can be aired in any order, and after saturation with deeply-serialized shows like *24*, *Lost* and others, some networks are backing off and looking for more procedurals too.

At first, viewers were watching densely plotted novelized series with the kind of passion network executives crave. Dana Walden, president of the Twentieth Century Fox Television studio, told the *New York Times* in October, 2006, "It did sort of filter into the ether. We were all having conversations about event drama, and an event drama *is* a serialized drama."

But how many hours will people devote every week to intense serialized dramas? And if you miss the first few episodes, it's like reading a novel beginning in the middle. Would audiences become commitment-phobic?

Several solutions exist: catch-up marathons (as HBO has always run), replays available on internet sites (more about new television outlets in the final chapter "In the Future"), and DVDs. In fact, sales of 24 after its first year validated the whole business of selling DVDs of entire seasons of series, which was just emerging at that time. On Showtime, *Dexter*, a character-driven psychological thriller, offers an interactive clues game on the network website to hold its fans. Still, networks wonder if it would be prudent to return to reliable procedural franchises.

And yet, those are volatile too. For example, the action-adventure franchise that thrived in the days of easy bad guys like *The A Team* and *Starsky and Hutch* has transformed to shows like *The Closer* in which a character said "I'm in America observing an empire on its deathbed, a tourist doing charitable work among the addicted and sexually diseased." In this context, Showtime's *Sleeper Cell* is an ambitious attempt to dramatize a range of characters and motives that are unfamiliar to most Americans. The action and adventure in shows like those emanate from the terrain, rather than having the franchise itself control the story.

Nor could *NYPD Blue* be defined solely by its franchise, though it's obviously a detective show. And obviously a family drama built on personal relationships among the ensemble. And obviously a spiritual quest built on the "dark knight" in search of redemption. Forget about detective work in the episode when Simone lay dying and viewers dramatically experienced his awesome spiritual transition. "Breakthrough" has been over-applied to various series, and when used for *NYPD Blue*, the accolade has sometimes missed the show's real strength by referring to its nerve to bare the rear end of a middle-aged man, when that's not where real innovation lies.

I haven't even broached the crazy notion that anyone would watch an insider series about politics, or the hybrids of "reality" shows mixed with dramatic storytelling. For instance, try mixing adventure, romance and even "family drama" with sci-fi/fantasy elements on *Lost*. A lot is going on!

Speaking of sci-fi elements, now there's a genre that has boldly gone where science fiction hadn't gone before on TV. While the Sci-Fi Channel (owned by NBC) continues a predictable roll-out of fantasy adventures like *Stargate SGI* and *New Atlantis*, which serve its niche audience without extending it, the channel also lucked into the critically-acclaimed *Battlestar Galactica*, which has sometimes been more a searing political allegory than even *West Wing* was, while occasionally venturing into contemporary relationships on the level of premium cable dramas. At the same time, *Heroes*, using a traditional sci-fi genre based on "graphic novels" (comic books), is a hit on NBC, attracting viewers who are not traditional sci-fi fans, featuring an international cast who struggle over having supernatural powers.

If I had to guess the frontier of science fiction writing on television, I would look towards the characters. In 20th-century sci-fi series, the leading edge was technology as used by fantasy heroes, usually "perfect," in action-heavy battles between good and evil, which tended to play to children and adolescents. Though contemporary sci-fi shows are as different as *Lost* is from *Heroes* or *Galactica*, they all follow flawed human beings, and the questions they explore involve relationships as much as philosophy; and they're watched by wide demographics. With so much range in this franchise, if you're interested in trying it, I suggest reaching up towards real dramatic writing based on honest characters, and leave cartoon-like thinking to the movies.

The vitality of 21st-century television drama has re-interpreted traditional franchises. But that doesn't mean they'll disappear. When I was a beginner freelancing any show that would give me a break, I landed an assignment on *Mike Hammer*, a network detective series. At my first meeting, the producer handed me two pages of guidelines. The first was titled "Mike Hammer Formulaic Structure." On the second were rules for writing Mike, for example, "Mike speaks only in declarative sentences." To be a strong man, he could never ask questions, you see.

The formula went something like this: At the top of the show, a sympathetic character approaches Mike for help. At the end of Act One the sympathetic character is found dead. In Act Two Mike is on the trail of the killer, only to find him dead at the Act break, and yet someone else has been killed (proving there's a different killer). In Act Three the real bad guy goes after Mike, and at the Act Three break, Mike is in mortal jeopardy. Act Four is entirely resolution, one-to-one, Mike against the killer. And guess who wins. As I started, I thought such a rigid form would be stultifying, but I discovered it was fun. Relieved of certain structure choices, I felt free to be inventive with the guest cast and the kinds of situations that could lead to the turns and twists.

Years later, an executive of the Children's Television Workshop (makers of *Sesame Street*) asked me to develop and write a pilot for a children's series, later named *Ghostwriter*, that would be structured like prime-time network dramas, complete with long character arcs, parallel stories, complex relationships among a diverse ensemble cast, and even references to controversial issues. I'd never written for kids, but I was intrigued. In forming the series with the CTW team, we began by identifying a general franchise — in this case, detectives because solving mysteries was a way to involve the whole cast and incite each episode's quest. Beyond that, we stayed close to what human beings truly care about, how they reveal themselves, and what makes people laugh, cry, be scared and fall in love — people of any age.

Ghostwriter was originally intended for kids around eight years old to encourage them to read. But CTW was astounded when research reported that the audience went from four years old to sixteen. That's not even a demographic. I think the show exceeded anyone's expectations because the realistic characters rested on a franchise that was so robust it could carry not only a very young cast but also some educational content while moving the stories forward with high tension.

But when is a franchise not a franchise? In 2004, Dick Wolf, creator of *Law and Order*, told *Entertainment Weekly*, "*Law and Order* is a brand, not a franchise. It's the Mercedes of television. The cars are very different, but if you buy a Mercedes, you're still getting a good car. *CSI* is a franchise — like the Palm Restaurant. *CSI* is the same show set in different cities, while the *Law and Order* shows are all very different from each other." No doubt, *CSI*, which competes head to head with *Law and Order* on several nights, would describe itself as an even bigger car.

When you're ready to plan a script as your showpiece for a series, ask yourself what the underlying franchise is. Even if the show is innovative and evolved beyond the tradition, the franchise may give you tips for constructing your outline (more on this in Chapter Four).

Ready, Set, Go!

Writing primetime TV drama series is an adventure into an expanding universe. If you rise above outdated ideas about television, and have pride in your talent so you never write down, you can create for the most powerful medium in the world. In the next chapters you'll find the tools you'll need, so get ready to jump on a moving rocket!

Summary Points

TV drama series have unique qualities:

• Characters continue over many episodes instead of concluding a dramatic arc as in a two-hour movie. Focus on depth of characters rather than looking for characters to change.

• Storylines may evolve over many episodes, especially in serials. Emphasize increments or installments of a series-long quest rather than tying up a plot. However, most shows have some stories that "close" (resolve) within an episode while other dramatic arcs continue.

• Network drama series are written in four, five or six acts marked by cliffhangers at commercial breaks, though off-network shows may not have formal act breaks.

• Certain franchises offer springboards that suggest hundreds of stories from a show's premise.

Adventurous cable programming and new markets have spurred growth and change in television, and provide fresh opportunities for writers.

GUEST SPEAKER: DAVID MILCH

David Milch is Creator and Executive Producer of *Deadwood*, and was Co-creator and Executive Producer of *NYPD Blue*.

PD: You went from writing and producing for a network to creating a show for HBO — what's the difference?

DM: As a practical matter, there isn't an enormous amount of difference because as time went on at the network I operated as I needed to operate... and the network accommodated that process, but it was not always that way. Structurally, HBO is built to accommodate the work process of the people who actually create the show, as opposed to networks which are antithetical to the proper needs of those whose vision it is that the show is intended to execute.

The predicate of a commercial network's existence is to appeal to as broad a segment of the population as possible. So their impulse is always to take the edges off of anything that might offend the audience. Once the network has bought the particular premise, immediately there ensues a leveling of that idea to make it as broadly appealing as possible. Now, one of the byproducts of that is the people who bring them their ideas internalize those expectations so they conceive shows that will appeal to as broad an audience as possible. There's nothing malevolent about that. It's just that the revenue base is advertising and advertising wants to sell to as many people as possible.

Since HBO just wants to sell to a particular portion of the audience by subscription, they are much more congenial to allowing people to execute their original visions. That would also be true of Showtime and some other places. The reason for that [approach], in addition to the revenue model, is that there is an idea at HBO about what constitutes quality programming.

In other contexts, there's a very simple way of analyzing the source of most behavior — it's either fear or faith. To the extent that any organization operates out of fear, mistrust of the audience or the people who generate the work, that's reflected in the content of the material. The opposite is also true in that if you believe in the material, you believe in the process, you believe in the programming, and you act out of that. It sounds so simple. But if you're able to do that then you maximize the chance of getting quality work.

PD: I find some similar themes, especially in the spirituality of your stories, in *NYPD Blue* and *Deadwood*.

DM: In the way I try to write, the theme is never separate from the character or plot. I think the moment you separate the elements out... if you take the fundamental idea of spirituality, I suggest that it would have something to do with an essential unity of all things. I would say all of my work is organized by either the sense of unity or the sense of separateness. That's another way of saying it's all fear or faith.

In *Deadwood*, due to the historical moment I was writing out of... I wanted to move back toward the genesis moment. And so I wanted to explore a world which has yet had no law of any kind. If *NYPD Blue* explored the life of people who, in the course of upholding the law lived outside the law, I wanted to move back in history.

Originally, I had proposed a series set in ancient Rome about the first guy who was arrested, St. Paul, who was taken to Rome for trial. HBO was very keen on it but was already developing a [similar] show. They asked me to think of another venue in which I could explore the same sort of environment. *Deadwood* was a purely illegal settlement, it was consciously outside the law, it was on Indian land, and they didn't want to pass any laws, so I studied it. That was how I came to that venue.

The idea is that the fundamental impulse that moves us toward some idea of civilization is that chaos is very uncomfortable. The absolute absence of individuation, as you're confused about who is who, and unrelieved and unrelenting profanity is really an assault on any idea of order. And it's tough when you experience that sort of thing. That's not where the world ends, that's where the world begins in earnest.

The question becomes, for the viewer, why stick around? Well, for the people of *Deadwood*, they have no choice. They have chosen that life. They have chosen to be outside the law. And that's why they speak the way they do. For the viewer, for whom the choice is volitional, it's a tremendous risk that you run being so inhospitable. My feeling was not to distort my sense of what the kind of primordial soup was in order to make the series more inviting. So those who came along, it's like going to war, it's a horrible experience, but people who have been through it feel bound to those who went through it with them. If you stick through an experience and you don't feel like you're being manipulated, and that the experience, however off-putting, is genuine, and you fight your way through, to my mind that's how America got born.

PD: As an artist, why did you choose television as your medium?

DM: Time. One of Robert Penn Warren's poems about Audobon, the guy who painted the birds, goes something like, "Tell me a story in this moment and century of mania. Tell me a story. Make it a story of great distances and starlight. The name of the story will be time. Tell me a story of deep delight." What we learn or fail to learn over time is what endows our experience with meaning, but to identify that as "theme" is to demystify the experience of life.

TV makes available the large canvas: the opportunity to portray lives over a big piece of time. For me, I have a pedestrian sensibility. I see things in small increments. I can render a moment without necessarily understanding its meaning. For that type of storyteller, the accumulation of moments is what ultimately shows the pattern of experience.

PD: From your early work on *Hill Street Blues* to *Deadwood*, do you see a historical evolvement?

DM: Every piece of work that I've ever done, which was successful, took place at a historical moment where everyone knew that the form or convention of the work I was doing was dead. *Hill Street Blues* was a show that was impossible to follow, that no one would ever watch, because it didn't have enough closure. When *NYPD Blue* came on the air, the one hour drama was dead. The police drama with continuing storylines was done. The last thing anyone thought would be successful was a western.

PD: What's next?

DM: When you begin to say "What's next" you've already lost your way. So you say "this will work, this won't work." What you have to do is submit yourself to the spiritual moment and you take what it gives you. It's the spirituality that you bring to the premise. If you're able to subordinate

Deadwood

yourself to bringing that moment alive, it's always going to work. You can't fake that stuff. The reason I won't give the network my scripts is because my responsibility is to the characters and the world.

PD: You don't show your scripts — they're cool with that?

DM: If they're making money, they don't care. They regard the artists as a necessary inconvenience anyway. Essentially, what they want is deniability. If it works, I thought of it. If it doesn't, it's not my fault. If you don't give them the script then it's not their fault.

PD: That's great.

DM: It's not, I've spent decades trying to sell out; I just couldn't figure it out.

PD: People reading this book may be college students or recent graduates. Would you say something to beginning writers?

DM: It is hard, and the first thing to understand is that it is hard. The moment of creation is antithetical to the things we need to live and breathe and put one foot in front of the other. You have to find a way to suspend the requirements as a living breathing person in order to give yourself to the requirements of your work. That's hard. In basketball, when a guy comes in to dunk the ball, and the defensive guy swats it away, they'll sometimes say, "don't come in here with any weak shit." If you're coming to the hole, you better come with everything you have. I would say that to any aspiring student. It's not a game and it isn't for sissies. If you want to do good work, doing good work must be your organizing passion. If you want to make a good living, and if you can do good work at the same time, great. You may make a good living or you may not, but you're certainly not going to do good work [unless it's your passion]. It's like having a child, or anything worthwhile; it's conceived and executed in blood and suffering. And if you want me to tell you something prettier, I will, but it won't be true.

This is the business of life which is the business of art to glorify. You struggle. And it's hard and, for the most part, daily, hourly, we fail. I fail and I fail and I live by failing and trying to find some grace in failure, and that's the nature of my work, and there is a kind of exultation in that and a consolation in knowing that you're doing, for better or worse, what you were born to do, but that's all it is. The rest is just conversation — the awards, the money.... If I could have chosen a different way, I would have. It's the way I'm built. You have to give yourself to that. It's the essence of creating art to do so in humility. You're giving yourself to something else. So those are all things that the beginning student ought to live into, and then, you know, in accepting that there's a kind of joy.

CHAPTER 2

HOW SHOWS GET ON TV AND THE TV SEASON

Fasten your seatbelt — here comes a heady two-year ride from the first glimmer of a new series twisting through one year of development and then barreling through a full season on the air. We'll be touring the traditional network cycle, though you already know from Chapter One that TV is changing. Currently, some cable stations premiere series in unusual months so they don't compete with the network season, and some networks are testing year-round production so they stay competitive with cable, especially during the summer. I'll discuss those variations at the end. But now, take a look at the chart (Chart 2.1).

"Year One" represents the months of forming and selling a new series. See the dividing line before May? That's when a new show first gets picked up by a network. In "Year Two," we'll follow a series that's in production. Month by month, you'll experience the process as if watching your own project grow up.

Let's begin by making believe you have a great idea for a television series. Screech! That was the sound of brakes. You're not likely to get your original show made if you're a beginner. At least, you're not going to do it by yourself. For decades, the custom has been to climb the ladder: You'd join a staff and go up the ranks until a network invites you to propose a series of your own. By then, the reasoning goes, you'd understand the way things work so you could reliably deliver an episode every week. No novice could have enough experience. Simply, no one would listen to you no matter how interesting your idea might be.

Chart 2.1 Traditional Two-Year Development and Production of a New Show

	Year One - Developing a new show												
	Apr	May	June	July	Aug	Sept	Oct	Nov	Dec	Jan	Feb	Mar	Apr
Create Proposal	■												▨
Production Co.		■											
Go to Studio			■										
Go to Network				■	■								
Pilot Script						■	■						
Green-Light									■				
Pilot Season											■	■	
Pick-Ups													■
Staffing													
Write Like Crazy													
Debut Show													
Finish Season													
Hiatus													

So let's back up and understand why beginners don't create new series. (I know, we haven't even gotten to the first month, but hold on, you will get on the track.) Consider what a drama series does: It manufactures hour-long films that air every week and continue (the producers hope) for years. Your ability to come up with a pilot (the first episode) doesn't prove you can write episode seven, or 20 or the 88th episode at the end of four years. It doesn't necessarily demonstrate that the series has the "legs" for anyone else to derive a full season, either. (Having "legs" means a show has the potential to generate enough stories to last a long time.) And it surely doesn't guarantee that you would know how to run a multi-million dollar business with hundreds of specialized employees (actors, set-builders, editors, office staff, directors, truckers, camera-people, electricians, composers… without even counting writers).

Television series aren't bought or sold on ideas, but the ability to deliver on those ideas.

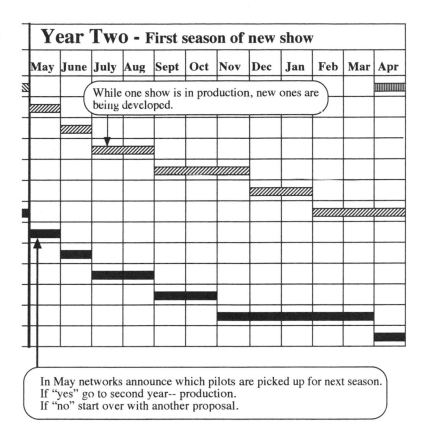

Now, don't freak. There are ways. The closed loop of staff writers becoming show-runners who hire staff writers who will one day be show-runners is loosening. Sometimes feature filmmakers who have clout but no television experience are paired with TV veterans. A second infusion of outsiders are the twenty-something producers. Since some outlets pursue teen audiences, they tend to prefer writers under 30. But could they have the experience to run a show? Here's how it worked at *The O.C.*

At 27 years old, Josh Schwartz, creator of *The O.C.*, became the youngest person in network history to produce his own one-hour series. He was a junior at the USC School of Cinema-Television when he sold a feature script for half a million dollars. A few months later, he sold his first TV pilot. And suddenly he was a TV producer, though he never spent a day on the staff of a series. Fox supplemented him with *Sex and the City* writer Allan Heinberg, who helped structure stories for the first 13 episodes, and Bob DeLaurentis, who'd spent two decades running shows. De Laurentis oversees all aspects of production while Heinberg runs the writing staff. As for Schwartz, he writes or re-writes many of the episodes. In an article in the *New York Times*, Schwartz commented, "It's not like writing a movie — you still have to learn how to map out a season, how to track characters. It's not something I could've done by myself for the first time. You need people who've been through it. Who know how to build to sweeps, or this is how a teaser works. I had to get educated."

That brings us to your starting point on:

YEAR ONE
APRIL

Create Your Proposal

So, here you are with your fresh idea — though I hope you have more going for you than that, even if you've never worked in television. For example, Aaron McGruder, creator of *The Boondocks* comic strip, teamed with film-maker Reginald Hudlin to create a series that attracted network interest. Not that you need a nationally syndicated strip, but do arm yourself with some-thing, at least accomplishment as a screenwriter. One of my former students (described in Chapter Seven), parlayed his credit on a quirky independent film *But I'm a Cheerleader* into several steps that led to writing a pilot for the WB (with his writing partner). Leverage whatever is special about you.

In this early stage, you're not aiming to shoot a series, only to land a meeting with a production company that has a track record. So your first goal is to be "adopted." For this, you'll need the same tool that will carry you all the way to the network, so everything else rests on square one, when you're on your own. Let's assume your idea has been percolating all winter, and now in April you're ready to form it into a presentation of some kind. But what kind? Actually, this stage doesn't offer the clear guidelines you'll find in the other steps. You'll need to discover the most compelling way to put across your unique concept. With that in mind, here are five possibilities:

(1) Write a TV Format

That term "format" can be confusing because it's used in different ways throughout filmmaking. "Format" may refer to a film stock or camera lens, to the way a script is laid out on a page, or even a genre or franchise. In this context it means a series proposal. Though a format isn't an exact process, certain components are advisable because you'll be asked about them in meetings anyway. In reality, most formats aren't even written except as notes for a network pitch. But I suggest you write everything, for now, to clarify your show for yourself and a production company. Lay it out this way:

Cover page: Find a title that grabs attention and suggests the tone of the show (funny, scary, dramatic, provocative, comforting, whatever). The title will probably change; think of it as a toe in a doorway. Underneath, identify the franchise or general category (i.e., teen drama, sitcom, political thriller, dramedy…). If it's based on something (book, play, movie, cartoon) you'd better say so, but make sure you have clear rights to the underlying work. Your credit is "Written By" or "Created By" and that goes on a separate line. Place your contact information at the bottom of the page. If you're represented by an agent or manager, of course, the cover is done by their office and your agent will be the contact.

Do register the completed format with the Writers Guild (specifics on that are in the Appendix). But do not put your WGA registration number on the cover — it's tacky. Also don't include any dates or draft numbers. Every draft you deliver is the first, untrammeled and never before revealed to human eyes — or that's what you'd like the producer to think. (No one wants something that's been rejected or gathering dust.)

On the top of page one, write a "Log Line." You've encountered that term in screenwriting classes, but did you know it originated in television? For decades, television station owners have been required by the FCC to keep a log of everything they broadcast. These had to fit on a line, like "Lassie finds lost boy." Then *TV Guide* and newspapers began printing short episode summaries like this one from *Joan of Arcadia*: "Joan learns the downside of vanity when God asks her to take a cosmetics class."

Soon the promotional tag found its way to movie posters, as in: "Tom Cruise stars as Nathan Algren, a heroic American military officer hired by the Emperor of Japan to train the country's first army. After being captured by his Samurai enemies, Algren becomes unexpectedly inspired by their way of life and fights to defend what he has come to love." Or, for a simpler example: "The women of Stepford have a secret." Before long, either full log lines (like the one from *The Last Samurai*) or "hooks" (like the one from *The Stepford Wives*) became necessary to pitch films, episodes, and series, not merely to log them or advertise.

A log line for a series may be less specific than the story summaries you'll use for individual episodes. The goal is to orient a listener (yes, listener, not reader) to your project, to catch an executive's attention. "MTV Cops" is a famous log line for *Miami Vice* from an era when MTV was new and hot. When he was first presenting *The O.C.*, Josh Schwartz knew the Fox network was looking for an updated *Beverly Hills 90210*, so he pitched his show as "90210 on the beach in Orange County," and later admitted that was a Trojan horse to set up a far more nuanced show.

Once your log line sizzles, take the first couple of pages of your format for an Overview. This is not a summary of the pilot (a common mistake) but an introduction to the world and the quest of the whole series, including location, style, tone, context, and, most of all, characters. Though full characterizations come later, the main cast must be mentioned up front. Use brief tags like "a single, middle-aged probation officer who adopts a child from one of her cases" (from Allison Anders' series proposal *In the Echo*); "a 29-year-old Congressional aide running against her boss" (from Rod Lurie's proposed *The Capital City*).

Within this Overview, suggest springboards for future episodes so decision-makers believe the series has legs. That is, state the source of future episodes, for example: Each week Joan gets a new challenge from God; each week the detectives pursue three cases, walking a thin line between vigilante justice and the job. As in any fiction writing, make 'em laugh, cry, be scared or angry or fall in love. The overview may be as far as you get in a pitch, so make it soar.

Follow the Overview with the centerpiece of any series: characters. If viewers don't root for your main cast, if they're not compelled to find out how the people are coping or loving or fighting back each week, you don't have anything. Remember, TV drama isn't really about the concept; it runs on the emotional fuel of endless character arcs, as discussed in Chapter One.

Take one page each for the few leading roles. I said few. Yes, you've seen excellent ensemble shows with casts in double-digits, but in a proposal, the listener's eyes will glaze over after you get past your third or fourth character. So focus on one fascinating, eminently castable character and engage us in her spirit and goals. You can do that again with roles for antagonists or partners, providing their connections to the protagonist are gripping. Beyond those few, summarize the secondary cast with only a tag for each, even if those parts will grow later.

(handwritten: for ASSIGNMENT: pilot in 2 page treatment -ish + 12 episodes — loglines 1-5 sentences each, (consisting) EP# 7 1-2 pages)

After the characters, you need to tell some stories. You might summarize a potential pilot in a couple of pages. (More about pilot writing in a second.) But networks really need the sense of a mid-season episode because that's a window to how the show functions every week. Some proposals focus on episode seven. Some list log lines for five to 10 potential episodes. Some describe the long arc and the end of the quest after five years on the air. Whichever method suits your series best, be sure you communicate an arena so rich that its possibilities seem endless.

That's it for standard components, but that's not it for a proposal. People refer to series pitches as dog-and-pony shows, and so far I haven't suggested any special enticements, furry or otherwise. Try photos, artwork, clippings, endorsements, biographies — come up with something fun. But don't do the baked goods angle; it's been tried, and readers get annoyed. You know, placing your proposal in a cake so the executive is sure to notice it. However, if your show is set in a bakery, maybe you should get cooking!

(handwritten: plus the special enticement (a $100?) Surveillance photos? 48 hrs?)

(2) Write a Pilot

Pilot scripts are assigned by networks in the course of development, and I'll tell you how that works when we get to September on the chart. (We're still only in April.) Normally, producers proposing a new series don't go in with a pilot already written because it's too expensive for something not likely to succeed (most proposals die, and so do most pilots). Also, network reactions might change the series. Why spend $30,000 or more for a script about a hermaphrodite in a beauty pageant when the network will only buy if the contestant is a poodle? But if your writing is not known, and you're passionate that a sample would convince readers, then speculating a pilot could be smart strategy.

J. Michael Straszynski, creator of *Babylon 5*, is said to have written all five years of his series while he was on the staff of a *Star Trek*, so *Babylon 5* was finished before he ever proposed it. But don't try that at home, folks. *(handwritten: !!)*

Short of writing 100 episodes, the worst you risk is another unsold script. If it's well-written, a pilot can serve as a writing sample along with any other screenplays or episodes. And as soon as you have clout (or know someone who does), you can take it off your shelf.

(3) Write a "Backdoor Pilot"

A backdoor pilot is a two-hour movie, and might be a clever way to propel a series. The game involves writing a pilot that masquerades as a movie, and, in fact, works as a closed story. But the seeds of subsequent tales and promising character developments are embedded in a situation that could easily spring many episodes.

You could offer it as a screenplay and be thunderstruck when someone else observes that it could lead to a series. Or you could come clean with your intentions up front. Depends on with whom you're dealing, but you certainly should tell an agent what you have in mind. Getting a television movie produced may be easier than a series, and a backdoor pilot gives a network a chance to hedge the bet. If the movie does well, you have a great shot at the series. If it doesn't, you still have a movie.

(4) Create a Presentation Reel

A show-runner once invited me to his office to discuss a series that had suddenly landed in his lap. He didn't have a clue about it, he said uneasily; it was loosely based on a hit movie and had been sold as a series on the basis of a 15-minute reel made by one of the movie's producers who didn't have time to do the show. So the newly anointed executive producer was hastily interviewing writers to find the series. The problem was that 15 minutes of "possible scenes" using the movie producer's actor friends (who would not be in the actual series either) didn't add up. Not that the 15 minutes weren't cinematic — they were beautifully atmospheric — but the people in the office were TV writers looking for the kinds of elements I've told you about: a) springboards suggesting where stories would come from; b) characters with potential for long arcs; c) some sort of quest or motor for the star. The reel turned out to be sort of a Rorschach test: everyone came up with a different show... which meant no show at all, finally.

Even if you're not a Hollywood movie producer who can sell a series off a few scenes, a reel might be helpful if used cleverly. Think of the dog-and-pony show, and imagine an executive in his office. It's 4 o'clock and he's been taking pitches every 20 minutes since his breakfast meeting at 8:00. You walk in with a DVD. Yes, I think he might wake up for that.

If you want to try, here are some tips:

Be careful it doesn't scream student film. You know: the long zoom in to the doorknob which is ever so beautifully lit and the reflective moments laden with symbolism. Often, student films aim at film festivals where their art is appreciated. In television, which moves faster, those same qualities may come off indulgent. So make sure your reel looks professional and suits the medium.

Keep it short enough so you have time to pitch before or after the film, including the set-up time. You may have only 15 minutes, total, in the meeting.

Do pitch the show. The reel is only eye-candy. Unlike the movie producer, you're not going to get away with not knowing how the series is going to work.

Have fun. Creative, original filmmaking can be an exciting calling card as long as the series would be able to sustain your approach.

(5) Attach a "Package"

A "package" consists of "elements" that enhance your project's profile. At one time, packages emphasized actors, especially ones who have succeeded in other series on the network, or movie stars. Certain "packaging agencies" still pride themselves in assembling all the creative talent (writers, producers, directors, actors) from their own shop and "attaching" them. Ah, there's another bit of jargon. When someone is "attached," that means he or she has committed to work on your show; that's a legal agreement, not just an "expression of interest," which doesn't count.

But the notion of packaging is changing radically in our volatile industry. Now studios are asking developers to include plans to exploit new shows on YouTube and MySpace. That request isn't casual; it presumes that someone who creates a TV series is simultaneously creating an Internet presence based on dramatic material, not merely advertising. It also places the emphasis on the imagination of the pilot writer/series creator rather than passing along ancillary markets to the production company. In fact, Internet episodes are at the core, not "ancillary" in this approach. So in the future you'll need to offer far more than a script.

Go ahead and try them all — one through five — if you have the time and money. But that would take another year. So to stay on our cycle, let's make believe you've created a terrific format, and backed it up with impressive writing samples. Now you move ahead to square two:

MAY

THE PRODUCTION COMPANY

You're on the hunt for a production company with your new series as bait. In May, you might get a producer's attention because the previous season has ended and work for the new one has not quite begun. If your proposal is ready sooner, you could also "put out feelers" in April during "hiatus." (You'll hear about the hiatus in Year Two.) Now, you need a company that can get you into both a studio and a network. Better yet, try to meet a show-runner who has an "open commitment" or "blind overall deal," which means a network is obligated to buy a show from him. Who knows, he just might be searching for something new.

But how are you going to find him? Through your agent; like it or not, that's how this industry works. Any competent agent knows who's willing to take series pitches, who is between shows, who might spark to your idea, who is willing to deal with a beginner, and who has relationships at the kinds of outlets that fit your show. The agent can put you in the room. So if you already have an agent, you can skip this section. NOT! Don't ever lie back and think an agent is going to do it all for you. To paraphrase: Agents help those who help themselves. If you don't have one, see Chapter Six, "How to Break In."

But what if you're determined to plow ahead on your own? It's not impossible to get to production companies, and in some cases they may be more accessible than agents. Read the "trades" (*Daily Variety* and *The Hollywood Reporter*) to scope who's interested in developing new series. If you have the magic bullet for a company who needs to get with the times and climb back to the top, or if you're young, talented, have some awards or credits, and an aggressive personality, you may well get past the receptionist. Part of the technique is finding the perfect match to your sensibility and your project. And part of it, quite frankly, is age.

I'll be candid with you about this issue. I'm sure you've heard about age discrimination in Hollywood. Some networks tend to chase young demographics, though not all are the same; in fact the top cable outlets and sophisticated network dramas prefer talent that has been honed. Still, the youth bias has created an opportunity for young writers. Very young. I know of a high school student whose home-made pilot was seriously considered, though it never sold.

At USC, my graduate screenwriting students range from mid twenties to mid thirties, so one year I joked to a class that they'd better not turn 30, just keep turning 29. Well, in the fall I got a call from Jennifer, a good writer who'd graduated the previous spring. She was upset because she applied for a writing job and the secretary asked her age. (That's illegal, by the way.) Jennifer, who had just celebrated her 30th birthday, remembered my joke and quickly answered "29." "Oooh, I'm sorry," the secretary cooed, "our ceiling is 26."

You may have heard about the writer who was hired on *Felicity* on the basis of being 18, and fired when she was discovered to be (gasp!) over 30. But the point for you is being young might help you get a meeting. After that, you'll have to wrangle not to lose your project to more seasoned writers, but right now we're talking about first steps.

Whatever your tactic, start by researching television production companies that do projects like yours. At the tail of each episode you'll see a list of producing entities. Sometimes several logos appear because an expensive series may spread the cost among various backers, so to find out who is actually developing series, try phoning the show or the network and asking. Other resources include websites, *The Hollywood Creative Directory*, the Library of the Writers Guild of America, and the Academy of Television Arts and Sciences. Information on all those is in the Appendix.

Once you have your targets, write to them and follow with a call asking to pitch your series idea. Don't mail the format, but if you can catch the reader with a beguiling few sentences, you may flush out someone curious enough to take a brief meeting. You don't need to wait for a response from your first choice before hitting up a second place. Contact them all at once.

At the meeting, you need to hook the listener quickly. Of course, you hope that listener is an executive producer or head of the production company. But if you're shunted off to an assistant, go ahead anyway. Make an ally so you'll have a chance to repeat the pitch to the decision maker another day.

What are they looking for? Energy. That's amorphous, I know, but it covers the sense that the series has possibilities. Remember, a series pitch is not the same as telling a movie story where the plot beats need to be in place. This is the first step in a long development process, and if this company becomes involved, they'll probably steer you toward revisions so the project will sell, or so it fits in a specific time slot, or competes with other series coming down the pike. They'll be watching how flexible you are, wondering if they'd be comfortable working with you for years, kind of a blind date. If you're defensive or reluctant to revise your precious property, they'll wish you luck trying to do it all by yourself — elsewhere.

They'll be checking whether the concept is viable; that is, whether they can physically produce it each week within a likely budget. But they won't ask that question unless you satisfy two other qualifications: (1) The show is completely new and unique, and (2) the show is exactly like what has succeeded before. Yes, it's a paradox. The solution is to be original within a franchise, even if that franchise is re-interpreted, as I discussed in the first chapter when I mentioned *Deadwood* as a contemporary version of the Western, and how *ER* differs from the old doctor series.

And, of course, you know what every TV series needs above all. Come on, you know the answer: Characters. The heart of your pitch is how fully you engage the buyer in the people you have created. But you already know that from your format, because you're well prepared.

So let's imagine you've pitched to a few executive producers and settled on one company that has everything: a studio deal, the juice to take you to a network, the ability to deliver the show, the willingness to keep you in the loop even though you're a beginner; and, most of all, they "get" your idea. You've found a creative home.

Maybe.

JUNE

THE STUDIO

Most production companies can't go to the networks by themselves. That's because network series are "deficit financed." Networks pay a fee to broadcast each program, around 75% of the cost of making it. For an hour-long drama which costs five million, the shortfall is around a million dollars per week. Every week. Companies don't have that.

Studios do. Think of the studio as the bank. From the point of view of a "suit," every time a studio endorses a series with one of the production companies on their lot they're taking a calculated risk. Four years will go by before they see any return on their investment, if they ever do, and most shows are cancelled before that. But, oh, when a show finishes the 88th episode, they hit what they call "the mother lode," "the jackpot,"

"Valhalla." Now they can sell the shows at a profit to syndication. A single hit underwrites years of failures. Will yours be that hit?

That brings us back to you. Probably, you have no agreement in writing with the production company. They're waiting to see if the studio will get behind this project. While you're away, the producer is talking to the Vice President for Dramatic Series Development of the studio where he has a deal. If the producer loves your show, he's pre-pitching it, maybe touting you as the next great thing.

Or not. He may be testing the waters to see if you're approvable before he sticks in his own toe. That might involve sending your writing samples to the studio executive, or even, quietly, to a contact at one of the networks. He may also test the general "arena" of the show, without specifically pitching it: "Any interest in a drama about house plants; I have a great fern." Prepare yourself, because if weak signals start coming back from the studio, he might drop the project; or he might keep the project but begin nudging you aside. You'll know you're being dumped if his conversation includes the term "participating," if he floats names of possible writers who aren't you, and if he talks up the title "associate producer." Sometimes that indicates an actual job, but it might be honorary, a way to shift you off the writing staff. Remember, you do have the right to say no and take your project elsewhere.

Let's imagine someone up there thinks you're interesting, at least enough to let you audition. So back you go to the studio lot. But this time, you and the producer will refine and rehearse your pitch, and together, you'll go to the V.P.

If your producer is powerful, and he has an open commitment or overall deal, the studio may let him make network appointments on his word alone. If he's not that strong, or he's not so confident of your show, he'll ask you to pitch your heart out again. Though your original format has been revised, you're essentially presenting what you developed in April. But now the producer is sitting next to you, and you're talking to a big desk.

Let's say you pass "Go." You advance to the next squares:

July and August

THE NETWORK

Traditional network television operates on the lemming model: All the creatures rush to the precipice at the same time and most fall off. You'll observe this behavior in most of the following stages.

All the networks "open" for new series pitches during the summer. They announce an exact opening date to agencies, and sometimes it's in the trades. Depending on their needs — that is, how many series are returning, how many slots they have to fill for the fall — some might begin meetings in June, and some might be hearing proposals as late as October. You want to get in there as soon as possible, before they're filled, though they're inundated no matter when you go. And the playing field isn't level. The big shots (companies with successful shows on the air) will have scarfed up prime broadcast real estate before your meeting is even scheduled.

The process is well-established and organized, though it looks like a shell game to an outsider. Each network may hear around 500 pitches during their open season. Out of those, each chooses 50 to 100 to become pilot scripts. Of those, 10 to 20 might be made into pilot films. Out of those, a few become series. Those numbers vary each year, but here's a simplified example from just one of the three major networks: Take 20% at each cut — 500 pitches yield 100 pilot scripts yield 20 pilots which yield five series (see Chart 2.2). That's a 10% overall chance of making a sale, if all else was equal, which, of course, it isn't.

Instead of dwelling on the odds, let's stay focused on your own opportunity. First, understand the human side of what you're walking into at a network. The Vice President for new dramatic programs, and the Director of new dramatic programs (along with a lesser title, Manager of new dramatic programs) are taking meetings all day, every day for three or four months. A parade of show-runners comes in and out of that office every 20 minutes or so. In fact, your own producer may be fielding other shows besides yours, which means they're in competition with you.

On the day of the meeting, everyone is dressed up. You'll gather in the lobby with your executive producer and possibly someone representing the studio, an agent from a major packaging agency (likely, the producer's agent), and other components of your package. That might mean a network-approved high-power writer who would guarantee the pilot script, or a television star.

I once went to a network pitch on a show where the lead actor was essential. When the day came, the actor was called to a dubbing session. And we couldn't change the appointment. So we went in with a blow-up of his head shot and sat it on a chair.

You'll have a cheering section in your meeting, and the first little while will seem like friendly greetings. Then the moment comes when the producer says, "You're on," the room falls silent, and all eyes are on you. Now, pitching to a network executive is a craft unto itself. Some execs nod, smile, and act interested. With others, it's like talking to Mount Rushmore. Regardless, keep your energy high. With the nice guy, you skip out of the meeting sure you just sold a series. With the mountain, you believe you failed. Neither might be true.

Chart 2.2 New Series Development at One Network (a hypothetical example)

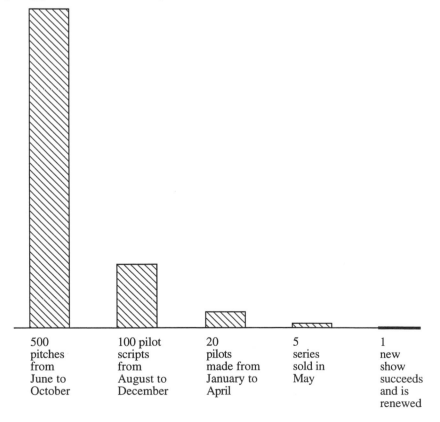

| 500 pitches from June to October | 100 pilot scripts from August to December | 20 pilots made from January to April | 5 series sold in May | 1 new show succeeds and is renewed |

If you haven't heard in a week or two, the studio (or your producer, depending on the network relationship) phones the network. They're usually pretty quick about saying no, and in that case, the studio will set up a meeting at the next network on the list. This can go on several times, but after three networks, and maybe a surreptitious call to basic cable, if you're not getting a nibble, they'll probably drop your project. Remember, the property is still yours at this point, and no one owes anybody anything.

But let's say you were funny and intriguing and fresh and unique — and the network thinks your show is just like another one that's a hit — so you pass "Go" again. Of course, you're not green-lighted to make a series — you know better than that by now. The assignment is only to write the pilot. That's the next group of squares:

SEPTEMBER TO NOVEMBER

THE PILOT SCRIPT

Whoever writes the pilot will have at least a "developed by" credit, and may even receive "created by" credit on the series. That will generate a royalty on every episode, and his name will appear on screen forever, even if the pilot-writer is long gone. Don't assume that's you unless your writing proves that only you can capture the style and world you've proposed.

Or have you already written the pilot? If you took a chance on it, the producer will wonder if it's going to hurt or help your prospects. That's a sticky situation because asking you to set aside your pilot in favor of someone else's draft is emotionally wrenching. But if you lose the whole deal because your pilot is less than mind blowing that's just as wrenching.

Some professional writers have built careers doing pilots for other people's shows. They're savvy about the ingredients any pilot needs, they bring a pedigree of successful series, and they know how to win over network readers. It's an oddity because these special pilot writers, who may earn up to half a million dollars for a one-hour script, usually are not the ones who will write the episodes each week, so network decision-makers are evaluating a hyped up version of the show. It's kind of a bait-and-switch where they're buying one writer's voice, but another will write the series.

Let's say they love your project because they love something about you — your hip writing style, insight into a subculture, your humor, your passion.

Or maybe you're just less expensive — $30,000 for the pilot script instead of half a million. Now the network calls the studio who calls the producer who calls your agent who calls you and you get a contract to write.

So, how do you do this thing? Pilots come in two flavors: **premise** and **ongoing**. A premise pilot begins with a "before" and propels the quest or situation the central character will tackle throughout the series. For example, *Northern Exposure* opened in New York City, where the lead character, Joel Fleischman, learns that his medical school scholarship requires him to work as a doctor in Cicely, Alaska. Joel fights to get out of this commitment but soon finds himself staring out a train window until he arrives at a frozen place where he's greeted by a moose. As we're drawn into his new world, we meet the characters who will become Joel's new relationships, and their arcs are set in motion.

In an ongoing pilot, the world of the show is in place and many of the characters are entrenched in their dramatic missions. The challenge is to reveal these characters and relationships without the aid of an outsider's introduction, which we had with Joel Fleischman. An example of an ongoing pilot was *ER*: a day in the life of an emergency room at a Chicago hospital in full swing. New characters arrived — Nurse Hathaway on a stretcher, and Carter as a young intern — but the elements of the show were already in play.

Whichever type of pilot you choose, you'll need the same ingredients. In addition to terrific writing, which includes building tension toward cliffhangers at act breaks and creating rich and provocative characters, just as you would in any episode (see Chapter Three for more about this), pilots have a special burden of exposition. Without the audience feeling it's being informed, you need to establish the rules of your world, the engine for future stories (springboards), and enough "backstory" (history) on the characters so their current situations are understandable. You want viewers riveted by the characters. Simply, your pilot has to make people tune in to episode two.

Some techniques are similar to beginning a feature, where audiences don't yet know the characters either. But features are easier because once people have bought tickets and are sitting in the dark, they'll give a movie time to unveil itself. Television has to grab people in the first minutes or they're clicking the remote. So, sure, use everything you know from theatrical screenplays in terms of presenting a new character, but start the story faster. Also, use everything you've learned about avoiding clunky exposition (bury it in an argument, play it in a scene instead of explaining, use visual evidence, parse it out in bits, reveal it as part of the plot instead of for its own sake, and so forth). If you're "living" your writing, instead of manipulating it, some of these problems may solve themselves. And if those central characters and your idea are as vibrant as the format you pitched, the pilot might come naturally.

Easy or difficult, 50 to 60 pages are going to be due at the network around Thanksgiving. From a network's point of view it will be the first draft. Of course, it won't. You will have gone through every step with your producer, and the studio may have read drafts as well. No one wants to take a chance this won't work, so if your drafts aren't delivering the spirit that landed this assignment, they'll bring in another writer, who will share the writing credit. So all through October and November you're rewriting like crazy — you and everyone else who's doing a pilot. And, true to the lemmings, everyone else's pilot is due at all the networks the same time as yours. All over town everyone is anticipating:

DECEMBER AND JANUARY

THE GREEN-LIGHT

Several possibilities: The network may send notes for a second draft of the pilot. If so, you'll gnash your teeth: What do they mean they don't like the central character — that's exactly who I pitched and that's who they bought! They wait until *now* to tell me they have another pilot too close to this, so we have to change everything! What am I supposed to do with a note like "not funny enough" when this drama was never supposed to be funny at all! No, I can't turn this drama about men in prison into a vehicle for Britney Spears! Huh???

After the gnashing, you'll sit with the producer and maybe your studio development person and figure out what you can fix, and what, if anything, may be left alone or argued. If they believe your situation is precarious, the studio may ask for a major rewrite. In any case, your finished script is due by Christmas — the same as everyone else.

And like everyone else, you're hoping your pilot script will be plucked out as one of the 20% or 30% that get "green-lighted." That means the network gives the production company the go-ahead to produce the pilot. These green-lights may be announced anytime from December through January. They lead to:

FEBRUARY TO APRIL

PILOT SEASON

Instead of snow, a climate of anxiety hangs in the sunny skies of Los Angeles in winter. It's accompanied by a giant sound of vacuuming, inhaling all unclaimed film crews down to the last grip and gaffer, all the sound stages, every available television director, and all the actors who cycle through pilots year after year in "holding deals" (contracts which hold an actor exclusive to a potential series). George Clooney was cast in 15 failed pilots before *ER*. Welcome to pilot season.

Though it begins with your script, the produced pilot is enhanced by "production values" (locations, techniques or personnel) that make it more expensive than a normal episode. For example, Disney spent a remarkable $12 million on the two-hour pilot for its 2004 series *Lost*.

When fully edited, a typical pilot will be 44 minutes long, the length of a network hour without ads. But once in a while a network asks for a 20 or 25 minute "presentation" instead, like a demo for a record company. That's bad news for you as the writer, because your finely honed 60 page script must be slashed to 30 pages, losing secondary story lines, nuance, and sometimes risking the sense of the show. Networks order these presentations anyway because they cost around two million, which is roughly half the cost of a pilot. If this befalls you, just sit down and cut the pages. You really don't have a choice.

Except for production revisions (for casting, location, timing, and so forth), the writer's work is essentially finished by February. Still, I advise you to stick as close as you can to the production. If the producers will let you, be on the set, see the "dailies," go to meetings. Of course, you know better than to breathe down the director's neck or stand in the way of rolling cameras. Just don't fade out after you've written "fade out."

By April, all the pilots in all genres at all the networks are edited and tested at the same time. This testing, incidentally, is a tribal ritual in itself. Unwitting tourists in Las Vegas (chosen because Vegas attracts visitors from all over the country) are given 10-dollar gift certificates in exchange for registering their reactions on an electronic dial while viewing a pilot. If something scores poorly, it may be re-edited; way too late to re-write, though. With the pilots done, it's time for:

MAY

PICK-UPS

All the lemmings arrive at the edge of the precipice at once — and off they go to New York by May. Isn't it strange that shows are (usually) produced in Los Angeles, and network and studio executives are based here, and the entire creation of the pilot happens on the West Coast, yet the verdict is rendered 3,000 miles away? That's because the decision is corporate, involving huge investments which impact parent companies and involve advertisers who (they hope) offset those costs. It's Big Brother time.

Once the pilots have gone, no one can do anything but wait. That doesn't stop studio executives from checking into top New York hotels and haunting lobbies where screenings are in progress upstairs. They can't really influence the outcome, can't attend screenings or discussions, so what do they hope to gain? Gossip — leaks, hints, a raised eyebrow that their show may go. Or die.

I once wrote a pilot for a company whose glory days were memorialized in posters of hit series lining the corridors. But the rooms off the corridors were empty. Every one of their series had concluded or been cancelled the season before. They fielded a number of possibilities, but only one went to pilot — mine. It was early May, and only one light was on in one office — the executive producer's. He went there every day and sat at the phone. He ate lunch at the phone. Waiting. Waiting for the call from New York. He sent his secretary to the city to listen for rumors, but she hadn't heard anything. I brought him lunch one day, but we didn't have much to talk about, staring at the phone.

Finally, in mid-May the call came: "We're not going to pick you up." There was no explanation — there never is — but post-game analysis guessed that too many similar shows were offered, or too many competing shops had early commitments, or too few slots were open, or none of the above.

But let's make believe your phone call is some version of "Pack your bags — we'll see you in New York." Your order will probably be in one of four categories:

• Full season

A network season is 22 episodes, though some shows do 24 or even 26. In reality, even an order for a full season is hedged: The pick-up (commitment to air) is "13 plus the back 9." That means 13 episodes will be broadcast, with the decision on the final 9 contingent on their performance.

• Short order

This is bad news for show creators. It means the network agrees to air only six episodes — or only four! If those hook an audience quickly, more episodes are ordered. But how many shows find their audiences in three weeks? With so many options, viewers might not even visit the newborn until week three. And some series take a while to get their legs. Historically, icons like the original *Star Trek*, *All in the Family* and other famously successful series took months before word of mouth alerted viewers to check them out.

Now, the heap of dead series, killed before people hardly knew they were on, casts a stench over creativity at the networks. Bottom-line network executives tend to avoid risks, but that policy backfires because fear-based decisions send some of the most creative producers and writers to cable where long orders are customary.

• Midseason

Midseason pickups may be the best news, some show-runners think. Though a late debut denies the show a spot on the fall schedule, and probably limits the number of episodes that would air the first year, some producers like it: Their show is removed from the crowd of September premieres and saved from the insistent pressure to be on the air in a few months. Networks also like midseason shows because they create an illusion of year-round programming which helps the network compete with year-round cable. And midseason replacements are a cushion against inevitable cancellations. If the network lets the show go ahead and produce a few episodes, pending a slot, you'll have the time to write as well as you did in the pilot.

That said, as the writer, you'll feel disappointed. You have to wait until late fall or early winter to find out when you're on the air. And it's hard not to wonder if you'll ever be given a place at all.

• Backup scripts

Backups are the smallest pick-up, accompanied by a better-than-nothing sigh. It means the network won't let you produce any episodes but would like to see additional scripts. They're holding on to the show because the concept interests them, but something in the pilot didn't work. It might be casting, tone, location, or something at the core — the direction of the stories themselves. This is a second opportunity to prove the series can work by actually writing up to five episodes, sometimes called "backup pilots." You, the writer, are in the spotlight, and assuming they haven't held back because the writing is weak, this can be your chance to shine.

Let's make believe you got a pick-up for 13 on the air. See the line before May in the diagram? Well, hold on because you're about to cross it to:

YEAR TWO

JUNE

Staffing

Hurtled out of the development chute, still tumbling, you land in June with three months to put an hour series on the air every week. That doesn't mean producing the first hour. It means scripts for the first five to seven episodes, plus three "in the can" (ready to air). But you have next to nothing. The sets have been struck and need to be re-built. You have no crew, no office, no production facility, no phones. And you urgently need a writing staff right now.

Shows that are ongoing or announced early aren't in this fix (and neither are cable series, but more about that at the end). Optimistic show-runners started reading sample scripts and speaking with agents as far back as February, especially if the pilot was attracting an industry "buzz." But without an actual order, they couldn't staff. And some producers are taken by surprise.

I was once hired on a staff in June and we didn't gather until the first week in July, though we were scheduled to premiere the first week of September. The executive producer, a highly regarded sitcom writer-producer, had done a pilot for an hour drama, outside his usual genre. Considered a "dramedy" (a hybrid of drama and comedy), it was a long shot. I think he was actually out of town on vacation when the pick-ups were announced; that's how unlikely he thought this would be. So there we sat in a temporary office lent by the studio — four adrift writers and the surprised show-runner. He opened with "Anyone have ideas for stories?"

But that's rare. With months to imagine winning this lottery, most show-runners are ready, and the instant the series goes, negotiations commence with writers. If you were in the mix from the beginning (if the concept was yours or you wrote the pilot), your deal is already in place. If you're trying to join a staff, June is when those jobs open and fill quickly, so your agent should have been pitching you in the months before.

The next chapter tells how a writing staff works, so we'll skip over that and assume by the end of June everyone is in place and writing has begun. It continues:

JULY AND AUGUST

WRITE LIKE CRAZY

Ditch the idea that summer is vacation time if you're writing for network television. July and August are the crazy-making months when the staff is turning out scripts as fast as they can. Though each show has its own rhythm, if you're in any writers' room, you'll be "breaking stories" around the table, dissecting outlines as they come in, and discussing early drafts by the other writers every week at the same time as you write your own. (In Chapter Four, I explain the steps of writing.)

Probably, the first episode exists: It's the pilot. But the audience might not discover your series the first week, or even the second. So in a way, the first three episodes will function as pilots. Episodes Two and Three have to reach a balance between orienting first-time viewers by reprising the overall "mission" and identifying the cast, while progressing the stories to hold people who watched before. If the pilot was a premise which deposited a character in a new environment or quest, then Episode Two is expected to deliver what happens there. It may be the most difficult and least rewarding episode on a show.

Think about it — the audience doesn't know the characters, so viewers are not yet emotionally invested. But neither do you have the benefit of the inciting situation or curiosity that sets the series in motion, since that happened the first week. Nevertheless, this "development" episode must sizzle with the tension and anticipation of the pilot. That calls for one of the more experienced writers — not you. Your earliest assignment might be Episode Four or Five, depending on the size of the staff.

While the staff is writing, production is rolling out shows. Probably, you'll be invited to sit in on casting guest stars in your own episode. Once shooting starts, "dailies" (unedited scenes) are screened almost every day. Go to the screenings, no matter how hard you're writing. After you hear how the dialogue plays, you might want to rework the cadence of a scene you're writing. Dailies also reveal the strengths of the actors. If chemistry between actors burns off the screen, you'll want to use it.

But don't get beguiled by stars. You've probably heard the joke about the starlet who was so stupid she slept with the writer. Well, that doesn't make sense in television where writers do have power, and smart actors know it. They'll want to have lunch with you to pitch stories for their characters. I was on one show where an actor researched each writer's birthday and sent exquisite hand-made cards; on another, an actor distributed coffee mugs personalized with each writer's name. Some show-runners warn new writers not to hang out with the actors, fearing they'll be too easily influenced. I say, go for it — talented actors contemplate their characters, and that can inspire you.

As the series evolves, the head writer must decide whether to let characters develop in a way he didn't foresee, or stick to the original plan. Some show-runners begin with a chart of story arcs for the whole season. In fact, one established series invites its large staff to a retreat in early June. On a whiteboard, they assign each character a color-coded marker and track the five main roles from episode one to 22 in a stack of horizontal lines. After all arcs are complete, they slice vertically, showing how the stories intersect (see chart 2.3). If you work for that executive producer, no one can abscond with the series.

But other show-runners have a freer approach. The team that headed *Northern Exposure* used to build their series "bible" as each script came along. In one episode, a writer would invent a brother for a character, or a secret past, or a private fear. These were listed as "facts to wax" and

Chart 2.3 Sample Character Arcs for a Season on One Series

Episodes

	1	2	3	4	5	6	7	8	9	10	11	12	13	14	15	16	17	18	19	20	21	22	Notes
Character "A"																							3 big arcs for series lead
Character "B"																							Begin major arc for next season
Character "C"																							Steady character
Character "D"																							Character "D" dies at end of season

distributed to the staff. After years, they accumulated a compendium of what various writers created — quite a different approach to a bible.

I used the term "bible" — no religious connotation (unless you worship the show). A TV bible is a document intended to help new writers and directors understand the rules of a series. Complete bibles contain elements similar to a "format" — a log line, franchise, an overview of springboards, tone, style, and the quest of the series, followed by character sketches and story guidelines.

The king of all series bibles was made for *Star Trek: The Next Generation*. At around 100 pages, it included intricate diagrams of the Enterprise, details on how the ship's bridge operates, definitions of technical terms, characterizations that not only summarized every crew member but also analyzed the relationship and history of each one with every other, an admonition of what to write and not write for the series; and it was accompanied by summaries of every story the show had ever aired, as well as every idea in the mill. *Trek* had to go this far because it was open to non-professional submissions. I think it was kind of self-defense against repeated questions from its many fans.

But that's extreme. Some bibles are just a few pages including the premise, character bios, and the kinds of stories they intend to tell. Others, like *Northern Exposure*, are amassed rather than generated. And, frankly, most shows don't bother with bibles at all. They take too much time when everyone is busy making the air date. But if one will be composed, now is the time.

While the staff writes and re-writes through the summer, network notes trickle down. Each episode is read by the network — Legal, and Standards and Practices, on top of the executive assigned to your show. Those notes go to the show-runner, so if you're a beginning writer he'll filter and interpret them; you won't interface directly with the network. Your boss is choosing when to fight the network brass and when to accommodate the notes. It's just part of the network landscape.

All this work leads to:

September and October

THE DEBUT

If it were a stage play, you'd have flowers and a party opening night. But in television, you're doing "post" on a later episode by the time the pilot airs. (Postproduction means everything after filming, like editing and scoring.) And that pilot was written a year ago, before the series was a glimmer in the eye of any of the current staff. Still, send up the fireworks in the parking lot after you watch it on TV like it was new.

Well, it is new, because once the show is broadcast, it feels like public property, out of the creative cocoon. "Overnights," which are quick national ratings, are on the show-runner's desk the next morning. He'll tell the staff to pay no attention to the numbers, just keep writing; and, indeed, lower level writers are shielded from marketplace pressures, temporarily. But how can you not feel buoyant if the show is liked, or disappointed if you played to an empty house? Just remember, it's not going to do any good to blame the network (look what they put us up against — of course we have no numbers), or blame viewers (they don't appreciate us because they're all... insert adjective), or blame your producer (he should've known the title sequence/opening scene/music/actor/whatever wouldn't work), or blame yourself (I have no talent). Hey, probably none of those is true. It takes time for a series to catch on. Assuming you really have 13 guaranteed on the air, and a few critics recommend the show in reviews, and the marketing people do their thing, and the audience does join you in Episode Two or Three, and becomes involved in the characters — then:

At Halloween — the end of October — the show-runner gets the call from the network: You've been picked up for the "back nine." You'll have an entire first season for the series to grow and stake its turf. Breathe out now.

NOVEMBER THROUGH MARCH

COMPLETING THE SEASON

When I used to work as a freelancer, I often made my whole year's salary between October and February. By then enough of the season is in place so some of the early tension is eased. Under an agreement with the Writers Guild, shows with full-season orders must give out two freelance assignments. These not only extend opportunities to new writers and those in "protected categories" (ethnic minorities or disabled, for example), but freelance scripts also can be auditions for the staff. They bring relief and fresh perspectives and stories to an exhausted staff. Or so the theory goes.

In reality, most shows are written entirely by the staff, and the few outsiders tend to be friends or writers coming off cancelled shows. Still, go ahead and pitch a freelance episode in the fall or winter. It's a good way to meet producers, and certainly a way to break in. (More about that in Chapter Six.)

In the absence of a written bible, if you're a freelancer needing the rules of a series, my advice is watch it a lot and check the Web sites. If the series is so new nothing can be found, and you've been invited in to pitch, the producer will messenger the pilot and some scripts to you. Maybe you'll get 10 minutes on the phone about their current story needs. Yeah, it's tough, but if they like your writing, and you bring areas the show can use, someone will guide you a little once you have an assignment.

Writing continues steadily until all 22 shows are in final drafts. Don't make Thanksgiving plans except dinner time. As for the winter break you had in school, you're not going anywhere this year. You'll have a few days off at Christmas and New Year's. Or maybe you'll be finishing a draft at home before the wrapping paper is off the floor.

Depending upon how well your series is pulled together (and that depends largely on the skill of the show-runner), you'll be slowing down at the end of February. In fact, your own episodes have probably been written, so you're sticking around for revisions, production, and polishes of scripts by other writers. Even if you're mostly done, follow everything through "post." Not only is the series very much alive with new episodes airing every week, but you want to preserve your position for the next year.

If the first season was a resounding success, the show-runner will have early notice it's been renewed. But plenty of first-time series are uncertain down to the wire, just like pilots. It's awful, from a writer's point of view. You want to create a season ender that entices viewers to watch in the fall, and yet if you're not being picked up for a second season, the impulse is to go out bravely and close the story arc. Not knowing, the producer will opt for the cliffhanger, while the staff hangs on its own cliff. This happens during:

APRIL

HIATUS

Vacation — yay! For a network series writer, spring is like summer and winter holidays rolled into a mass getaway. The hiatus might last three months from late March until July, or be as limited as a month and a half — April to late May. If the staff is assured it's coming back, this is a fling of freedom. If everyone's worried, the agents sniff around for a jump to another show. In any case, the break is total. Many shows lock their offices and leave nothing but an answering machine; even the receptionist is gone — far away, after 40 weeks non-stop.

This brings us all the way back to where we started, as the cycle spins around and around and around.

An Alternate Universe

That traditional network paradigm is broadly accurate for, well, traditional networks. But in the alternate universe of cable television you'll encounter different patterns. For example, *Deadwood* on HBO did 12 episodes per year, not 22. The entire season was written in winter and spring, so all scripts were finished before any production begins. They started shooting around the end of July, which is actually similar to networks, but *Deadwood*'s next season didn't begin airing until the following March, when many network shows are winding down. You'll read more about this in the "Guest Speakers" sections, where David Milch, the show's creator, comments on how doing a series for HBO after years at a network affects him as an artist.

Similarly, in the "Spotlight on Writing Procedurals" following Chapter Three, Melissa Rosenberg of *Dexter* reveals several differences she experienced at Showtime after years writing for network shows.

Here's another configuration: In 2000, Showtime optioned a British series with the strange title, *Queer as Folk*. Everyone assumed the American version would be so diluted it would lose the guts that made it worth buying. After all, nothing like that had ever been done here. Then, one Sunday, writers Ron Cowan and Daniel Lippman, who had struggled to create television movies about gay life within network standards, happened to read about this option in a newspaper. They got in touch with Showtime, and said they'd do it, if they got complete creative freedom — unimaginable at a network. Not only did Showtime give them their freedom, but also a full 22-episode order. In the Writers Guild membership magazine *Written By*, Cowan and Lippman said, "The handcuffs had been removed; we'd been released from the prison of network television. And the question posed to any newly freed man was posed to us: 'Now that you have your freedom, what do you plan to do with it?'"

In the future, you'll be entering an industry whose long-established systems are no longer as certain as in the traditional model. The predictable cycles are changing, and new outlets are experimenting with different ways of making and delivering stories to an expanding audience. So ask yourselves a version of Cowan and Lippman's question: Now that you'll have choices, what do you plan to do with them?

SUMMARY POINTS

Creating a new TV show follows specific steps from concept to network sale.

Once on the air, a show also relies on definite steps of development from a pilot, through writing and producing, to being renewed.

In the earliest stages, a show creator might write a format or pilot script in the hope of getting a green-light to produce the pilot, which is a prototype for the series. The pilot together with a "package" competes with other new series for a time slot, known as a "pick up."

A full 22-week traditional season would occupy the writing staff through an intense 40-week schedule before hiatus. Some new series get only "short orders," though.

On cable stations, the seasons and production times may differ but the general development process has the same creative components and opportunities for writers.

GUEST SPEAKER: STEVEN BOCHCO

Steven Bochco is creator and executive producer of *NYPD Blue* and many other series including *Hill Street Blues*.

PD: You're generally regarded as a pioneer, from *Hill Street Blues* all the way up to some exciting experimental stuff. Of the other cop shows you've done — *Hill Street Blues*, *Murder One*, *NYPD Blue*, *Cop Rock* and *Brooklyn South* — do you see any trajectory in what you want to do with television, from *Hill Street on*?

SB: Yes and no. I don't think we started *Hill Street* with any grand notion of changing the medium. I mean, we just created the show and then, at some point in the process, the show began creating the show. And by that I mean that certain things that we committed to conceptually forced us to do other things that complemented the original things we'd done.

When you end up creating a show with seven, eight, nine characters — in response to that, ask yourself how can you appropriately dramatize that many characters within the framework of an hour television show? And the answer is that you can't. So you say, okay, what we have to do is spill over the sides of our form and start telling multi-plot, more serial kinds of stories. Even though any given character may not have but three scenes in an hour, those three scenes are part of a 15-scene storyline that runs over numerous episodes. So that was simply a matter of trying to react to the initial things we did. The show began to dictate what it needed to be. Probably the smartest thing that Michael [Kozoll] and I did was to let it take us there instead of trying to hack away to get back into the box. We just let it spill over the sides.

PD: So you didn't go into it thinking you were going to have 14 characters?

SB: No, we just sort of started out knowing what we didn't want to do. We didn't want to do the typical cop shows that we'd been involved in writing and producing for years because we didn't feel like we had a lot more to bring to that kind of programming. So the idea of focusing, to some degree, on these cops' personal lives was appealing. But that's all we had when we started, and it just kind of organically evolved.

PD: It's generally considered the progenitor of a whole wave of television that is not necessarily about cops at all.

SB: The next show that adopted our style was *St. Elsewhere*. That came on the next year with my friend Bruce Paltrow. They were downstairs, we were upstairs. One of the reasons people, to this day, erroneously credited me with *St. Elsewhere* is that it had so much similarity in style and form.

But then it's time to move on. When we started looking at *NYPD Blue*, I didn't have a lot of interest in doing another cop show unless I could do something with the form that would really change television. That was the only time that I really, consciously thought, here's an opportunity to do something in the medium that could change it.

PD: What were some specific things you wanted to change?

SB: It was nothing exotic. I just really wanted to expand the language and visual palette. And a cop show seemed a more legitimate canvas on which to do it rather than a family or legal drama. There's just something so gritty and blue collar about a cop show that the language seems organic. So I thought, if you're going to fight that battle, you have to justify doing it on the grounds that not doing it is really less than realistic.

PD: I think that's what's struck me about all of your shows. Above all, they're honest and real. These people are the way people are.

SB: Some of them are racist and some are cowards and some are frightened and some are mean spirited, and you know, some people just don't like each other. It's politics in the workplace, so that's the stuff you always go to. And, you know, David [Milch] and I had always wanted to work together again. He wanted to do a cop show. I was less interested in a cop show but wanted to do this thing to change television. I didn't want to do it in a vacuum, but there really hadn't been a one-hour hit since *L.A. Law* in 1986 and here we were in 1991. The hour drama was in the toilet and that's my business, so my business was in the toilet.

I thought the only shot we had at reviving the form is if we were willing to compete with cable television. So that was my pitch to ABC when they wanted a cop show from me. I remember Bob Iger [now President and COO of the Walt Disney Company, which owns ABC] saying to me, "I made a huge deal with you because I wanted another *Hill Street Blues* and what did I get — a 16-year-old doctor [*Doogie Howser*] and a bunch of cops who sing." So I said: I'll give you the cop show you want, but be careful what you wish for, because the price is this, the language and the nudity. It's one thing to say yes to that theory, and it's another thing to get that script, and you've got something that's never been seen or heard before in television. Originally, the show was supposed to go on in the fall of 1992, and it didn't because we couldn't agree on language and sex. I refused to water it down. I said you take it as it is or we'll move on. So it got postponed a year.

I remember flying... with the president of our company and my attorney and we had a meeting... with all the creative, legal, broadcast standards executives, and they spent an hour and a half saying why we couldn't make the show. And we spent an hour and a half explaining why we couldn't make it any other way. I flew back home convinced that it was a dead show. And, finally, they came around. I created a real paper trail along the way, [knowing] that given half a chance, they'd renege. And they did try on various occasions, but I'd been so conscious about the paper trail, I could always go back and say here it is.

In the months before the show went on we were getting thousands and thousands of pieces of mail — they were coming in sacks every week, from the religious right who'd spent a million dollars taking out full-page ads in major newspapers in America, beating us over the head for being pornographic. But, of course, no one had seen the show, which was very offensive. It would have been one thing if they'd seen it and taken issue with it. But these ads were so cynical, manipulative, and untrue about the content of the show — I mean, everything I wanted to do, I wanted to accomplish.

Interestingly, we succeeded, not by the show itself but by the panic-stricken religious right because they created a stir that no publicity machine in the world could duplicate. And thank God they did because given all the anxiety about the show, if we had faltered a moment in the ratings then I think we would have been gone in three weeks. But we came out of the shoot huge.

PD: Do you think that the same story could be told today if someone went in with something the religious right opposed in the same way?

SB: No I don't, I don't. Not today. Maybe next year, maybe five years from now, because all that is cyclical. A lot of it is tied to election cycles. More than anything right now, it's a function of corporate terror. As the television industry has become more and more vertically integrated, all the networks are now divisions of huge corporate entities, and in that environment they're fearful of the government and of advertisers and of their own stockholders, that it's just fear of not rocking the boat, it's just get the ratings, make the ad time, get the dollars. Ultimately, it's a self-defeating attitude.

PD: Which brings us to the question of cable: David [Milch] mentioned having more power at HBO. You took a shot at a cable show too...

SB: We developed a show for F/X about the war in Iraq, which was a very different experience. They really have a creative model that's 180 degrees opposite from the broadcast networks. They want to be different. They want to be controversial, edgy, out there with stuff that isn't being done anywhere else. It puts them in a position of being an alternative universe and so, with the exception of the available dollars because it's still a small dollars universe, there aren't too many differences in what you can do at F/X compared to what you can do on HBO. So it was a lot of fun.

There are very bright network executives over there, terrific guys and committed to their shows, which is very refreshing — they've got *The Shield*, *Nip/Tuck*, and *Rescue Me*. They're trying to find shows that are unique, that brand them in a certain way. And they came to us with this idea. My initial impulse was, "Gee, I'm the wrong person to do that." I've never been in the military.

PD: You've never been a cop either.

SB: True. It's why I rethought my position, among other things. I also have a political point of view about the war that I don't have about cops in general. I've always maintained, for myself, a very strict prohibition of using these shows as any kind of a platform for my own political positions on anything. I'm not going to say it's wrong to do that, I'm just not comfortable to do that. Norman Lear was always unabashed on his political positions both personally and professionally. And that's great. I just never wanted to politicize my shows in any way. I've had a show on primetime continuously for the last 24 years, since January 1981, and, you know, that's a real responsibility and a real trust. And I just personally, am not comfortable using that position to proselytize.

PD: What do you think you owe the audience?

SB: A good story.

PD: And a good story to you means...?

SB: A good story to me means all kinds of things. First, a good story has a beginning, a middle, a complication, and resolution. In some fundamental way, that gives the audience a certain pleasure and satisfaction in having spent their hour in a worthwhile pursuit; and if, in addition to that, it makes them think about something or gives them a different point of view about something, then great. If it engages their sensibilities in a way they haven't anticipated — great. Those are all wonderful bonuses but that all stems from a good story.

PD: I got more than that from the best episodes of *NYPD Blue*.

SB: You know why? The good ones all have good stories, and the great ones have great stories. And when you're telling a great story, the inherent elements in great storytelling are complex thematic moral and ethical ambiguities, considerations of big human elements and conditions. Those are the kinds of big theme issues that are embraced when you are telling great stories.

But it always starts with the story. If you say, "I got to do an episode about free speech" then you're [lost]. You're starting from the wrong place. You tell a great story and themes emerge, so that's just "Writing 101." I'm just a nut about story, story, story, story.

PD: At one point you were developing three shows at the same time. How could you stay close to all of them?

SB: First of all, I've been doing it for over 30 years, so I've learned how to be really good at it. And also it's just an issue of time management. I'm good at managing my time. Every one of those shows is at a different part of its evolution, so a show like *NYPD Blue* requires a fraction of a time that the new show requires because all of us speak a common language. The show has such a long and complex memory to think about that you don't have to invent what's there. My only chore in the last season of *NYPD Blue* was to make sure we finished the series in a way that's really satisfying to an audience and make them feel like they didn't get schmucked.

And, again, storytelling, except it's a different consideration of story. You're not considering story events, although you have to, as much as you're looking at character arcs. How do you take all of these characters on a season-long journey that organically spins them into their next life? So the audience goes, ah, that felt good, and I'm sad but I get it and I'll miss these people. But that's a different type of thinking, and that's been going on in my head for a long time. The time that I'm spending with the writers now is almost exclusively devoted to character arcs because they'll come up with the stories, and we have a well of stories from cops we collected, so that part of it will almost take care of itself.

A new show requires a lot of effort because it's new guys and new concepts, but it's always fun with a good new show because you get to turn over cards. It takes about two years, maybe three, to turn over all your major cards in a new show — gross character revelations in a drama, oohhh, he's a drunk, ohhhh, she's gay. After three years, the job changes, the task of maintaining a show is a different task. So at the beginning, when everything's working right, and this one is; it's huge fun because it's invention.

PD: How do you keep your edge?

SB: I had a wonderful mentor years ago who said to me, Steven, you either have to have "f you" money or "f you" attitude. And I didn't have "f you" money so I had to develop an "f you" attitude which wasn't that hard to do. And once I got it, I just thought, well this works. I'm much more selective who I say that to these days.

PD: I'm wondering if there's anything you'd like to say to students in film schools who are thinking about television careers.

SB: Go to medical school. Not to be a doctor, go to medical school, so that when you go back into television you'll have something to write about. Have a life. It's my one beef with most young writers. If you want to be a director or producer, that's one thing. Those are skills you can learn. But, to be a writer, you got to have something to write about. Not that everybody doesn't, we've all lived lives, but when you're twenty-one, you know, you haven't lived much of a life unless you've had an extraordinary experience to write about.

Unfortunately, most really young writers form their sense of life from watching television so what you end up getting is this sort of "Xerox" of life which is never the substitute for the real thing. So I always tell students, pursue your dream but in the meantime, get a real job and have a real life.

PD: Why do you do television instead of movies?

SB: Easy. Easy, easy, easy. It's a better medium. Even with all the bullshit of television, it's still a more provocative medium than the movie business. The movie business is basically appealing to kids and cretinous teenagers. That's essentially what the movie business is. Very few are, in any serious way, committed to making thoughtful, provocative medium to low-budget movies that fill a real niche in the movie going experience. Everybody's looking for *Spider-Man* and *Batman* and all those other men, and big high concept. Those are fun and, in the summertime, kids flock to them, but that's not what I do.

Believe me, for any writer, you're going to have more fun and learn more and be more productive writing in television than in the movies. You're not going to have to share credit with 15 other idiots. You're not going to be abused and disrespected by 15 jerks in suits who have too much time on their hands and all they want to do is eat lunch. Television is a job — you got to get it on, you got to get it out, the writers are going to write their scripts, they're going to get on the tube. And that's great. If you're lucky enough to get on a successful show, you're going to do more credited writing in two years than most movie writers do in a lifetime. So it's a much more satisfying medium for writers.

POSTSCRIPT

In 2007 Steven Bochco launched an Internet series, "Café Confidential," which runs on the video site *Metacafe*. After decades of making 60-minute shows, Bochco's new "episodes" are closer to 60 seconds. But the heart is the same: it's all about characters and their stories; storytelling on the frontier.

CHAPTER 3

How a Classic Script Is Crafted

Constructing your episode may seem daunting at first, but hour dramas — especially primetime network shows — follow a general template. Your insights into character, talent with dialogue, inventiveness in storytelling, and the depth of meaning are all creative qualities beyond any system. But I've found that using a basic pattern can actually release your artistry because you don't have to worry whether the underlying skeleton will hold up.

Initially, I even advise students to try to separate their right brain and left brain functions — the creative and the analytical. We know how we are as artists, ready to run off with the circus, or an emotional explosion. Those moments when passion takes over are gifts, and if you're touched by a cinematically hot encounter between characters, go ahead and write it down. The best writing is like trying to catch the wind anyway. But then put that piece of writing aside and return to engineering your script in the cold light of the left brain.

Even if you could somehow begin at page one and steam your way through to page 60 in a single creative breath (and I don't think anyone can), television series don't work like that. As you'll discover in Chapter Five, you'll be collaborating with a staff and will have to submit an outline or beat sheet (more about those in Chapter Four) prior to writing your teleplay.

The Dramatic Beat

Before we go further, keep in mind the nature of a screenplay scene, as I'm sure you've learned in screenwriting courses or books. A dramatic scene is the essential building block of storytelling on screen and should have a complete dramatic structure. That means each scene has a motivated protagonist who wants something and drives the action to get it through conflict with an opposition, usually an equally motivated antagonist. That's just a basic statement of story plotting. If you're stuck on this point, then take a break and refresh yourself on screenwriting before you move on to TV. Seriously. Writing television drama isn't easier than theatrical movies, even though it's shorter; actually it's more difficult because it requires all the same elements compressed in a tighter form.

When you look at the sample script pages that follow you'll notice numbers at the sides. Those are automatically generated by screenwriting software in preparing a "shooting script" (that means the final draft which goes into production), but you should not have numbers on your presentation draft. I left these numbers in to help refer to sections as I discuss them (and because these really are from shooting scripts). The numbers indicate "Slug Lines," also called "Scene Headings," but they are not scenes in the dramatic sense I'm using. For example, an establishing shot outside a building is not a full dramatic scene, though it is a location that physical production needs to plan. For our purposes, a dramatic beat may encompass one or more slug lines; the key is identifying a step of the story, not a shot. You'll see more examples when I talk about the script segments.

A, B, C Stories

We're going to look at a show that uses parallel storytelling. In this sample, the three story lines are not sub-plots, but independent tales each involving distinct guest cast. Since they occur within the same arena — a New York detective precinct — and they feature the same main cast, the stories are sometimes interwoven, sometimes blended, sometimes juxtaposed. Clearly, in style and tone they are part of the same show, and you might find a theme linking all the stories within an episode.

The largest (or most resonant) story is called "A." The second most important story is "B." And the third, "C" story is sometimes comic relief in an otherwise serious show, or may be a "runner," such as a recurring incident or character issue. Like any description of writing methods, those distinctions are flexible. Among variations, you may find A and B stories that are equal in weight, shows where a C story in one episode is a seed beginning a major arc in subsequent episodes, and shows that normally have three stories but might turn up with two or four. Again, I'm giving you a sense of the overall design, not laying down the law.

Some series usually have more than three stories — *ER*, for example. And some are "A" story only, for example *Monk* and *X-Files*. Before you speculate a show, carefully study how it's crafted.

Each series has its own ways, but I've come up with a generic grid that fits many network shows. I use it to analyze sample episodes in my classes, and here's a blank one you can apply to the excerpts printed in this chapter. For practice, try it while you're watching TV. Once you get the hang of it, you can also use this simple chart in the early planning stages of an original script (Chart 3.1).

Chart 3.1 Basic Four-Act Grid

	ACT I	ACT II	ACT III	ACT IV
(T)				
1				
2				
3				
4				
5				
6				
7				

Chart 3.2 Sample Six-Act Grid

Approximately 20-24 scenes total

	Act 1	Act 2	Act 3	Act 4	Act 5	Act 6
1						
2						
3						
4						
	8 to 10 minutes (replaces teaser)	8 minutes or less	8 minutes or less	Less than 8 minutes	6 to 8 minutes *might have only 3 scenes*	Around 5 minutes (replaces tag) *might have only 2 or 3 scenes or very short scenes*

◄— NOTE:
First three acts
may be longer

Chart 3.3 Seven-Act Concept

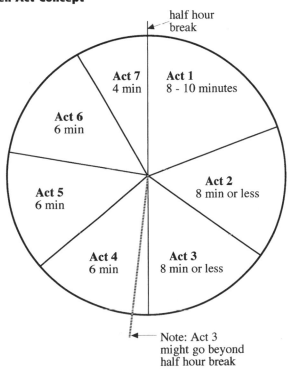

half hour break

Act 7
4 min

Act 1
8 - 10 minutes

Act 6
6 min

Act 5
6 min

Act 2
8 min or less

Act 4
6 min

Act 3
8 min or less

Note: Act 3
might go beyond
half hour break

Four Act Grid

The titles on the top are the four acts of an hour episode. Remember from Chapter One that on network television (but not on premium cable like HBO) commercial breaks occur roughly every 13 to 15 minutes. Dividing 15 minutes into 60 minutes gives you the four acts. Now, an hour drama doesn't really run an hour — it's actually less than 50 minutes after commercials. And each act isn't really 15 minutes — more like 12. But for planning a script, figure that Act One ends around page 17 or 18 if the show has a teaser (more about teasers in a minute); Act Two ends around page 30; Act Three at 45; and Act Four around 60 (or anywhere from 55 or so to 65).

On the left of the grid you see numbers one through seven. Those are the scenes in each act. Why seven? Well, you won't always have seven, in fact. Five solid scenes could fill out an act in some cases, and in "vignette" shows where scenes are quick, you might find yourself counting up to nine or ten. The basis for the list of seven is the two-minute scene. Back to arithmetic: If an act is 14 minutes, and each scene is around two minutes, 14 divided by 2 = 7.

Five and Six Act Structure

In 2006 some network and basic cable shows including the popular *Grey's Anatomy* and *Lost* went to five acts, and then ABC network mandated six acts for all its new shows, so they became six acts. You can guess why: more commercial breaks. I don't know any writers who like this change which seems pushed by desperation to pump revenues when network advertising rates are declining and the audience has discovered the mute button, not to mention all the people who record shows to omit commercials altogether. Not every show is guilty, though. *House*, on Fox, is still four acts (plus a teaser) for example. But elsewhere, potentially interesting shows such as *Nip/Tuck* (on FX) are so chopped up the drama begins to feel like decoration between the ads.

Like it or not, you need to find out if the show you're speculating has four, five, six or even seven acts, and how to re-configure your structure. I suggest you begin with the four-act idea. Then take what used to be the teaser and lengthen it to around ten pages to create a new Act One. Be sure you open directly into the story with jeopardy or action or a provocative issue because this is where you need to hook the audience (and the reader).

Each of the succeeding acts will be shorter than in a four act plan — roughly 10 pages each. In a six-act structure, you might have only 20 scenes in the entire hour, with acts only around eight pages long. Try thinking in terms of Act Six being a tag or the final shoe dropping, or a twist. You might see an Act Six that runs as short as five minutes. On *Nip/Tuck*, to use an example of a six-act (or teaser plus five) show, the writers often complete all dramatic arcs at the end of Act Five (which is the same as a show with teaser plus four), and use the short sixth act to add a surprising twist that, in a way, might be considered a teaser for the next episode because it incites a new issue or challenge rather than concluding the current storyline.

Seven Acts? You Gotta Be Kidding!

Just as I was finishing this Second Edition, a producer-writer colleague stopped me on campus at USC and uttered, his voice aghast, "I saw a seven-act script." Well, I'd written two-hour television movies that were seven acts, which isn't unusual for a movie, so at first I didn't understand his alarm.

"No," he pressed, "it was an hour episode of..." and he named a major network show. They'd shown the bizarre script to him as a sample, just that morning, inviting him to consider joining the staff. He still hadn't recovered.

"They're crazy," he seethed, "this is the golden age of television; drama has never been better; and they're chasing everyone away!"

As I talked him down from the ledge, we tried to reason out the seven acts. No mistaking the problem, though. At seven acts, dramatic material would occupy 40 minutes or less. The remaining 20 minutes would go to ads and promotions which would be flashier than the show, produced on a higher per-minute budget, and hard to escape, leaving the drama looking like scraps between the commercials. The once-interesting series might lie in shards.

We both knew why the network forced this structure. Their advertising revenue was down because so many other options (and viewers) are available on cable stations and the internet. It's easy, but faulty, accounting:

If a buyer used to spend a dollar to get the attention of ten people, but now only five people are watching, he might ask for twice as many advertising spots for his same dollar. Of course, viewer attention doesn't really work like that. The five remaining viewers are asleep, or avoiding the ads by recording shows and fast-forwarding through them, or buying whole seasons of shows on DVDs, or surfing other channels.

Of course, I'm exaggerating. Networks are still much larger than cable stations or any other venue for drama. Nevertheless, for many writers, artistic death by a thousand cuts isn't worth the network advantages.

My colleague was swearing off writing for networks altogether, "I'd rather make a fraction of the money and do a fraction of the season for a fraction of the audience on Showtime."

Now, that's good news for guess who: YOU! If you're just beginning, the sound of television's top writers receding in the distance towards the many creative opportunities off-network might leave some room for you to break in. So, in the spirit of thinking positively, I've included a hypothetical seven-act illustration. Once you think about it, the structure becomes less weird.

For example, the three acts in the first half hour are not very different from the traditional two acts plus a long teaser. Then, if you knock off that seventh act as a tag, you really have only acts four, five and six — one more act in the second half hour than in traditional shows. Think about how many cliffhangers or twists you can generate in fast-moving stories for your ensemble. With all those "reveals," clues and relationship conflicts among a large cast, you can probably come up with a rhythm that both advances the stories and leaves viewers wanting to un-mute the television after the break.

In other words, no matter what they throw at you, make it work. A clever writer can create seven gripping acts by staying rooted in the characters. See, that's not so different, after all.

THE TWO-PAGE SCENE

I use the two-page scene as a target for students partly because inexperienced writers have difficulty accomplishing a complete dramatic beat in fewer pages, and when they write longer than two pages, their scenes tend to lose focus or become redundant.

Historically, screen scenes used to be long, more like stage plays. If you look at great movies from the 1940s, like the ones starring Humphrey Bogart, you'll see some scenes that run five or even seven pages. They reflect a different era where the slow evolvement of a dramatic moment, gradually experienced, was part of the pace of life. Whether the change was caused by the 15-second information module of *Sesame Street*, or TV ads where a one-minute commercial is long and 30 seconds is normal, or the speed of computers, where you're growling at the screen if a function takes two seconds — an electronics-savvy populace is quickly bored. If audience attention drifts, or is way ahead of where you're going with the story, you've lost your moment. On television today, a one-minute beat is more welcome than a three-minute scene, and if you're starting page four of a single encounter, that's a red flag.

Notice also that I'm using the words "minute" and "page" interchangeably. That's just shorthand. A minute per page may be an average, but it's not always accurate. Pages of dialogue move faster, while action eats up lots of time. As with all my construction advice, I'm pointing out a general design, not policing whether you color outside the lines!

Using the Grid

If you're using a four, five or six-act grid to help you understand the form of an episode on TV, I suggest you begin by recording the show. Watch it all the way through and name the A, B and C stories (or whatever number of stories your show has). Attach each story to one of the main cast, and then summarize that particular arc in a sentence. Keep going, creating a "log line" for each story.

Once you've figured out the stories, re-play the episode. This time, write a letter in each of the boxes on the grid. For example, if Act I, Scene 1 is about the "B" story, put a B in that box. As the grid fills out, it will probably look sort of like a checkerboard with A,B,C (or other) stories following each other in a somewhat random pattern.

You'll notice that the cliffhanger that occurs at the end of an act might not always be a suspenseful moment in the A story; it might be a turning point in the B story, for example. You'll also see that sometimes one of the stories continues for several beats in a row, especially if it's following a "line of interest" the writer didn't want to interrupt. On other occasions, you'll see one story interposed between beats of another; this might be used to convey a sense that time has passed between the beats in the first story (this skipping is also called an "ellipsis").

No rules exist for how this "checkerboard" should look, so don't get hung up trying to match the order of scenes. You're serving the dramatic tension of the stories, not some outside system. The point is to recognize the way parallel stories complement each other.

The grid may also help you track the arcs, and especially if your show is part of a serial, you might be surprised that one of the storylines ends in Act Three, or the C story doesn't begin until Act Two, or Act Four is entirely about resolving the A story. That's all okay. Again, the structure serves the story within the general parameters of a four act episode with cliffhangers. So learn from other shows but don't copy.

If you're using the grid to create an original script, your first foray into the grid might be to jot notes about key points in the boxes: how the show opens, the "worst case" cliffhanger which is ¾ through a drama, and how the show will end. (That ¾ pivot occurs at the end of Act Three if you have four acts, or in Act Four or Five if your show is divided into more acts.) You might do that for the A story only, or for both A and B stories, leaving room to think about the "C" later. Particularly with the act breaks, it's helpful to reverse-engineer, stepping backwards from the cliffhangers to the beats right before to fill in the actions that led to the jeopardy or collision. That reverse technique may help you figure out your outline. (I'll explain more about outlining in Chapter Four.)

TEASERS

The excerpts you'll read in this chapter are from a show that opens with a "teaser," though not all series begin with one. A teaser, also called "a cold opening," refers to dramatic material before the titles (before the name of the series and credits). It may be a one-minute "hook," or as long as ten minutes that includes several small scenes, making it nearly as full as a traditional whole act. In any style, it exists to grab viewers faster than the enemy, which is the remote. The notion is to open the hour with an action, image, situation or character that provokes enough anticipation to keep viewers through the title sequence and into the first act.

However, increasingly, title sequences along with theme music have been dumped by networks preferring to grab viewers with uninterrupted drama. The "tease" is the story itself, and titles scroll over Act One.

Often, a teaser sets out the problem of an episode. For example, on a detective show, the crime to be solved may be enacted or discovered in the teaser. But even within the detective franchise, each show is unique. Looking back at the classic *Miami Vice* series, the lush teasers featured life in Miami and a provocative crime in progress in a textured environment usually involving drugs. The main cast never appeared in the teaser. Similarly, in *The X-Files*, a mysterious phenomenon occupied the cinematic teaser, though Mulder and Scully didn't learn about it until they were contacted in their office in Act One. In contrast, both *Law and Order* (classic) and *NYPD Blue* usually opened with the detectives arriving at a crime scene after the deed is done.

In many law and medical shows, a case arrives and incites the events of the episode. But in *ER* and *Grey's Anatomy,* where emphasis is on the ensemble cast and episodes usually cover a single day, teasers have sometimes shown the continuing characters waking, getting ready for work, or traveling to work, launching their personal stories that will spin out in the episode.

HBO's *Six Feet Under* always opened with someone dying (as bizarrely as possible) who turned up in the Fisher family funeral home in Act One, underlining the show's notion that life is random. But that teaser was rarely a component of the episode's drama; its link is thematic. The prison drama *OZ*, which used to run on HBO, also opened with theme rather than continuing story — a philosophical monologue, in fact. Even the classic sitcom *Cheers* was an example of a teaser that reminded viewers of the show's world (a neighborhood bar where "everybody knows your name"), instead of beginning a dramatic arc.

If you're a new writer, though, I recommend sticking with story rather than message. A swiftly propelled dramatic tension will lure a reader to turn the page and a viewer to see what happens next. Real storytelling is difficult, and I've seen too many students fool themselves into thinking they can impress by opening with a weighty theme or abstruse philosophy, when they're actually avoiding the challenge of impelling an arc. The best teasers tend to be the best drama.

ABOUT THESE EXCERPTS...

With appreciation to Steven Bochco, Executive Producer of *NYPD Blue* and many other great drama series, who graciously gave permission, here is the Teaser and Act One of each of two Emmy-winning episodes that ran four years apart. I've chosen these historic examples partly because they're so clearly crafted that you can easily grasp the structure, and also because they've stood the test of time.

The first excerpt is from "Simone Says," which aired at the beginning of 1995; story by Steven Bochco, David Milch, Walon Green; teleplay by David Milch, Walon Green. This episode introduced the character of Bobby Simone (played by Jimmy Smits) in the middle of the second season. Other main cast — Andy Sipowicz (the acclaimed Dennis Franz), Lt. Fancy, Detectives Lesniak, Martinez and Medavoy, Asst. D.A. Sylvia Costas, and receptionist Donna, were established in the series at this point; the remaining names are guest cast. Read and try to identify the stories and think about the form. Following the script pages, I will analyze its dramatic elements.

After that, you'll see another episode segment, along with a discussion.

NYPD BLUE
"Simone Says"

FADE IN:

1   EXT. PRECINCT - DAY   1

        To establish --

2   INT. LAVATORY - LOCKER ROOM - DAY   2

        SIPOWICZ enters from the hallway wearing his jacket and
        carrying a small paper bag from a drug store. He goes to his
        locker, opens it takes his jacket off and hangs it on the
        open locker door. Crossing to the sink with the bag, he
        glances around as he steps in front of the mirror, removes a
        pair of drug store reading glasses from the bag and puts them
        on. A large tag hangs from the glasses, dangling against his
        cheek as he unhappily studies himself in the mirror. Sipowicz
        snatches away the glasses and stuffs them back in the paper
        bag as someone comes in.

        He turns and sees BOBBY SIMONE moving to the bank of lockers
        to the left of the door, checking a small piece of paper in
        his hand on which a locker number's been written.

                          SIMONE
                'Morning.

                          SIPOWICZ
                How's it going?

        Sipowicz steps over to him --

                          SIPOWICZ (CONT'D)
                Andy Sipowicz.

        Simone regards him, smiles and extends his hand --

                          SIMONE
                Bobby Simone, nice to meet you,
                Andy.

                          SIPOWICZ
                Yeah.

        Sipowicz clears his throat, steps to the door and exits. Hold
        a beat on Simone, crossing Kelly's name off the locker,
        inscribing his own, then --

                                                    CUT TO:

2.

3   INT. SQUAD ROOM - DAY   3

Sipowicz crosses the Squad Room directly to Fancy's office.

4   INT. FANCY'S OFFICE - DAY   4

FANCY looks up to see Sipowicz.

                         FANCY
                'Morning Andy.

                         SIPOWICZ
                That's no good. That's not gonna
                work.

                         FANCY
                What isn't?

                         SIPOWICZ
                I just met this new guy.

                         FANCY
                Simone.

                         SIPOWICZ
                Yeah that's not gonna work out.

                         FANCY
                What happened?

                         SIPOWICZ
                    (waves dismissal)
                Don't get me started.

Fancy watches Sipowicz pace. BG In the Squad Room we see
Simone meeting Medavoy, Martinez.

                         SIPOWICZ (CONT'D)
                The whole attitude's wrong. "How
                you doing," this type of thing.

Fancy's phone rings. As he picks up the receiver --

                         FANCY
                He asked how you were doing?
                    (into receiver)
                Lieutenant Fancy.
                    (beat)
                Okay/
                    (hangs up)
                We're got a homicide.
                    (MORE)

                                                        3.

                         FANCY(cont'd)
                 (beat)
            You're senior in the Squad. I want
            him with you, at least till he
            learns the precinct.

Sipowicz shakes his head, disaffected with his entire lot --

                         SIPOWICZ
            I need glasses and everything else.

Off Fancy, as Sipowicz exists his office --

5   INT. DONNA'S DESK - DAY   5

Donna looks up from her desk to see JAMES ABRUZZO.

                         ABRUZZO
            Yeah, I'm here to see Adrianne
            Lesniak.

                         DONNA
            Your name is ...

Abruzzo ignores her question, crosses to LESNIAK at her desk.
Lesniak, just arrived, is putting her things away. She sees
him and a look of weary desperation crosses her face --

                         LESNIAK
            Jimmy ...

                         ABRUZZO
            What? It's not like you give me a
            choice.

Lesniak faces him from her desk --

                         LESNIAK
            Not here. Please.

He settles in a chair facing her --

                         ABRUZZO
            Then where? I can't talk to you
            outside work 'cause I don't know
            where you're staying anymore, I
            can't call you here, 'cause you've
            told that bitch at the desk not to
            put me through ...
                 (louder)
            Where am I supposed to talk to you?

4.

                    LESNIAK
          We've got nothing left to talk
          about.

Abruzzo sees Donna staring at him ==

                    ABRUZZO
          What are you looking at?

Donna looks back to her desk. She lifts the phone.

Abruzzo leans close to Lesniak, grips her wrist --

                    ABRUZZO (CONT'D)
          You don't know how much I love you.
          You don't know what I'd do for you.

                    LESNIAK
          You're drunk; Let go.

She tries to snatch her wrist away as Fancy steps up behind
Abruzzo.

                    FANCY
          All right, you get up and you get
          the hell away from Detective
          Lesniak.

Abruzzo slowly turns his head and looks at Fancy.

                    ABRUZZO
          No, you get back. I'm holding a .38
          pointed straight at her guts.

                    LESNIAK
          Jimmy.

                    ABRUZZO
          Let's go. You want to keep this
          private, we'll talk in private.

He brings her to her feet.

People in the room are frozen until Fancy lunges, grabs
Abruzzo's gun hand and swings the pistol toward the ceiling.

A shot is fired, but Fancy hangs onto the gun, preventing the
cylinder from rotating to fire again. Abruzzo punches at
Fancy who hangs on with both hands.

Sipowicz lunges for him but a kick from Abruzzo catches him
in the stomach, he's hurled back and his lower spine slams
against a desk.

                                                        5.

Abruzzo is pulling at the gun, swinging it wildly from side
to aide while Fancy hangs on.

From over a desk, Simone flies through the air and hits
Abruzzo with a tackle that hurls him to the ground. Fancy
pulls away with the gun as Simone spins Abruzzo around and
twists his arms behind him.

As Sipowicz comes forward with obvious lower back pain,
Simone cuffs Abruzzo. Abruzzo is hauled to his feet in the
circle of people.

                         LESNIAK
                    (miserably protective)
               He's from the two-seven,
               Lieutenant, he's on the job.

                         FANCY
               He's under arrest.
                    (to Donna)
               Get a D.A. down here.
                    (to the newcomer)
               You're Simone?

                         SIMONE
               How you doing Lieutenant?

                         FANCY
                    (to Simone and the other
                    Detectives)
               I got this, get to your homicide,
               Thirteenth and Third.

                         ABRUZZO
                    (to Lesniak)
               Are you happy? Look what you've
               done to me now.

                         FANCY
               Shut up!   •

                         SIMONE
                    (to Sipowicz)
               Are you hurt?

                         SIPOWICZ
               I'll live.
                    (beat)
               C'mon, ride with me.

Off which --

                                        SMASH CUT TO:

MAIN TITLES

6   EXT. STATION HOUSE - DAY   6

Sipowicz and Simone move toward Sipowicz' car as in b.g.
Medavoy and Martinez do the same.

                    SIMONE
          Lesniak and Abruzzo were going out?

                    SIPOWICZ
               (nods)
          She broke up with him, got
          transferred, he went half-wacky.

                    SIMONE
          Looks to me like he made the whole
          trip.

                    SIPOWICZ
               (beat)
          What was your last assignment?

                    SIMONE
          Intelligence. I drove for the
          Commissioner.

They've reached Sipowicz' car, are about to enter --

                    SIPOWICZ
          You were one of those guys got
          grade promotions?

                    SIMONE
          Yeah.

                    SIPOWICZ
               (flat-voiced)
          That was nice.

Off Simone, getting in, taking the hit --

                                        CUT TO:

7   EXT. 13TH STREET AND 3RD - DAY   7

Sipowicz' van pulls up at the crime scene and parks beside
Medavoy's car, from which we see Medavoy and Martinez
exiting. Sipowicz and Simone get out.

In front of a remodeled apartment building, a body is on the
street half under a bloody sheet.

7.

Two units are parked with their bubble gums flashing and a paramedic van is at the curb. Sipowicz and Simone step up to the body.

A man in his thirties, dead in a blood-soaked linen suit.

                    SIMONE
          Anyone check for I/D.?

                    UNIFORM
          Waited for you.

                    MARTINEZ
               (to Sipowicz)
          Want me to get started on the
          canvas?

                    SIPOWICZ
          Yeah, and have a uniform run the
          plates on these parked cars.

During which Simone has pulled his gloves on, crouched to look in the D.O.A.'s pockets for I.D. Sipowicz also crouches effortfully beside the body.

                    SIPOWICZ (CONT'D)
               (to Simone)
          Two in the chest. You see any other
          hits?

                    SIMONE
          No.
               (reads I.D.)
          Raymond Alphonse Martarano, Jr.,
          Bensonhurst.
               (looks up)
          The wise guy's son?

                    SIPOWICZ
          Or someone too stupid to change his
          name.
               (to Medavoy)
          Greg, find out if the M.E.'s
          responding and let Fancy know we've
          got a mobbed-up stiff.

                    MEDAVOY
          Yeah, all right.

As Medavoy moves off --

                    UNIFORM
               (to Sipowicz)
          We found a shell over by that curb.

                    SIMONE
          I got that.

Simone turns to go check it out, remarks to the Uniform re
the on-lookers --

                    SIMONE (CONT'D)
          Could you move the crime scene back
          twenty feet and get me a traffic
          cone to put over this shell?

                    UNIFORM
          Sure.

Meanwhile Martinez has approached Sipowicz, points to a man
on the sidewalk.

                    MARTINEZ
          That man's the super, he said the
          victim knew one of the tenants.

Sipowicz steps over to GOLDMAN, a middle-aged man in a blue
baseball jacket.

                    MARTINEZ (CONT'D)
          Mr. Goldman, this is Detective
          Sipowicz.

                    GOLDMAN
          Yeah, hi ...

                    SIPOWICZ
            (re body)
          Did you know this man?

                    GOLDMAN
          Mr. Big Shot Ray Martarano Jr.?
          He'd tell the lamp-post who he was
          if nobody else was around.

                    SIPOWICZ
          Who did he know in the building?

                    GOLDMAN
          2C ... Miss Anderson.

                    SIPOWICZ
          You know where we can find her?

                    GOLDMAN
          She's a model. I'm supposed to call
          her agency number for emergencies.

9.

                    SIPOWICZ
          I need that.

Suddenly O.S. Shouts. Sipowicz turns. Across the street a
woman shouts from a doorway --

                    MISS SAVINO
          Help me! ... Help! My mother's been
          shot!

From the street, Simone races toward the building. He faces a
woman, thirties who is standing in the doorway of an
apartment. Her hand is covered with blood.

                    SIMONE
          Where's your mother?

                    MISS SAVINO
          In there ... in there ...

8   INT. GROUND-FLOOR APARTMENT - DAY   8

Simone rushes into the ground=floor apartment. In the room by
the window, an elderly woman is sitting in a chair, her head
to one side. Miss Savino stands in the doorway as Simone
rushes to her mother.

                    MISS SAVINO
          I was at the grocery store.

Simone looks at the woman, who is obviously dead.

                    MISS SAVINO (CONT'D)
          She's dead, isn't she?

                    SIMONE
               (puts his hand on the
               woman's shoulder)
          She is. I'm sorry.

                    MISS SAVINO
          She was in our own apartment. She
          was at her own window.

                    SIMONE
          Why don't you sit down.

                    MISS SAVINO
          That's my mother.

                    SIMONE
          I know, I'm sorry.

Miss Savino raises her hands to her face and sobs as Sipowicz
comes through the doorway slightly out of breath, followed by
E.M.S. personnel, who go directly to the body.

                    SIPOWICZ
          What happened?

Simone pushes back the window curtain. A hole is revealed in
the glass where a shot entered, killing the woman.

                    SIMONE
          Stray from the street.

Off which --

                                              CUT TO:

9   EXT. PRECINCT - DAY   9

         To establish --

10   INT. SQUAD ROOM - DAY   10

         Fancy clears the stairs, enters the Squad, approaching
         Lesniak at her desk. He keeps his voice quiet.

                    FANCY
          How are you feeling?

Lesniak gestures defeatedly -- doesn't say much so she won't
cry.

                    LESNIAK
          I'm upset.

Fancy nods.

                    FANCY
          I.A.B. Just took him to Bellevue on
          a seventy-two hour evaluation.

                    LESNIAK
          And he's a collar, right?

                    FANCY
               (nods)
          I alerted the D.A. and Corrections,
          if he goes into the system we're
          going to be notified.

A beat, then --

11.

                    LESNIAK
          What happened, that's the thing I
          kept seeing in my mind. I kept
          being afraid that was going to
          happen.

                    FANCY
          Adrianne, you want to put a twenty-
          eight in, try it again tomorrow?

She shakes her head no.

                    LESNIAK
          I'd like to try it today.

                    FANCY
          Pay attention to how you're
          feeling.

                    LESNIAK
          Okay. Thanks.

Fancy nods, moves off, joining the just-arrived Sipowicz. Off
Lesniak --

11   ANGLE - SIPOWICZ AND FANCY   11

                    FANCY
          I heard there was a second D.O.A.

                    SIPOWICZ
          Eighty-two year old woman sitting
          at her window.

                    FANCY
          The world's coming up here 'cause
          it's Martarano's son. Organized
          Crime, Intelligence ...

                    SIPOWICZ
               (sarcastic)
          Now I know the case'll clear.

                    FANCY
          Anything off canvass?

                    SIPOWICZ
          No witnesses. He was banging a
          model lived in the building.
          Simone's finding out where we can
          pick her up.

They look toward Simone at Kelly's old desk --

                FANCY
        How's that going?

                SIPOWICZ
         (re Simone)
        You know he drove for the P.C.?

                FANCY
         (nods)
        I saw that was his last detail.

                SIPOWICZ
         (more trying this attitude
          on than genuinely
          irritated)
        I take twenty-two years making
        second grade, he gets it for
        shooing away squeegee-bums.

Fancy lets it go, heads for his office. Sipowicz moves to
Simone at his desk.

                SIMONE
         (covers the receiver with
          his hand)
        The agency told me where she's
        working. Give me half a minute.

Sipowicz nods, looks to where COSTAS has just entered, moves
to her --

                SIPOWICZ
        How's it going?

                COSTAS
        I was just seeing to Abruzzo.
         (re Simone)
        Is that the new Detective?

                SIPOWICZ
         (nods)
        Simone, what kind of name is that?

                COSTAS
        First or last?

                SIPOWICZ
        If it was his first he'd be a girl.

                COSTAS
        Last name Simone sounds French.

13.

                    SIPOWICZ
          Yeah, maybe.

They're both looking toward Simone, react as he raises his
voice -

                    SIMONE
          Hey, I went through a lot of effort
          getting that red cock. I don't want
          to lose its color.
               (beat)
          I don't want to argue about this.
          You tell Billy he can't be around
          my place with his blue-barred cock.
          Okay thanks.

Simone hangs up. He sees them looking at him --

                    SIMONE (CONT'D)
          I breed birds. Racing pigeons.

Costas nods. Then quietly, to Sipowicz --

                    COSTAS
          Tell him you keep fish.

Sipowicz shakes his head no. Simone's collected his
materials, approaches--

                    SIPOWICZ
               (indicates Costas)
          Assistant D.A. Costas.

                    SIMONE
          How do you do?

                    COSTAS
          How do you do.

                    SIPOWICZ
               (to Simone)
          They gave you that address?

                    SIMONE
          Yeah, she's working on Seventh
          Avenue.

A beat, then --

                    COSTAS
          Must be interesting raising
          pigeons.

14.

                         SIMONE
                 It's a lot of fun, gets you
                 outdoors.

                         COSTAS
                 You people and your hobbies.

                         SIPOWICZ
                         (to Simone)
                 Let's go.

        Off which --

                                                CUT TO:

        12   INT. A GARMENT SHOWROOM - 7TH AVENUE - DAY   12

        The place is chaos, hung with cigar smoke as buyers move
        among sellers and brokers beside a flood-lit ramp, where
        models parade a spring line. Sipowicz and Simone push their
        way through, following THELMA LEVY, a tailored fiftyish
        woman, wearing a no-nonsense expression.

                         LEVY
                 How long will this tie her up?

                         SIPOWICZ
                 We won't know till we talk to her.

                         LEVY
                 And it couldn't wait until after
                 she finishes work.

                         SIPOWICZ
                 NO.

        She leads them into --

        13   INT. A DRESSING ROOM - DAY   13

        Sipowicz and Simone can't help but look around as they are
        suddenly amidst a plethora of nubile bodies in various stages
        of undress. Dressers move excitedly in front of them as
        clothes are whipped on and off. Ms. Levy stops them.

                         LEVY
                 Wait here, I'll get her.

        The work is so concentrated and frenetic that for the most
        part they are ignored by the nude models attended by ranks of
        fey male dressers and a few female fitters.

15.

The talk level is deafening. As Sipowicz mops his brow Simone observes good-humoredly --

                    SIMONE
          What a country huh?

Ms. Levy appears with PAULA ANDERSON, good-looking, lots of make-up and a pill-assisted figure.

                    LEVY
          Make it as quick as you can.

Levy moves off --

                    SIPOWICZ
          I'm Detective Sipowicz, this is
          Detective Simone.

                    PAULA
          What's going on?

                    SIPOWICZ
          Do you know Raymond Martarano, Jr.?

                    PAULA
          Yes.

                    SIMONE
          When's the last time you saw him?

                    PAULA
          We partied last night, then I had
          to come to work.

                    SIMONE
          You left him at your apartment?

                    PAULA
          What's going on?

                    SIPOWICZ
          He was murdered this morning
          outside your building. Your
          downstairs neighbor was killed by a
          stray bullet.

Paula takes this in.

                    PAULA
          Which downstairs neighbor?

                    SIPOWICZ
          Mrs. Savino.

16.

It seems like a struggle for Paula to keep her hard edge.

                    PAULA
          I don't know anything about it.

                    SIPOWICZ
          Why don't you come to the Station
          House so we can get the background
          on this.

                    PAULA
          I'm working.

                    SIPOWICZ
          Well, now you're not working. Now
          you're coming with us to the
          Station House.

Simone holds a robe out for her to cover herself --

                    SIMONE
          Why don't you get dressed Paula?

The tone of which seems to circumvent her resistance. As
Paula puts the robe on --

                                   FADE OUT.

                    END ACT ONE

Analysis

Before we get into content, notice that a TV drama script looks just like a theatrical screenplay. This might be news if you've written sitcoms because half-hour comedies use a unique form. Most screenwriting software will give you format options, so choose "standard," "screenplay," or whatever term your system uses for writing movies. And, of course, you know better than to use a divided page or anything called "video."

Now, I said this show starts with a teaser which precedes Act One, yet you see no heading. Some series do write TEASER in the beginning, then they FADE OUT at the end of the teaser and start a new page headed ACT ONE. Other shows start with ACT ONE at the top of page one, whether or not there's a teaser. The only way to know what a particular show does is check out one of their sample scripts. In any case, Acts Two, Three and Four will begin on new pages and be headed ACT TWO and so forth, centered at the top.

OPENING SCENES

Look at #1 which simply establishes the Precinct building. Is that a scene? No! Remember, I told you a scene is a dramatic beat, not a production location. This kind of shot merely tells viewers where we are.

#2 opens the action with a personal detail that speaks volumes without dialogue. Think about what is revealed when a man tries on reading glasses for the first time. What do you suppose is in the character's mind? Notice how he hides them the moment Simone enters. In Chapter One, I spoke about the essential intimacy of television, and here it is: In his private moment, Sipowicz is self-conscious about aging. Insecurity that his eyesight is weakening gives viewers a window to his need to prove his status in this episode.

The Simone character is played by a younger man — tall, handsome Jimmy Smits. In comparison with Sipowicz — fat, balding and now needing glasses — the rivalry is set in motion from their first appearance. The script doesn't spell out how each man looks — that's not necessary in a TV series where everyone working on the show knows who the actors are. In fact, character tags, which are common in features, are slight, if they're included here at all. Still, everything you need emotionally is on the page in this tiny moment.

Notice also that dialogue begins on page one. That's normal for television, though you might have read features (especially older ones) where description, atmosphere, and action without speech occupy the first few pages. Look at the kind of dialogue on the first page, though. It seems like they're saying nothing except hello. That's not really what's going on, though, is it? You want to aim for dialogue that is both natural and withheld. In other words, let viewers sense the meaning under the surface without hitting it on the head, as much as you can.

You could analyze that the first scene of this teaser ends at the bottom of page one when Simone crosses off the name of Sipowicz's former partner and writes his own. It's a gesture of power in a beat that's all about relative power. But to understand the dramatic flow, I'd rather turn the page because the same tension continues into the outer rooms.

From having "lost" the unspoken battle with Simone (which is only in his own mind), Sipowicz barrels out to his boss, Lt. Fancy in #4, and complains about the new guy. From a dramatic point of view, this page could be interpreted as a whole scene too because it has conflict between characters, however subtle: Sipowicz wants to reclaim his power by getting rid of Simone, but Fancy resists. At the end, when Fancy worsens Sipowicz' problem by ordering him to work with Simone and teach him, Sipowicz reasserts his theme that started on the first page, "I need glasses and everything else."

Though you could argue that two distinct scenes start this story, I'll group the first two and a half pages (slug lines 1 through 4) into a single beat to help you visualize the storytelling. Let's name this story "A," because it has the most resonance for the series as a whole (even though it actually doesn't occupy the largest proportion of pages in the full script). On page 62 at the very end of the episode (not printed here) this opening moment is paid off when Sipowicz allows Simone to see him put on the new glasses, and he allows himself the vulnerability, "I got to wear glasses now." Their arc won't really end for four years, but this episode accomplishes a full step.

If you're filling in the grid, you would write "A" in the space next to the "T" for teaser. The "log line" for story "A" might be something like: "Sipowicz feels threatened when his new partner Simone arrives." Other wordings are also possible, of course. The point isn't what you call a story but how well you attach it to the drive of a continuing character.

The teaser's not over, though. Here comes the Lesniak story that I'll call "C." Without the full episode, you'd have no way of knowing where this one is going or how it measures against the rest of the script, so I'll just tell you. Detective Adrianne Lesniak is a continuing character whose problems with her ex-boyfriend (Abruzzo) appeared in previous shows, and this beat is part of her ongoing struggle to be free of him. But it really does more in this episode: Thematically it leverages a story with a guest cast which will begin in Act Two. That "C" story will require Lesniak to deal with women who have been abused by a man. As those female characters struggle to find courage to defend themselves against their abuser, Lesniak's personal search gives the case a deeper meaning for the audience.

The entire Lesniak/Abruzzo encounter runs almost three pages under scene heading #5, but you'll easily see it has several smaller components: the initial conflict between Lesniak and Abruzzo, then the fight which also involves Sipowicz and Simone, and finally the resolution with Lt. Fancy. By the time this scene is done, not only is Lesniak changed, but Simone has also been introduced to the squad in a dynamic way, and through the fight the balance between Simone and Sipowicz has budged a bit too.

If you're keeping notes on the grid, you'd write "C" next to where you wrote "A" for the teaser, because this opening has two beats.

The only way you know this scene ends the teaser is the transition "SMASH CUT TO" (at the bottom of page 5 in the script) and "MAIN TITLES" (at the top of page 6). ACT ONE begins right after the main titles, though this series doesn't state that on the page.

Act I, Scene 1

#6 is a whole scene even though it's less than a page long. Read it again and find the dramatic elements: Who is the protagonist? Who is the antagonist? What does the protagonist want which is opposed by the antagonist? Where is the climax of their conflict? How does it resolve? No, I'm not going to tell you the answers. This is good practice for tight scene writing and to grasp how character arcs are progressed. You might ask those same questions about every scene you write. Notice also that no scene exists merely to explore character. Simone and Sipowicz are on the trail of a murder while this beat happens.

Clearly, this is what we're calling the "A" story, so if you're doing the grid, put "A" in the first box in Act I.

Scene 2

In #7 the "B" story begins, and it would be routine police work at a crime scene except that we bring to it another level: the underlying jousting between Sipowicz and Simone. Clearly, the scene has three main components: first, the rising tension as they discover Matarano is "a mobbed-up stiff;" second, a guest character who leads the detectives to the next beat in their search. That construction might be flat, but the end of the scene is the third "beat" which spins the action in a new direction with the surprising shouts for help from Miss Savino. (On the grid, put "B" in the second square.)

Scene 3

#8 is an additional scene from the "B" story. You see, it's not necessary to checkerboard the order of these; it's more important to follow the line of audience interest. And that leads directly to the twist in this scene that raises unexpected questions about the crime. As in any mystery, the audience doesn't know which clues to value and which are red herrings, and neither do our characters — that's part of the fun of the genre. ("B" goes in the third square.)

Scene 4

Why bother with an establishing shot of the Precinct in #9? Think of a reason before I tell you. Okay, here are a few: It helps re-orient viewers to "home base" after several beats in the field; it signals the beginning of a new sequence; and it creates an ellipsis — that is, an impression time has passed — so that characters who appeared in one beat are separated from their reappearance in a next beat when they couldn't have actually traveled that quickly.

Why does the episode return to the "C" story in #10? It's not as if this beat that runs less than a minute advances the plot in an important way, so why bother? I recommend you take a shot at questions like that because they stretch your writing muscles, even though I can't hear your responses.

A few answers: It keeps that "C" story alive in viewers' minds, especially since it won't return until Act Two; it raises tension about Lesniak's state and invests us in her emotional challenge; and it delivers some information that was left unresolved in the teaser. On this last point, no scene should be written for exposition only. If you need to communicate facts, set them within an emotional context, as happens here. (Write "C" in square 4 on the grid.)

Scene 5

Notice that the next scene is set apart merely by an Angle within the same time and place and doesn't have a new slug line such as "INT. SQUAD ROOM – DAY." You couldn't use INT. SQUAD ROOM anyway because it belonged to Scene 4, so "Angle" — which is a literary device, and doesn't intend to tell the director which angle to shoot — flags that this is a new story beat.

#11 lasts almost three pages — a little long when the material has no external action. What's actually going on? Well, first you need to know that Sylvia Costas, the Assistant D.A. is Sipowicz' girlfriend (and in later episodes becomes his wife). Costas is beautiful, sophisticated, intelligent — a step up for Andy Sipowicz. She loves him, though, and tries to help, even if he's too proud to accept advice. Now picture the smooth, attractive, newly arrived Bobby Simone in the same room. With those dynamics in mind, re-read this scene.

Look for Sipowicz' motive, his vain efforts to knock down Simone, Costas' curiosity about Simone, and how the implied threat of her interest results in lines that don't seem to be about much at all while we can almost feel Sipowicz boiling underneath. Obviously, this is the "A" story, so "A" goes in square 5.

Scene 6

#12 and #13 together make up scene six, which returns to the "B" story by introducing Paula, a guest star who may have the secret to the murder. Using resistance to the cops as they enter the showroom, and Paula's reluctance to reveal what she knows, the scene builds conflict.

This takes us to the end of Act One, which ought to be a cliffhanger. The anticipation of more unexpected turns in the Matarano case might generate the kind of dramatic tension to keep an audience through the commercial break. However, this is not such a tremendous act ender, though the "B" story has certainly been advanced. I think what holds viewers to this episode is the arrival of Bobby Simone and curiosity how he'll affect the whole series.

After you write "B" in the box for scene six, you'll notice the number of scenes in Act One doesn't go to seven. That doesn't matter. And if you add the two scenes in the teaser to these six, that's actually eight scenes within the first 14 minutes or so. In the original script, Act One was 16 pages, including the teaser, and set three stories in motion, so it certainly accomplished a lot of storytelling.

THE SECOND EXCERPT

Four years later, the "long narrative" of the many-faceted relationship between Sipowicz and Simone comes to a close with Simone's death. "Hearts and Souls" (story by Steven Bochco & David Milch & Bill Clark; teleplay by Nicholas Wootton) stretched the boundaries of episodic television as it followed Simone through a kaleidoscope of flashbacks to the afterlife, delivering an emotional and spiritual dimension rarely seen on screen.

In the Teaser and Act One we'll observe the interplay of comedy and tragedy and a gradual build of suspense before the show takes its surprising turns in Acts Two, Three and Four. Read it before moving on to the analysis.

NYPD Blue

"Hearts and Souls"

FADE IN:

1   EXT. HOSPITAL - MORNING   1

       To establish --

2   INT. HOSPITAL WAITING ROOM - MORNING   2

       Present are SIPOWICZ, KIRKENDALL and MARTINEZ. Given the
       configuration of the room and its proximity to the door
       exiting the Cardiac Care Unit, Martinez has the prime vantage
       point for viewing Simone's departure and waving greeting,
       this to Sipowicz' simmering chagrin. After a beat --

                         SIPOWICZ
                You're gonna monopolize that
                position?

                         MARTINEZ
                   (defensive)
                I didn't see anything yet.

                         KIRKENDALL
                   (to Sipowicz)
                He wants to wave to Bobby.

                         SIPOWICZ
                That's why we're all here Martinez.

                         MARTINEZ
                Andy, I ain't moving.

                         KIRKENDALL
                I brought a harness so I could
                dangle from the ceiling.

                         SIPOWICZ
                Yeah, that's funny.

       Medavoy's just arrived in a mood of happy anticipation.

                         MEDAVOY
                I take it the grand departure
                hasn't taken place yet?

                         KIRKENDALL
                Hey Greg.

2.

Sipowicz looks away, disgruntled. Medavoy surveys the room.

>   MEDAVOY
> You're in the garden spot, huh
> James? Greet Bobby without exposing
> him to any bugs.

>   SIPOWICZ
> Yeah, he came 'two in the morning
> with a pup tent.

Martinez snorts at Sipowicz. Medavoy remains sanguine --

>   MEDAVOY
> Plenty of good spots.

Sipowicz paces. Off which --

>   CUT TO:

3   INT. SIMONE'S HOSPITAL ROOM - MORNING   3

SIMONE is sitting in a chair. His pants and shoes are on.
Emaciated from his illness, Simone swims in the shirt RUSSELL
is carefully buttoning. Russell, in whom we identify
excitement layered over physical and nervous exhaustion,
studies her husband with a hovering solicitude.

>   SIMONE
> Are you done?

>   RUSSELL
> Am I hurting you?

>   SIMONE
> No no.

>   RUSSELL
> One more.
>   (completing her task)
> You've got like a little drainage,
> I wanted to go slow buttoning over
> the bandage.

>   SIMONE
> Now I'm going to lean back a
> second.

>   RUSSELL
> You set the schedule Bobby.

He tries to manage a smile of reassurance.

                                            3.

                        SIMONE
            Not used to all this action.

She forces a smile in return, watches as he privately tries
to measure his feeling of growing malaise. After a beat --

                        RUSSELL
            Dr. Swan said you might get a
            little drainage from your stitches.

                        SIMONE
            Was my bandage wet?

                        RUSSELL
            No, it was a little yellow
            drainage.

Simone nods. After a beat --

                        RUSSELL (CONT'D)
            I wonder where Dr. Swan is.

                        SIMONE
            We got time.

                        RUSSELL
            It's just he was supposed to
            discharge you twenty minutes ago,

Simone closes his eyes. Though Russell has tried to sound as
if she's dealing with a minor irritation, in fact she's
growingly, irrationally afraid that if they don't leave soon
they're not going to be able to leave at all.

                                        CUT TO:

4   INT. HOSPITAL WAITING ROOM - MORNING   4

Sipowicz has conceived an excuse to improve his position --

                        SIPOWICZ
            I'm going to make a phone call.

                        KIRKENDALL
            You want the cellphone?

                        SIPOWICZ
                (shakes his head no)
            Personal, I better use the
            payphone.

He heads out. The others watch.

                    MEDAVOY
                (admiring amusement)
            You know what Andy's doing, James?
            He's improving his position.

                    MARTINEZ
                (nods)
            He could lose five years from his
            pension, making that lame an
            excuse.

Sipowicz has reached the phones. DR. SWAN exits the
elevators, moves past. Sipowicz, feigning dismay at
discovering he lacks the proper change, keeps his head down,
re-examining this phenomenon as he moves toward the Nurses
Station.

                                        CUT TO:

5   INT. SIMONE'S HOSPITAL ROOM - MORNING   5

Simone and Russell react as Dr. Swan enters, utters his
standard discharge line.

                    DR. SWAN
            Understand you want to get out of
            here this morning.

                    SIMONE
            Absolutely.

                    RUSSELL
            Bobby has a little drainage on his
            bandage.

                    DR. SWAN
                (nods, not overly
                 concerned)
            Some of your stitches may be slow
            in absorbing.

                    SIMONE
            Diane was saying.

Russell emulates Dr. Swan's tone of unconcern.

                    RUSSELL
            He just has a little yellow
            drainage.

                    DR. SWAN
            Let's have a look.

5.

Dr. Swan keeps his tone casual, though in his lexicon "yellow drainage" translates "big trouble." He begins unbuttoning Simone's shirt. Simone fills this silence --

> SIMONE
> Diane's talking about hanging her
> shingle out 'her time off The Job.

> DR. SWAN
> Good, I'm looking for an associate.

Dr. Swan's undone Simone's shirt, does his best to dissemble his reaction on noting a spreading stain on Simone's bandage made by yellow pus seeping from his incision.

> DR. SWAN (CONT'D)
> You do have some drainage.

> RUSSELL
> From his stitches dissolving?

Dr. Swan keeps his voice neutral -- as if discussing an interesting chess problem --

> DR. SWAN
> I'm not sure. I'm going to use a
> little Q-tip, check Bobby's
> incision.

The camera positions itself consistent with beginning a discrete revelation of Simone's incision as Dr Swan removes the bandage. Off which --

                                                    CUT TO:

6   INT. HALLWAY OUTSIDE SIMONE'S ROOM - MORNING   6

Sipowicz has inched forward to the Nurses Station, glances back one last time to see if he's under scrutiny from his colleagues, then takes the last few steps necessary to gain a view of Simone's room, reacting with sickened shock on seeing Russell and Dr. Swan helping Simone back into his bed.

The eyes of the two partners meet. Sipowicz puts up his hand to Simone, waves weakly; Simone nods acknowledgement as Sipowicz moves back to the Waiting Area.

                                                    CUT TO:

7   INT. HOSPITAL WAITING ROOM - MORNING   7

Medavoy spots Sipowicz coming out the closed door of the
C.C.U.

                    MEDAVOY
                (almost chortles)
            To Andy, rule-obedience is a
            totally foreign concept. Went up
            the hall to wave.

Martinez won't concede his own position's been supplanted.

                    MARTINEZ
            What I'm here for, watch Bobby
            enter that elevator.

Sipowicz re-enters.

                    MEDAVOY
            You went to wave to Bobby, didn't
            you Andy?

                    SIPOWICZ
            They're putting him back in bed.

Kirkendall reacts with silent dismay.

                    MARTINEZ
            Is that some temporary precaution?

                    SIPOWICZ
            He don't look good.

                    MEDAVOY
            He went through major surgery ten
            days ago Andy.

Kirkendall's seen Russell approaching.

                    KIRKENDALL
            Hi Diane.

                    RUSSELL
            We have to stay awhile more.

                    MEDAVOY
                (emptily)
            Yeah huh?

7.

                    RUSSELL
         Bobby has some wound infection they
         have to identify. He needs a C.A.T.
         scan and then they're going to
         debride him.

                    MARTINEZ
         Andy said he was lying back down.

Russell nods --

                    RUSSELL
         You should go on to work. I'll call
         if there's any news.

                    KIRKENDALL
         Sure, call when you get a chance.

The Detectives put on their best face when Russell leaves.
Before she's out the door Russell gives a passing half-smile
to Sipowicz. A beat. Sipowicz seethes --

                    SIPOWICZ
                 (to Martinez)
         Want to come back or you want to
         keep your spot?

They're all devastated, troop out. Off which --

                                        SMASH CUT TO:

MAIN TITLES

8   EXT. PRECINCT HOUSE - MORNING   8

      To establish --

9   INT. SQUAD ROOM - MORNING   9

      Sipowicz is the first of the Detectives to return from the
      hospital. He's solemn, dour; moving as though weighted;
      FANCY's going over materials with DOLORES at her desk; it's
      clear they know of Simone's turn or the worse. As Sipowicz
      hangs up his coat --

                    FANCY
         Your ex-wife's here Andy, she's in
         the lavatory.

                    SIPOWICZ
         Is she all right?

8.

                        FANCY
                    (noncommittal)
              Yeah, she seems all right.

Sipowicz nods; even this unexpected information can't refocus
his thoughts.

                        FANCY (CONT'D)
              Did you see him at all?

                        SIPOWICZ
                    (nods)
              I saw him from out in the hallway
              for just a couple seconds.

                        FANCY
              Did he look like he was getting
              sick again?

                        SIPOWICZ
              I don't know.

Sipowicz sees KATIE SIPOWICZ, his ex-wife and mother of Andy
Jr., As she exits into the hallway. She's skittish, clutches
her handbag.

                        KATIE
              Hi Andy.

Sipowicz moves to join her in the hallway.

                        SIPOWICZ
              Are you all right Katie?

                        KATIE
              Yes, I just had to use the girls'
              room.

                        SIPOWICZ
              I mean what're you doing here?

                        KATIE
              Is this a bad time? I can talk to
              you some other time.

At this point Sipowicz is pretty sure he's smelling booze on
Katie's breath.

                        SIPOWICZ
              C'mon, let's talk in the Coffee
              Room.

9.

Because she's been drinking, Sipowicz decides to take her the
back way to the Coffee Room. As he begins to shepherd her in
this direction we see Medavoy and Martinez ascending the
stairs.

10   INT. HALLWAY - CONTINUOUS   10

Follow Sipowicz and Katie --

                        KATIE
              It's not the worst, right Andy? The
              worst already happened.

Sipowicz' embarrassment at her condition distracts him from
what she's saying.

                        SIPOWICZ
              What're you talking about?

                        KATIE
              I'm in a problem, but Andy J.
              dying's the worst that can ever
              happen.

                        SIPOWICZ
              Katie when in hell did you start
              drinking?

                        KATIE
              What?

                        SIPOWICZ
              C'mon in here.

As they enter.

11   INT. COFFEE ROOM - CONTINUOUS   11

He brings her to a chair.

                        KATIE
              I had one small drink. It's coming
              to the City and seeing you. I had
              one small drink.

He's poured her some coffee, puts it in front of her, in the
next instant reacts with gruff sheepishness --

                        SIPOWICZ
              You still take milk?

                              KATIE
                    Please.

Sipowicz provides this, watches her.

                              KATIE (CONT'D)
                         (barely audible)
                    I'm in some trouble, Andy. I was
                    arrested in Seacaucus for a D.U.I.

                              SIPOWICZ
                    On your way in to see me?

She shakes her head no.

                              SIPOWICZ (CONT'D)
                    So the small drink today wasn't
                    your first small drink.

She starts to cry, holds her hand to her mouth --

                              KATIE
                    Please don't bully me.

                              SIPOWICZ
                    All right. All right.

Katie tries to compose herself --

                              KATIE
                    I'd had a glass of wine, one glass
                    and the Cop says I rolled a stop
                    which I did not. The person in
                    front of me rolled the stop.

                              SIPOWICZ
                    Did you blow impaired? Did you take
                    a breath test?

                              KATIE
                         (shakes her head no)
                    I always heard you say never agree
                    to tests.

                              SIPOWICZ
                    And you told this Jersey Cop your
                    ex-husband's on The Job?

                              KATIE
                    It didn't do any good.

                    SIPOWICZ
        And Andy J. you told him about --
        that he'd been on The Job in
        Hackensack?

                    KATIE
        I couldn't bring myself to say
        about Andy.

                    SIPOWICZ
        Give me this Cop's name. When did
        this happen?

                    KATIE
        Nine weeks ago.

                    SIPOWICZ
            (shocked)
        Nine weeks? When the hell's your
        trial date Katie?

                    KATIE
        This afternoon.

He stares at her in angry bafflement.

                    KATIE (CONT'D)
            (apologetic)
        I was so embarrassed to come to
        you.

                    SIPOWICZ
        Were you too embarrassed to go to a
        lawyer?

                    KATIE
        I thought maybe you could help me
        keep it from that.

He slams his hand on the table --

                    SIPOWICZ
        How the hell was I going to help
        you Katie if you didn't tell me
        about it?

All his old frustration at her timidity and fear and
defeatedness wash over him. She winces as she always did when
he would shout or slam his hand down.

                    KATIE
        Oh Andy.

He looks at her cower; his hand goes to his forehead. He
looks away --

                    SIPOWICZ
          You got the paperwork?

Gaze averted, she produces the summons and trial notice from
her purse. He looks at these a beat, then --

                    SIPOWICZ (CONT'D)
          Drink your coffee and let me see
          what I can do.

                    KATIE
          Am I too embarrassing to you to
          stay here?

                    SIPOWICZ
          Katie, drink your coffee.

Off Katie, as Sipowicz exits --

12   INT. SQUAD ROOM - CONTINUOUS   12

Medavoy's with Martinez at Martinez' desk. They barely note
Sipowicz' exit from the Coffee Room, his brusque movement
toward his desk. After a beat --

                    MEDAVOY
          I'll tell you James, I never had
          the wind so completely taken from
          my sails.

                    MARTINEZ
          I got as much enthusiasm doing a
          day's work as stepping on a nail.

Sipowicz peers at Katie's paperwork, picks up the telephone.

Meanwhile MICHAEL WOLFF, 28, in sport coat and slacks, has
entered the Squad. He's carrying a manila file folder.

                    WOLFF
               (to Dolores)
          My name's Michael Wolff. I need to
          speak with a Detective.

                    DOLORES
          Just a minute.

Dolores has checked the Catching Board, heads for Medavoy at
his desk.

                    DOLORES (CONT'D)
Detective Sipowicz is catching but
he's with his ex-wife --

                    MEDAVOY
What's the guy's problem?

                    DOLORES
He didn't say.

                    MEDAVOY
I mean did it seem like an urgent
problem?

Dolores, as distressed as the others by the turn in Simone's
condition, allows herself some small exasperation.

                    DOLORES
He didn't say. He's got like a
bruise above his eye, I don't know
if that's part of it or not.

                    MEDAVOY
Yeah, all right.

Martinez gives his partner a commiserating look as Medavoy
gathers his energy, starts toward the Catching Area.

13   NEW ANGLE - SIPOWICZ   13

Into receiver --

                    SIPOWICZ
My name's Sipowicz, I'm a Detective
in the Fifteenth Squad in Manhattan
-- you wrote my ex-wife up for a
rolling stop last September 8th ...

Medavoy's reached the Catching Area --

                    MEDAVOY
                (to Wolff)
Can I help you?

                    WOLFF
I was assaulted.

                    MEDAVOY
Uh-huh.

Wolff points to his eye --

14.

                    WOLFF
          My name's Michael Wolff. The son of
          one of my tenants gave this to me,
          and I've had just about enough.

                    MEDAVOY
          You want to press charges.

                    WOLFF
          Yes I want to press charges.

                    MEDAVOY
          For that half-a-shiner there,

                    WOLFF
          Yes.

Medavoy abandons the forlorn hope Wolff may dematerialize --

                    MEDAVOY
          Okay, c'mon.

As Medavoy shepherds Wolff toward his desk, <u>hold on</u> Sipowicz.

                    SIPOWICZ
                (into receiver,
                 incredulous)
          She don't tell you till you're in
          the Station House? You'd already
          turned the work in?
                (listens, nods)
          No, I can . . .I don't doubt what
          you're saying.
                (confiding)
          I'll tell you, we had a son on The
          Job in New Jersey got murdered --
          if she was impaired wouldn't
          surprise me if her drinking's
          ensued connected with that ...
                (rubbing his neck)
          Anyways, are you going to have a
          problem if I try reaching out to
          the Prosecutor?
                (beat)
          I appreciate it. All right, thanks
          a lot.

Sipowicz disconnects, punches in Costas' number --

                    SIPOWICZ (CONT'D)
                (abrupt)
          You know anyone in the D.A.'s
          Office in Seacaucus?
                (MORE)

15.

                SIPOWICZ(cont'd)
          (listens; angrily)
       I told you what I know on that --
       they kept him in and he's got a
       complication.
          (listens)
       'Cause my ex-wife took a collar
       driving drunk, Sylvia -- all right?
       -- and she don't let me know till
       three hours before her trial, and
       in between being criticized by you
       for my tone I'd like to try keeping
       her out of a jackpot. Now do you
       know any prosecutors in Seacaucus?
          (beat)
       All right. Thanks.

He hangs up. During this conversation, through the atrium
window, we've seen Katie, having exited the back door of the
Coffee Room, make her way to the landing through the rear and
side hallways, descend the stairs.

Now Sipowicz rises, starts toward the Coffee Room; as he
transits, <u>hold on</u> Medavoy and Michael Wolff --

                MEDAVOY
       Before we make this a case, Mr.
       Wolff, have you considered how
       filing charges against her son's
       gonna affect your tenant's
       willingness to pay rent?

                WOLFF
       I'm in my last year at Stern, which
       is the N.Y.U. Business School --

                MEDAVOY
          (who gives a shit?)
       I see.

                WOLFF
       I'm managing this building while my
       uncle decides if he likes living in
       Florida; I could care less how
       bringing charges against this
       steroid case affects his mother's
       paying rent.

Having found the Coffee Room empty, Sipowicz returns to the
squad --

                SIPOWICZ
       Son of a bitch!

16.

This declaration is made in proximity to Wolff; Sipowicz
moves into Fancy's Office --

14   INT. FANCY'S OFFICE - CONTINUOUS   14

He's behind his desk. Sipowicz enters.

                    SIPOWICZ
          I need lost time.

                    FANCY
          All right.

                    SIPOWICZ
          I need to go find my rummy ex-wife.

Sipowicz starts for the door, stops --

                    SIPOWICZ (CONT'D)
          I need the cellular.

Fancy nods; Sipowicz collects the cellular, exits --

15   INT. SQUAD ROOM - CONTINUOUS   15

He heads for the door, stops at Dolores' desk.

                    SIPOWICZ
          I got the cellular.

                    DOLORES
          Okay.

                    SIPOWICZ
          If my wife calls, or there's news
          on the other front.

Dolores nods. Sipowicz exits.

16   NEW ANGLE - MEDAVOY AND WOLFF   16

Medavoy's begun filling out a 61; Wolff corrects Medavoy's
spelling of the tenant's name --

                    WOLFF
          U, not O on his name, and two l's --
          Bullinger.

Medavoy looks up, considers Wolff, shakes his head and
laughs.

17.

                    WOLFF (CONT'D)
          What's so funny?

                    MEDAVOY
          Nothing, Mr. Wolff.

                    WOLFF
          I guess you and I don't share the
          same sense of humor.

                    MEDAVOY
          I guess I don't really care about
          that, okay. Let's just you and me
          fill out your complaint how his guy
          only hit you the one time while you
          dunned his mother for her rent.

Off which --

                                        FADE OUT.
                    END ACT ONE

ANALYSIS

Let's start by naming the stories. "A" is about Simone dying; "B" is Sipowicz and his ex-wife Katie; "C" is Medavoy and Wolff. I've used simple tags, and that's fine for identification, but when you plan your own script, I suggest you create real dramatic log lines. That way, you'll be sure your stories have conflict - that they're actually stories, not just situations. Using the example episode, you might phrase log lines something like this:

A: As Simone's death becomes imminent, he fights until he ultimately makes peace with his memories. Within this arena, Russell, Sipowicz and others have story arcs from denial and anger to acceptance.

B: When Sipowicz is challenged by Katie's drinking and desperation, he must overcome his anger, guilt and his own alcoholic history to be able to help her.

C: Medavoy struggles to stay professional while an arrogant man's complaints escalate.

Notice in each case I've stated the stories as issues for main cast, not the guest cast, though the guests (Katie and Wolff) are bringing the inciting incidents.

COLD OPENING

This teaser is entirely "A" story (slug lines #1 through #7), though it's comprised of several beats. In planning an important opening like this, I would begin by making a mini-outline, planning each beat to build suspense. See if you can make your own list of the turning points in these first pages that end with "SMASH CUT TO," which signals the end of the teaser.

Did you get these beats?

• The Detectives spar with each other in anticipation;

• The first reveal: Russell discovers the drainage;

• Sipowicz schemes to find out what's happening;

• Tension mounts when Dr. Swan confirms the problem;

• Sipowicz discovers it; we see his personal stakes;

- Sipowicz and Russell reveal the crisis to the detectives, who leave, apprehensive.

Those six beats ramp quickly into the drama using a basic storytelling progression: Anticipation — Expectation — Surprise. That is, viewers are led to *anticipate* an event, which holds people through the set-up. As the action advances, we come to *expect* certain outcomes. Instead, the story turns (twists), generating a sense of *surprise* which then begins a new sequence of suspense. You can readily create tension on screen that way, as this teaser demonstrates so well.

Also, consider the use of humor in this heavy episode. Here's another age-old practice: increase the impact of tragedy by setting it against a comic foil. Shakespeare played his fools and foolishness — sometimes for belly laughs from the audience of his day – in his most tragic plays. Here, the episode begins with a moment so light it's almost silly — jockeying for position at a window. Then, as the drama moves into Act One, an outrageous fool appears in the person of Mr. Wolff. With all that in mind, let's get into the first Act.

Act One

The "B" story about Sipowicz and Katie (#8 to #12) begins with several beats that are emotionally challenging to Sipowicz in the midst of the already-heartbreaking news his partner isn't getting better. I just spoke about the value of comic relief, yet here's more stress. So why do you think the writers chose to come out of the title sequence and open Act One with this?

Here are some possibilities: While the Simone illness is suspenseful, it does not involve action for our continuing cast — except, of course, Simone and Russell, though even for them, the conflicts are internal, and their decisions result mainly from reflection. In dealing with Katie's very tangible distress, followed by her wandering off, Sipowicz is able to vent the claustrophobic hospital.

Katie's story also provides an opportunity for Sipowicz to externalize his feelings about Simone (including his anger), without which he'd be stuck brooding. Throughout *NYPD Blue*, a prominent quality of Sipowicz as a character is his determination not to yield to helplessness even in the face of the dregs of society, or, in this case, death. Often, Sipowicz fails, but here, Katie's needs provide a way for him to be the rescuer when he cannot rescue Simone.

See if you can discover other reasons for choosing this "B" story in this episode, and why it's an effective opening for Act One.

Throughout this Act, take note of the fluid blend of scenes within the Squad Room. In the first sample script, the scenes tended to be easily separated. Here, you'll find multiple scenes in the same time and place, choreographed directorially. For example, at the end of #9, while Sipowicz takes Katie into the hallway, we see Medavoy and Martinez ascending the stairs. The point is that we don't lose the persistence of the other characters and dilemmas. The action directs the camera to "Follow" them, moving our attention with this scene, but we're also aware of material which is concurrent in the room we've left.

Similarly, the "C" story with Wolff commences as Sipowicz goes towards his desk in #12. In fact, notice that the "B" story is literally interspersed with the "C" story in #13. Towards the end of #13, you'll see multiple visual layers: While Medavoy and Wolff move to Medavoy's desk, they pass Sipowicz at his desk, and while Sipowicz speaks, we see Katie sneaking away in the background, followed by Sipowicz crossing the room, leaving us holding on Medavoy and Wolff. It's a complex, but elegant way to create depth (multiple levels) on screen.

This layering style — scene on scene in the same time and place — is found in many other sophisticated series too, so watch for it. In writing your own script, though, I suggest you separate the stories when you plan them initially, and weave them together only when you're ready to go from outline to teleplay. (You can read more about this technique in Chapter Four.)

WHAT YOU SHOULD DO NEXT

Read and analyze all the good television scripts you can find from many different series. Sure, you've watched TV all your life, but observing how episodes are crafted on the page prepares you to work as a writer.

If you'd like to see how these two example shows turned out, they can be read and watched at the Library of the Writers Guild and at the Museum of Television and Radio. Both institutions have award-winning shows available to the public. (You'll find those and other resources in the Appendix.)

Once you have a solid sense how the best dramas are constructed, you're ready for the steps to write your own, which I'll show you in the next chapter.

Summary Points

Many (though not all) drama series use parallel non-sequential stories denoted by letters A, B, C, and so forth. Three stories per episode are typical, though some shows have more. Each story is usually "driven by" one character in the main cast.

Scenes tend to run two minutes or less. Six or seven scenes comprise an act in a classic network drama. With four acts, that adds to around 28 scenes total in an hour episode. However, certain shows that have quick dialogue-intensive scenes have more beats per act; shows with action sequences might have fewer. Shows with five or six acts may have as few as 20 scenes total.

A "teaser" is a prologue to an episode and may incite one or more of the stories.

By analyzing a quality show using the "grid," you can see its structure at a glance.

The best television shows demonstrate the principles of dramatic art that apply to all quality screenwriting.

Spotlight on Writing Procedurals
Model and Anti-Model

with Guest Speakers Ann Donahue of *CSI: Miami* and Melissa Rosenberg of *Dexter*

Ann
Donahue

CSI is "the most successful franchise in television history," according to Les Moonves, president of CBS, the network that broadcasts the shows. With the seminal series flourishing season after season and two chart-topping progeny, *CSI: Miami* and *CSI: New York*, not to mention off-network re-runs, the franchise is inescapable, not that the tens of millions of viewers are trying to escape. When all the other "procedural" series are added, this genre, broadly defined, occupies around half of all hour drama series on network television.

Why?

Ann Donahue, co-creator and show-runner of *CSI:Miami* said it's because in a way, procedurals are simple. People want stories resolved, to see the solutions that aren't really available in life, to be assured at the end of each episode the bad guy gets caught.

Not that *CSI: Miami* is simple — the investigations have multiple twists, the science is intricate, and the forensic visuals are startling. But from the viewpoint of dramatic construction and the intention of the series, the format is predictable. That brings us to a general definition of "procedurals": shows that crack their cases each episode, where the emphasis is on the puzzle more than arcs for the continuing cast. Investigation — crime-solving — is key in *CSI* and other police/detective procedurals, though *House* is an example of a medical procedural that also uses a succession of clues to reveal the culprit (in that case, a disease).

Procedurals have been around since the era when only three networks existed and they all required closure on every show every week. In the 1990s, *Law and Order* infused the genre with serious issues, "ripped from the headlines." But *CSI* raised the entertainment ante when it appeared in 2000. Anthony Zuiker, a writer who had no television experience at the time, had done tremendous research, even ridden with crime scene investigators in Las Vegas to create the pilot. The network brought in experienced producer-writer Carol Mendelsohn, who in turn brought in Ann Donahue, who had won an Emmy for *Picket Fences* and had worked at Steven J. Cannell Television at the same time Mendelsohn did.

From the beginning, *CSI* was a complicated procedural with science that none of them knew and inserts showing incised flesh pierced by bullets (later dubbed "meat shots"). They had five technical advisors and had to figure out how to write the exposition and hide it.

Mendelsohn told *Written By* magazine in 2002 that their fidelity to fact continued as the series grew. The three executive producers searched newspapers for accounts of murders that inspired plots, and boned up on forensics. They went on to create the *CSI* style using super close-ups of microscopic evidence and unusual visual and sound techniques that dramatized changes of perspective, passage of time, or mood. Mendelsohn said, "The minutiae are the real essence of *CSI*. The interesting stuff is the real facts."

The challenge in writing procedurals is how to get beyond the technical to the heart. Donahue says: "The mistake we all make, including me and all of our writers on the first draft, is we do load it up with clues and we go to plot. Here's the thing: no one cares about plot. No one ever has. But story — story is not the same thing. You look around and it's the story of the guy who doesn't want to lose or who wants to go the distance. That's something people care about. Usually, that's the A story. The B story of that is his love — does he get the girl or not?

"With our shows, the A story is investigation, but the B story is the emotional line. How does one of our characters on *CSI* feel about the case and what is it doing to them personally; or one family member of the victim is involved and how can we help them through this tough time? We have to keep switching back and forth between the investigative A story and the emotional B story. If you have Act One and it's nothing but a clue takes you to this character, and that clue takes you to the next character, and our characters are only confronting them with evidence, you're failing.

"We're working on a story right now about a babysitter and there's a murder in the house where she's babysitting. We get prints of a man in the neighborhood. He says 'I went in there to steal something.' Yeah, well, why were you hanging around? Why was your nose pressed up against the window? 'Well, I was dating the babysitter, that's why.' Well, suddenly, it's not just a guy who was stealing something, but he's telling us something about our suspect who we heretofore thought was so innocent. Now we find out she's covering up the murder for her boyfriend. We find out later, they're covering up for each other. The point is you're not just interviewing the neighbor who says, yeah I robbed; I was a bad person. It's what we call upping the stakes. Someone who presented herself as innocent is having a guy over for sex. Later, that whole story becomes a 'Mrs. Robinson' story because the babysitter's mother was also sleeping with the boyfriend.

"Every person your characters investigate — and it has to be based on forensic evidence — doesn't have to be guilty but they have to give you something else so the story builds, builds, builds. The other rule is you have to have a warm body by the end of Act One, within the first 17 pages. You have to have a real suspect that informs the audience about the story they're watching.

"A show's job is to entertain. It's plot-driven, and the writer should commit, tell the story and let nothing get in the way — not educating the audience or political correctness or 'arias.' The hero must have desire. He must be thwarted. There must be complications.

"The difference the *CSI* franchise brought in was our production values. Each show, if it's done right, is always going to be visually intriguing and ultimately satisfying. The filmmaking is changing, but filmmaking will never replace storytelling. What I find heartening is what's always going to matter is the story and the execution of the story. When you get to the end, a good ending is surprising and yet inevitable. That's what people are waiting for.

"So every story, whether it's a medical show or a cop show or a soap opera is a mystery. A secret is going to be revealed. When are other people going to find it out? How do we see a certain person get a comeuppance? And I don't think that's ever going to change. We want it the way we always wanted it to be. We want the ending we couldn't get in our formative years."

After speaking with Ann Donahue I wanted to put the procedurals giant and *CSI: Miami* in perspective, so I had a conversation with Melissa Rosenberg, Co-Executive Producer of *Dexter*. That show is also set in Miami, also uses forensics (the character Dexter is a blood-spatter specialist), and also has a murder each week. But *Dexter*, which debuted in late 2006 on Showtime, is different in every other way.

Rosenberg had written and produced series that included character-driven dramas and dramedies, and, unlike Donahue who brought well-honed experience in procedurals to *CSI*, Rosenberg had never done one. "So it was interesting in *Dexter* that there was a forensic element," she said. "Generally, I do not watch procedurals, so I've stayed away from them."

PD: But the *CSIs* are wildly popular.

MR: All of the procedurals on every network are wildly popular.

PD: Why do you think they are?

Melissa
Rosenberg

MR: I think people love a mystery and they love to see it unfold.

PD: *Dexter* may be a mystery but it isn't really a procedural, is it? The episodes don't have closure, and it has a strong serial element.

MR: During our first season it changed. When we all came on, we thought it's a cop show. True, the main character is a serial killer, but there's a procedural element. We had a choppy beginning because we were figuring out what the show is. Finally we figured out it's about this fascinating character.

PD: How did that change from procedural to character drama dawn on the staff?

MR: After we kept banging our heads on the wall trying to figure out the stories. We realized it's not about solving mysteries. It was about exploring this character. That's the big difference. There was an overall mystery of the season: thirteen episodes of who's the ice truck killer, and that's an ongoing mystery. But the week in week out shows weren't like that. There are too many shows on television like *CSI* or a zillion others.

We don't do procedural stories. If we're getting into one, we say, oh, wait a minute. We have to start over because we're not doing a *Dexter* story, and we have to find our way back to character. My nightmare show to work on would be *House*. That's such intricate procedural writing and research. It's a complicated, long medical mystery.

PD: Comparing *Dexter*, *House* also has a strong central character, unlike *CSI* which has an ensemble cast. How is *Dexter* different?

MR: *House* solves a disease of the week, so every episode can stand alone. They've kept an ongoing story throughout the season, but it's very much background. For us, whatever the crime of the week is, well, we don't really have crimes of the week. There's Dexter committing the crime of the week. He follows some criminal, so there's that procedural element but we don't have a formula where at the beginning and end of every episode we do the same thing. One of Showtime's requests of us was to not have a formula. It was funny coming out of network television, used to being on shows and trying to find their formula, then to go on to a show where you don't have to do that.

PD: That's very different from most network shows. Ann Donahue felt strongly about the structure; by 17 minutes in, at the end of Act One, there had to be, as she called it, "a warm body," somebody who was a likely suspect they'd go find. Every week it has to be that way, and at the end of the show you'd come to the end of it; there isn't a series-long arc, though viewers do care about the main characters and they do have relationships with each other.

MR: Our very first conversations are the season arc. We track where we want to go. Then we start breaking it down until we

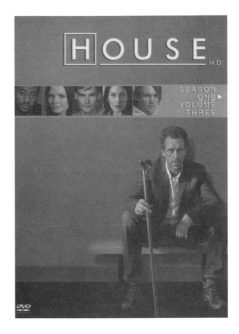

get to the individual episode. Showtime said the objective was really not to be network television. They wanted serialized episodes.

PD: How has the pressure differed at Showtime compared to networks?

MR: Less. So much less. Cable is the place to be — twelve episodes and out, compared to 22 or even 26 that a lot of network shows have, and the pressure of slamming it out there every week. My first *Dexter* script I finished a month before prep. There was time to think about storytelling. I never had that on any show; it's just wonderful.

Another difference was in the notes. My last show was on CBS and when we had a notes call there would be maybe fifteen people on that conference call. I wasn't even sure who all of them were. But at Showtime: three people, our two executive producers and the writer. You could actually have a conversation; you could discuss a story whereas everything at the network was by committee.

PD: Dexter is basically a vigilante murderer? Did the ethics come up in discussion?

MR: He's our lead, so you have to get people invested in him. We try to take people along with him, rooting for Dexter, and then reveal what a monster he is. We hope the audience goes ooh, I wasn't ready for that.

The other show that does that extraordinarily well is *The Sopranos*. You get deeper and deeper into Tony and then he does something horrible, and you remember, oh yeah, this guy's a sociopath. As writers, we bring people in, seduce them with the character and then shine the mirror on themselves, because we all have these very disturbing aspects that none of us wants to look at. That's what storytelling is all about.

PD: I wonder if this kind of show could have been on the air in another era. On *CSI*, for example, the good guys always get the bad guy, and he is a really bad guy. And that's satisfying to a large part of the audience. Now this is the flip side: Dexter, the killer, invites you to see the world from another point of view. I wonder about this being on the air at this time.

MR: True, *Dexter* is of its time. I don't think this would have been on the air around 9/11 either because we needed a couple of years to believe things were black and white. But it's not that simple.

CHAPTER 4

WRITING YOUR OWN EPISODE

HEARING VOICES

(The following impressionistic essay appeared in *The Journal* of the Writers Guild of America.)

> "…Trumpet at his lips, he listened to the notes bounce from brick rooftop to rooftop until, finally, he knew the rhythm of the echoes. He'd based his music on those intervals. People called him a genius, but he knew what they could not understand — that he had merely listened."

That's from a short story I wrote in college, when I believed music exists before it is played, that a statue is inside the marble block and the sculptor cuts away whatever is not the statue, and that for writers … now we come to it … characters exist beyond what is written, with larger lives than fit on film. They'll talk to you. You merely have to listen.

You catch a character the way a surfer catches a wave, waiting in still water until it wells up from a source as invisible as it is powerful.

Whaddya want? That was a kid talking.

Okay, okay we know what it's really like. In some scripts, catching a character is more like catching a bug mid-flight on your windshield.

Working writers have to hear other voices. "You want it good or you want it Friday?" Yeah, yeah, I know, good *and* Friday … and it better be Friday.

The voice of my first movie business boss plays in a perpetual loop. Greenly arrived from the East Coast, I had landed a studio development job. I brought the boss a script by a New York friend and naively blazoned it with the kiss of death. I called it beautiful. I can hear the boss now, over his thick cigar, "Don't tell me that shit!" He's making boxing moves like Norman Mailer. "Man to man! Action! Action! Get it? Mano a mano!" He's snapping his fingers in my face. "Is it going to make 100 million? Is it? Is it? That's what you tell me. You come in here and prove it's going to make 100 million." A sucker dare. No one can prove any movie will make a dime. But I didn't know.

He didn't snap his fingers in your face. You're over the top, and that character is running wild. Stop him!

Okay, okay. He didn't snap. But the rest is true. I soon left the studio job for a writing career. The denigrated New York author went on to win a Pulitzer. And the executive retired richer than both of us.

What's that got to do with the voices?

They don't come easy. Sometimes you have to snare them.

My field is television drama. I've had the chance to learn from a few great writer-producers who provoked their staffs to what drives a real person, not just what gets a laugh or twists the plot. Where else do you find a 22-hour narrative of evolving characters? Immediacy. Intimacy. Power. Like a hard-charging river. But we all know what's along the banks: some cesspool shows.

When I was a beginner, I went for an assignment on one. It wasn't exactly a cesspool, just stagnant. The series characters were moved like toys to fit a franchise. While the producer described contrivances he wanted me to write, the characters in my head screamed, "Can we have the bathroom pass?" With enough craft, you can do an assignment like that. Fake it. Kind of like a worn-out love affair, and as deadening.

Then, in the midst of the script, a character surprised me with a line that could only have come from her. Gotcha! The sound of her voice was like having her address. And once I knew how to find her, she forced the characters who answered her to be as real. And they made their world whole. Once you've had it good, you don't want it any other way.

Right, like you do that every day.

No. Staring at the computer screen with a belly full of caffeine and terror, I know what it's like to have nothing on a character besides every *thing*. Facts. Stuff that has to happen at the act break. Wind whistling on deserted shores. But I've learned something: craft can be a tugboat that pulls you out to where you can hear the voices.

So, you gonna get to Joan of Arc, or what?

Not Joan. But there is a connection. The high when you're flying with a scene rolling out like it's alive — that euphoria is worth putting up with the detractors and distractions. It's like an all-nighter when you can't get enough of each other, you and the characters, and no one wants to sleep again ever, and it's already all there... just listen.

* * *

I decided to begin this chapter about preparing you to write your own script by quoting that article so we don't lose sight of the source — where writing really comes from — as we focus on the nuts and bolts of craft.

FINDING YOUR STORIES

Whether you're setting out to write a spec script or you're on a staff vying for an episode assignment, you'll need to choose subjects which (1) fit the medium, (2) complement the specific show, (3) contain events that will play on screen, and (4) express your unique experience or fresh insights. Yes, you can do all four.

Ideas that will work on television have the scale and intimacy I discussed in Chapter One. So look for character-based subjects that benefit from scenes with dialogue.

To fit an existing show, you need to have watched that series so much you can hear the characters' voices in your head. And you'll have figured out the kinds of springboards the show uses to impel stories, and its pace and style.

As you know, externalized actions are basic to any screenwriting. Just as in a feature screenplay, you plan your structure around things that happen. That sounds simplistic, and I wouldn't bring it up but I've seen otherwise-sophisticated students become so involved with the psychology of TV characters they forget that character is expressed in a series of events on screen.

Finally, what do you bring to the party? Of course, you'll consider ongoing relationships among the cast; those kinds of continuing stories are called "on series," and are fine to write, but be warned: the large turns in a season's arc are planned by the show runners. It would be naïve to spec an episode where the Gilmore girls get married, or an episode of *Monk* where the character is cured of his obsessive-compulsive disorder, or a *Dead Like Me* where Georgia proves to her family that she's still alive. Don't do episodes that change the central characters or the course of the show.

Instead, think about incidents you know (or know of), and then play them out in the world of the show. If that's scary, you're not alone. Even Aaron Sorkin, creator of *The West Wing*, *Sports Night*, and movies including *A Few Good Men*, sometimes has difficulty beginning. He confided at a Writers Guild Foundation seminar in 2004: "It's bad enough trying to have ideas. When you really start you're trying to get one. Every day you're flipping through instantly dismissible ideas, so my head is like the worst movie you've ever seen. Horrible, horrible ideas that go nowhere. It's like being bludgeoned with your own inadequacies."

One way to break the logjam is through research. Some writers maintain files of clippings from quirky magazines and small town newspapers; others hit the Internet or books. For example, if you were planning a *CSI*, you'd be smart to investigate scientific clues that can be visualized under a microscope. If you're researching for *Carnivále*, dig up a sub-culture in the 1930s which inhabits a town the carnies would visit. For a *Law & Order*, you might come across a topical issue on an op-ed page and angle it with an unexpected interpretation of the law. Now, none of that means you should rely on gimmicks. Clever bits of information do not make stories. But they might turn your own creative wheels.

And here's how they turn: Make your subject live and breathe through the experiences of your continuing cast. That's key. The most common error is to tell the story through the guest cast. I'm going to repeat that in other words because it's so important: Don't write a story that can be told without your continuing cast. If your story could work as a movie without your show, then you haven't made it work for your show.

Here's an example of wrong and right ways to approach your story. Let's make believe you're planning an episode for a series about Jane and Sally, who are detectives, and you've come upon an item about a woman cat burglar who scales tall buildings to steal Manolo Blanik shoes.

A *wrong* log line would go like this: Portia Pedi, a former rock climbing champion, attempts to scale the Trump Tower at night to acquire the world's most expensive stilettos, but her clever plan is foiled when she's caught by Jane and Sally.

A better approach to an episode log line would be more like this: Jane confronts her fear of heights on a ledge of the Trump Tower at night when she must rescue Sally who has been taken hostage by a woman cat burglar, and together Jane and Sally foil the plan to steal the world's most expensive stilettos.

See the difference? In the wrong version, the guest cast drives the action of the show and leaves the main cast as mere witnesses or pawns of the guest. In the second version, the challenge, jeopardy, and viewpoint belong to the main cast, whose decisions create the turning points.

Once you've identified a subject for your spec episode, write it as a log line. (Log lines are discussed in Chapter Two, in case you want to refer back.) That's easier said than done because in order to state your story in a sentence, you need to know the whole dramatic arc. I understand that's difficult, but I advise you not to skip ahead. Once you're clear about your story's conflict you'll be secure you really do have a plot, not only a premise.

If you're working on an A-story series, you can move on as soon as you have a single log line, though you'll need to make sure your one story has sufficient substance for around 28 scenes. If you're doing a show with three or more stories, you'll need separate log lines for the B, C, or other stories, and you do have to figure out each one. With that done, you're now ready to get to work.

BREAKING YOUR STORIES

"Breaking a story" means identifying the main turning points. On network TV it involves structuring the episode so strong cliffhangers occur at the act breaks and the story engine runs all the way from the inciting incident in the Teaser (or the beginning of Act One) to the resolution in Act Four.

It's not a process to take lightly, and even experienced writing staffs wrestle with stories for hours, even days. In addition to placing the act breaks, apply these two basic dramatic tests:

(1) Credibility: What would real, normal people do in the situation? Are you forcing the plot twists by contriving actions that stretch believability, or do the actions and responses of the characters follow naturally from the jeopardy or conflict? What's honest here?

(2) Rooting interest: Do you care whether the characters succeed? Are the stakes clear enough and high enough to make an audience root for your protagonist? Will people be emotionally involved?

Once you've settled on your essential stories, you can sneak up on the structure by figuring out some tent-poles. The easiest may be your opening because the event that propels the episode is often what attracted you. But even with the most obvious story, you'll have options: Do you want to open with the guest cast who will present the challenge, or with an internal problem for one of your main cast, or with a goal for one of your main cast which becomes subverted once the guest cast arrives?

Aaron Sorkin told the Writers Guild Foundation seminar how he starts: "I have an idea for the first page and a half for *The West Wing* — which, by the way, no joke, if I know what the first page and a half is of something, I don't want to say I'm half way home, but I can see the house."

Whatever it takes for you to see the house — the voice of a character, picturing a place, coming upon a crime scene, getting a case, or confronting a conflicted relationship — close your eyes and make that come to life. Then you'll be centered in your show's world, which makes it easier to be real about what happens next.

The second easiest tent-pole is probably the ending. When you chose this subject the final outcome might have been inherent. The body is found at the beginning and the real killer is the one who reported it, or the nice witness, or the secret lover, or whatever. Your challenge is how to arrive at that ending through the main character's process of discovery or growth, not mainly to solve a crime or cure a disease or manage to survive. So even when you know the ending, you have to get to it, and therein lies the craft of storytelling.

The third tent-pole occurs at the end of Act Three. It's the "worst case." Remember, in drama, the worst event is whatever opposes the protagonist's goal (or the triumph of the antagonist), not necessarily bad stuff that happens. For example, in the hypothetical show about detectives Jane, Sally, and Portia the shoe burglar, the worst case might be that Jane, who is afraid of heights, is forced to venture out on a ledge to rescue Sally. The jeopardy here is not only to Sally, who has been taken hostage, but that Jane has to confront her darkest demons in making herself climb out, and is shaking so badly because of her fears she's going to blow her one chance at the rescue. That's the cliffhanger before the Act Three break.

Here's another example: A doctor fears his wife doesn't love him anymore and is struggling hard to win her back. During the episode, he has a patient who needs surgery. At the same time it's raining outside. From a dramatic viewpoint, the worst case is that the wife rejects him, not that the patient dies or the rain turns into a flood, though those circumstances could certainly complicate the character's quest.

When you know the Act Three "worst case" you've nearly solved your basic structure because you can begin figuring backwards to how your characters arrived at this crisis. Even if you can fill in no more than one or two beats prior to the act break, you'll begin to feel the progression.

Now you want to pin down the cliffhangers at the ends of Act One and Act Two. Developing the antagonist might give you some clues. Often (but, of course, not always) the second act is where the opposition that began in Act One gains strength. You know that at the end of Act Three this opposition will appear to have won, so see if you can come up with two surprises. You might discover that the protagonist underestimated the antagonist in the first act but is forced to fight back after a reveal at the end of Act One. In Act Two, maybe the antagonist is not exactly what was expected, or your characters follow a red herring, or they even believe they've won, when the antagonist (or problem) re-asserts itself at the Act Two break.

Using our make-believe Jane and Sally show, you might introduce the challenge that someone is stealing shoes in Act One and reveal at the Act One break that the culprit is a woman cat burglar who scales skyscrapers … and that brave Jane is paralyzed by this case because she's afraid of heights. So in Act Two Sally has to go it alone as Portia becomes more and more bold, endangering many shoes. In fact, Jane's inability to work on the case leads to Sally being taken hostage at the Act Two break. As the jeopardy deepens through Act Three, it becomes urgent that only Jane can save Sally, and that she has to go out on that ledge or all is lost at the Act Three break. Act Four is pure resolution, and would emerge naturally from the "worst case."

Of course, that's a silly story, but I'm trying to give you a broad sense of how to find the big bones of your structure. Your writing is more subtle, more complex, and doesn't rely on cartoon-like action, right? Still, these "tent-poles" can help you plan:

THE GRID

Yep, here it is again, doing an encore since the last chapter. This time, though, you're not noting the various stories of someone else's script. Now, you can use the grid for your own rough ideas by filling in the major beats I've just described — opening, ending, worst case, Act One break, and Act Two break.

One caveat: You wouldn't bring this to a meeting, and I've never seen anyone use it on a show. The grid is something I've created for myself because it helps me see the entire hour at a glance in the earliest stages of figuring it out. If this doesn't help you, don't worry about it. The grid is just a planning tool because everybody has to start somewhere, and a blank page might be daunting. Make copies and play with it if you'd like. Vary it for five or six acts if that fits your show.

Chart 4.1 Basic Four-Act Grid

ACT I	ACT II	ACT III	ACT IV
(T)			
1			
2			
3			
4			
5			
6			
7			

THE OUTLINE

The first step of writing involves listing the scenes in your script. This process has several names in addition to "!@#$%^&*()+," which is what you might want to call it when wrestling down the structure. Actual names include "outline," "step outline," "beat outline," "beat sheet," and "treatment," but they all amount to figuring out the order of events in your teleplay.

"Treatment" has a specific definition, usually observed only in the breach, and it's not a word you'll hear much in television. Technically, a treatment would be a half to two-thirds the length of a finished script written in prose (not screenplay form) that includes every scene in the order it occurs, as well as tone, style, and descriptions, and is virtually the entire script lacking only dialogue. Believe me, nobody writes treatments like that. If someone asks you for a "treatment" of your story what they really mean is a few pages that summarize it. Even for full-length features, I've heard the term "treatment" apply to a three-page pitch. Don't bother with it unless you're asked.

A "beat sheet," as used by some producers, is mid way between a treatment and an outline. It parses your show into acts and describes the big story elements, though it doesn't spell out specific scenes. So we're talking about seeing the dramatic turns, not a diagram for writing.

"Beat outline" is sometimes used interchangeably with "outline" because it's a list of what's actually written in the teleplay, and usually those "beats" are scenes. On one show where I worked, the producers asked writers for a very full outline (like a treatment with numbers), but when the staff met, they would reduce the narrative in the outline to a more skeletal list they called a beat outline so the construction could be analyzed.

For example, an outline scene might say something like "While Jane clings to the ledge, frozen in fear, desperately trying to convince Portia to release Sally, Portia taunts Jane to climb out to get her." The simplified beat might say "Jane on ledge — Portia: "Come get her." It's an internal cue used for planning though it might not make sense to an outside reader.

This brings us to your outline. As you know from Chapter Two, an outline is a step in the professional development process. It's a contracted stage of writing that generates "story by" credit and pays almost as much as a whole script. If you have a contract with "cut-offs," you might get no further if the outline doesn't work; but a successful outline means your option for a first draft will be "picked up" (you'll go ahead to write the script).

What if no producer or payments are involved, though? Un-fun though outlines may be, you really should write one, even if you're working alone on your spec. I advise: Don't travel without a road map — hour episodes are too complex, especially if you're juggling multiple storylines. If you're on your own, though, hand-written notes might be enough, and initially you could get away with being vague, noting only what you need to accomplish for the characters within a scene. Personally, I've found that the time it takes to type a complete outline and weigh each beat saves me oodles of time writing because I'm not worrying about being lost or redundant, and it saves me from writing scenes I'll have to delete because they don't move the story ahead. To me, grief-avoidance is worth the effort.

HOW TO WRITE YOUR OUTLINE

Nobody launches into an outline at number one and trucks on to number 28 in a straight line. Instead, start with the tent-poles I mentioned and fill in the grid until it's complete enough to write the scenes as an outline. Or you could begin with index cards, as many writers do. Cards are wonderful because they're not threatening. If you don't like an idea, toss it out. If your order doesn't make sense, re-arrange the cards. And you can "down-load" your thoughts in any order, which lets you reach creatively to scenes you'd enjoy whether or not they fit next in the script.

One technique is to choose different color cards for each story. If you do all the beats of the yellow story, then the green one, then the blue, and assemble them, you'll see at a glance whether you've lost your green story in the second act, and whether the blue is paying off in Act Four or if it petered out in Act Three (which might be okay, but at least you'll have a chance to ask the question).

Remember, in a multiple-story show, the stories are probably uneven. So, if you'll have around 28 scenes in an hour episode, and your "A" story predominates, it might have as many as 12 to 16 beats; the "B" could have eight to 12 beats or so, and the "C" has whatever is left, as few as three or four beats, up to maybe eight. Of course, if you're dealing with vignette writing, with seven or eight parallel stories, you might have a whole little tale in a single beat, though that's not typical of most dramas. Understand, I'm not suggesting exact numbers of scenes that should go with any story. I'm illustrating the kind of planning you might do.

Let's say you start with your "A" story. Make cards for every scene that tells your story. Count them. If you've got 40 cards you have a problem. Maybe the cards are fragments rather than whole scenes. See if you can condense many of them together until you have 10 to 20 cards. Or maybe your story doesn't fit in an episode. What portion of this story is the essential conflict that could work within an hour? Or maybe you're rambling, including backstory or side incidents that aren't part of the forward motion. Whatever doctoring you need to do, get that A story down to size.

What if your beats are too few? You can trouble-shoot by asking the opposite questions. Maybe you have combined a few scenes on one card. See if you can separate them into two-minute blocks, and then see if this story becomes the right size. Or maybe you don't have enough material for a major story. If it truly doesn't have enough meat, then you might look for a larger story to "marry" with it. Or maybe it does have fine potential but you haven't yet spelled out the moments that would unveil it on screen. Again, see if doctoring will get you to a useable scale.

After you do that with one story, go to the next and the next. Some scenes from different stories may play at the same time and place, so you'll actually get more mileage out of your screen time than you'd have if each story was a free-standing little movie. And once you weave them, you'll discover interesting contrasts, where telling one story enables you to ellipse time in another, or a scene from "A" resonates thematically with "B" in an interesting way. Putting the stories together can lead to discoveries, so you want to be flexible here.

After your individual stories are filled out, and you've ball-parked which beats occur at the act breaks, read the cards through with the feeling of watching on screen. Don't kid yourself. If you're bored, the audience will be too. But they're only index cards — change anything you want at this stage.

Once your basic structure is in hand, write it out. Here is a cheat-sheet for how a standard outline looks:

"Title of Episode"

TEASER
Summarize the teaser in a few lines, usually with more description or tone than the beats that follow. In shows where the teaser is a single scene it's one paragraph.

   -- However, complex ensemble series may begin several stories in the teaser and break them into separate blocks.

   -- Teasers with two or three (or more) distinct scenes may have two or three (or more) segments like this.

ACT ONE

1. EXT. LOCATION - TIME
The beats of the outline are numbered, beginning with #1 in each act, and headed by slug lines, as in a script. Keep them short like "log lines" for the scenes.

2. INT. LOCATION - TIME
Each step is a scene with dramatic structure. Every scene has a protagonist (a character who drives the scene), a goal, and an antagonist or opposition to the goal, even in scenes one minute long, even where conflict is subtle.

3. INT. SAME LOCATION - LATER
These are dramatic scenes, not production scenes. In other words, beats are determined by the content, not merely by time or location. If in the same location you have a new conflict it is a new outline beat.
   However, in a show where multiple stories converge at a single moment, and you use a fragment of a different arc, it may be easier to follow if you note it after the scene.

4. EXT./INT. A FEW LOCATIONS - DAY TO NIGHT
A single dramatic scene may cover several places, beginning when characters meet, continuing with them in and out of a car, concluding elsewhere. In this case use an inclusive slug line, as above, though you wouldn't do it in a script.

5. INT. SQUAD ROOM - DAY
An example: Jane arrives saying a mantra about her fear of heights just as Sally accepts a dare from Pedi to try on the stolen shoes if they meet her on the roof right now.

6. 7. See if you can fit one Act per page. The hour outline would then run around four pages total. However, every series has its own pace and style.

If you use that outline form to specify locations and times for each scene, it will help you be real about what's actually on screen. Here's an example of an *incorrect* beat in place of #5 on the sample:

INT. SQUAD ROOM — DAY
Jane says the mantra to herself while driving to work and stopping to feed the pigeons. While petting one, then releasing it, she thinks about how scared she would be to fly like the pigeons. Meanwhile Sally gets a call from Pedi, who is trying on shoes on the roof, inviting Sally and Jane to join her up there, where we can see her dancing in high heels. Sally worries whether Jane would be able to go up there too. When Jane enters, saying her mantra, Sally tells her etc.…

That's awful, right? That example is like one of those children's games where kids try to pick out all the things that don't belong in a picture. Before I tell you the answers, find the mistakes, yourself. … Okay, ready?

- Engage each scene as close as possible to its conflict or problem. Here, Jane meanders while screen time ticks away before we get to the purpose of this beat.
- Animal wrangling is expensive and consumes production time, so it's an example of the kind of material TV series spend for only when essential to the drama.
- If you're inside the squad room, you can't see Jane outdoors. All that would be exterior (EXT.) action. In an outline, you can use an inclusive slug line, but if you really mean to place the dramatic conflict in the squad room, omit the driving.
- Jane's fear of flying is not visible on screen. Don't put it in the outline if you can't put it in the script. If you do intend to put it in the script, though, indicate how you'll show it.
- A similar problem recurs with visualizing Pedi on the roof. Sure, there should be a place in the script to establish Pedi. If this is it, be clear in the outline — and give it all it's due as a meaningful location — or omit it from this scene and allow Pedi's dare to be heard on the phone or communicated in Sally's dialogue.

Once you delineate your usable beats, you can easily turn your index cards into an outline a producer (or you) could track. Or maybe not so easily. When you move from hand-written notes to a typed structure you'll probably realize some facts slipped by: You've indicated a scene is in daytime. Oh, it can't be day because the scenes before and after are at night. But it doesn't make sense for the characters to be at work at night. Okay, should you move this scene elsewhere? Or can the other scenes occur in the day? If so, how does that change the tension? What day of the story is this anyway?

That's just a hint at the reality-check awaiting you, but better to resolve it in the outline than after you've written 60 pages!

ALTERNATE OUTLINE FORMS

Not every show, or every writer, does outlines so detailed or specific. Some prefer to plan the characters' arcs but leave the actions (where, when and how the characters play out their conflicts) to whoever writes the scripts.

I once wrote for *A Year in the Life*, which began as a beautiful "limited series" (which is like a miniseries) that followed a Seattle family in the aftermath of the mother's death. The short run proved so successful the family drama was picked up for a full season. The show-runners, Josh Brand and John Falsey (who also created *Northern Exposure* and *I'll Fly Away*), had planned complete character arcs for the season, and since this was very much a serial, all episodes were like puzzle pieces that had to fit a larger picture.

The first outline Brand and Falsey handed me was unlike anything I'd encountered at the time. It followed the psychological and emotional progress in the hour but suggested only a little that could be termed "plot" or even incidents. Yet, it was an important point in the season. In the "A" story, the family patriarch, widowed for less than a year, proposes marriage to an independent woman who has a fulfilling life as a doctor and no need to marry. The "B" story dealt with the teenage granddaughter who is arrested for driving without a license. In the "C," the newly married daughter-in-law tries to get a first job; and she and her husband have a fight. So it's not as if the hour was devoid of contents, but the outline I was presented had hardly any guidance about how to relay these stories.

For instance, one beat said something like: "Coming into the kitchen after arguing with his wife, the son wants to confide in his father, but can't. The father's proposal has just been turned down, and he'd like to tell his son, but he can't confide either. During the scene neither man ever says what is on his mind, though they comfort each other." That was all.

I loved the challenge, but before I could write that scene I had to create a mini-outline for myself. In this case, the scene was set in the family kitchen late at night, each man surprised to find the other there, not wanting to show vulnerability. I kept the dialogue entirely "off the nose" (indirect), each man emphasizing his strength for the other, while they comforted themselves with food. No chase scenes or car crashes or anything larger than two people at a table, but the delicate moment did have tension because the audience knew what was being withheld. I tell you, this is the most difficult kind of scene to write because you have no external jeopardy to lean on; the conflict comes entirely from character, and much of the opposition is internal.

Because it was so difficult, I made notes for the turning points within this tiny scene — the optimal place to enter, when to take the milk from the fridge, exactly when the son would ask what happened with the proposal, the moment he'd let his dad off the hook by mentioning football tickets, the spot where the father would sigh and pointedly reveal nothing, and so forth. It helped me to have that map even though no one else saw it.

Many writers use outlines somewhere between the specific, detailed "cheat sheet" and the loose emotional agenda from *A Year in the Life*. On *ER*, for example, the outlines don't tend to have numbers but each step is a fully realized scene with dramatic structure. That's especially impressive when you consider how short the scenes on *ER* may be. Here is a fragment of an actual *ER* outline of the Emmy-winning episode "Love's Labor Lost" written by Lance Gentile. I'm grateful to Warner Brothers, Executive Producer John Wells, and writer-producer Lance Gentile for permission to print it here.

Episode 18

TEASER 7:00 AM

-- ROSS and GREENE toss a football outside the ambulance bay. An ambulance races past, a familiar face in the window. "Was that Benton?" Ross goes long for a pass as a car careens down the street and a bloody gang member is tossed out into the street.

-- Ross, Greene and HATHAWAY race the gang member down the trauma hallway, passing HALEH, who takes us into Trauma One, where she finds a distraught BENTON. The old lady with the broken hip is MAE BENTON, his mother.

-- In Trauma Two, CARTER and JARVIK join the heroic resuscitation of the trauma victim. Carter witnesses Greene at the top of his game, impressed.

-- Mae is shy about her son seeing her naked, exposed and in pain. Haleh reassures him that she'll give her special attention. Benton wants to write out the orders as Haleh has been insisting. She lightens up on him: "Don't worry - I'll take care of it. Go see if Greene needs any help."

-- Benton enters Trauma One as Greene is prepping for a thoracotomy. As Benton pulls on a trauma gown to do the procedure, Greene says he doesn't need any help — go be with your mother.

-- When orthopedic resident JANET BLAIR arrives to admit Mae, Benton insists that the chief of orthopedics be called in.

-- Greene and Hathaway escort an OR team out of Trauma Two. As Hathaway heads home from the night shift, she passes DR. GREGORY NELSON, chief of orthopedics, steaming into Trauma One.

-- Nelson, none too happy about being pulled from his department meeting by Benton's persistent calls, does agree to do the case. Benton tries to get him to say that he, not the resident, will actually do the case. Nelson flatly refuses, and he and Blair take her off to OR. When Benton tries to get on the elevator, Nelson flatly forbids him to go anywhere near the OR.

All that occurs in the first several minutes, so you can see how fast television storytelling needs to move, how packed it is with dramatic stakes, and why you'd need to be at the top of your craft to write a show like *ER*. The episode you're writing might not be as intense, but you can learn a lot from *ER*'s skillful blending of the arcs and the way this outline blasts each story out of the opening like cannonballs.

For example, in the very first beat, a peaceful "status quo" is immediately broken by the inception of the "A" story when Benton arrives in an ambulance, but rapidly diverts attention to the urgent "B" story when the gang member is tossed onto the street. Talk about grabbing attention!

Re-read your own outline and read it to friends until it's as powerful and clear as you can make it.

Sonny's List

One of my former MFA students, Sonny Calderon, told me he taped reminders around his computer, mostly tips that came from my response to someone's work in class. He thought these four might be useful as you begin your first draft.

- Every beat is an action. A character "realizing" something is not a scene. Each scene involves a character who wants something but faces resistance.
- The antagonist must be as strong and motivated as the protagonist. The more equal the sides, the more suspense. See the world from your antagonist's viewpoint also.
- Aim at the turning point where the protagonist must make a difficult choice, a moral equation which is nearly balanced.
- Anchor your story with the Worst Case Scenario three-fourths through. This is where the protagonist seems to fail and must overcome his internal problem to deal with the opposition.

Your First Draft

How close should you stay to your outline? That depends how close your outline is to what works on screen. If you're on an assignment from a show, you will have vetted your outline with the head writer (and maybe the whole staff), so you're sent off to your first draft with an implied contract to deliver what they expect. Sometimes an outline is considered "locked," which means you're committed to the beats on the page and you'd better stick to them. In hasty or ultra-low budget productions, some companies have been known to start prepping (pre-production) based on the outline. (That may mean scouting locations and rough scheduling, for example.)

But what if you come upon something you want to fix? Say, in the outline, a beat exists to reveal a character's secret, but while writing, you realize the secret is already apparent from a previous scene, so you need to cut the extra beat. Or you might want to make a larger change: The guest cast pops out, speaking in a way that's more interesting than appeared in the outline, and the "voice" of the character demands that certain scenes be angled differently.

If you're doing a spec, absolutely go for the revisions if you're sure of them. You don't get points for sticking doggedly to an outline that doesn't make sense! But if this script is for a producer, it's better not to make large changes without asking. I made that mistake once. I was doing a script for a show and had thoroughly worked out my outline with the show-runner. But as I approached Act Four, I was inspired by what I thought was a more clever resolution, so I went ahead and wrote it.

Well, one day after I delivered the script, the producer was on the phone complaining I hadn't given him the ending we'd discussed. Surprised by the emotional tenor of his reaction, I listened silently as he went on about this single point before I appreciated what he was really saying. The original ending had been his idea. Whether or not my version was better, his feelings were hurt — not just because I hadn't used his suggestion, but because he felt I'd disregarded him. This was about respect. Aha, I made a mental note: In the future, pick up the phone and ask. If you get the boss on board, he'll probably say okay to write what you think is best.

Now, how do you actually do the script? You've written screenplays before or you wouldn't have reached this point, and this one is not so different. Once you get past the structural requirements of the hour format, and you've told your stories via the show's continuing cast, the next special factor is speed. Episodes are usually due two weeks after the outline is approved, and that feels fast if you're used to mulling over a feature for months. Of course, if you're speculating, no one will know how long you took to write, but a concentrated schedule is a habit you'll need if you're going to work in television.

I'll show you how easy it is to deliver in 14 days. Let's say you have an outline with 28 beats (four acts with around seven scenes in each). I like to follow my outline exactly, so I write just two scenes each day. Voila! 14 X 2 = 28. When I'm writing at home (not on staff), I begin each morning reading over what I wrote the day before, fine-tuning it. Then I take a breath and get ready for the first scene of the day. I approach it as if these next pages are the single most important piece of writing I'll ever do. I want to bring to this screen moment the richest experience, full of subtext and nuance, while delivering the action in the tightest way I can. I might imagine the whole scene before writing a word, or take a walk and jot down ideas, or close my eyes and wait for the characters' voices. Whatever it takes. Then I write two or three pages. And stop.

I find that pushing on diminishes quality, and I want to come to the next scene fresh. So I'll take a break. Lunch, errands, gym, calls — I try to take my mind off it, though when I'm most relaxed, not even trying, I'll have ideas for a way into the next scene or a perspective on one I wrote. Much later in the day, in the afternoon or night, I'll re-read the morning's scene and revise it. Then I repeat the process of finding, forming, and writing the second scene of the day. And stop.

I've found that by the time I reach the end of the script, my first draft has already been edited because I refine my work each day. Of course, not everyone works like this, nor should they. I have a writer friend who starts work at 4:00 A.M. and smashes through as many pages as she can before she runs out of steam, hardly looking back. She tells me she'd never let anyone see that "mess" that rambles, repeats, and wanders into tangents. She regards it as raw material which she edits away after she arrives at the end. You could think of it as the difference between painting and carving a sculpture: The painter pays attention to each brush stroke, adding one after another until the picture is formed. The sculptor begins with a hunk of material, and cuts away "everything that isn't the statue," to paraphrase Michaelangelo. One method isn't better than another — whatever works for you is right.

If you're frightened by a blank page, put something on it — anything. A painting teacher once taught me that as I stood staring at a blank canvas. He walked over and threw ink on my pristine surface, and that got me moving, even if only to clean up the ink. Some writers break the emptiness with automatic writing or anything a character might say, even if it's not the way to open the scene. Some people write by hand for the visceral feel of words flowing from the mind onto paper. Others talk into a tape recorder.

Aaron Sorkin commented to the Writers Guild Foundation Seminar: "When I try using a tape player, I freeze up immediately. It's walking around and talking to myself; it's driving and talking to myself. Ultimately, it's about typing. The problem I have with these new fangled computers is that they don't make a good sound. It used to be... a typewriter makes a sound like you're working. I like the clack."

So do whatever spins your wheels. But stick with professional form when you turn in your draft. You already know you need specialized screen-writing software, and you ought to be up on how scripts look. It might help to refer to the samples from *NYPD Blue* in Chapter Three. And in case you need a quick refresher, here's a "cheat sheet" on standard form.

ACT TWO

FADE IN:

DAY or NIGHT

EXT. LOCATION - TIME OF DAY

The action is in a paragraph at the outside margin and goes all across the page, single-spaced.

When you introduce a character for the first time, use capitals. Example: CHARACTER ONE enters. But when Character One is mentioned again, that name will not be upper case (except when heading dialogue, of course).

                    CHARACTER ONE
          Dialogue. Try to keep this to under
          5 lines per speech, and always
          condense to minimum.

                    CHARACTER TWO
          Responses can include pauses, often
          indicated by...
               (beat)
          And then the dialogue continues
          after the parenthetical.

                    CHARACTER ONE
               (parenthetical)
          The parenthetical above should
          modify or describe how a line is
          said, but not give a large action.

If you want Character One to go across the room and do something, that belongs here in action, not in a parenthetical.

                    CHARACTER ONE (CONT'D)
          When the same character continues
          speaking after an action, indicate
          it with (CONT'D) after the name.

INT. LOCATION - TIME OF DAY *DAY/NIGHT*

Give only enough description to build dramatic tension or reveal an essential insight into character or plot. Do not indulge in set decoration.

                    CHARACTER ONE
          Notice that after a new slug line,
          you don't need to write "CONT'D"
          though the same character is
          speaking.
               (MORE)

2.

                    CHARACTER ONE (cont'd)
        When dialogue goes on long like
        this and breaks in the middle of
        the page, use "more" and "cont'd"
        as illustrated. Do not write long
        dialogue speeches like this though!

SECONDARY SLUG LINE

A secondary slug line might include ANGLE ON A DETAIL, or one
specific room or part of a scene, such as CLOSET.

In spec scripts and all first drafts, do not put numbers on
the scenes nor "continued" on the tops and bottoms of pages.
That happens only in the final shooting script.

And when you reach the end of each Act and the end of the
script...

                                    FADE OUT.

Get S/W software —
Movie Magic
or
Final Draft

Remember, you're writing a "selling script," not a "shooting script." You want to entice a reader, especially if this is a spec, so write what will keep someone interested. Mr. Sorkin shared this insight at the Seminar:

> "...The selling script is the most important right now. I'm not writing a script right now for a line producer to sit and budget, for a DP [Director of Photography] to work at. I'm writing a script for you to read, to sit there at night — you can't stop turning the pages, this is so much fun. Even now in the scripts that I write, I only, frankly, describe what's important for you to get that moment. It's possible that I'm going to describe, 'and the camera pushes in and pushes in and pushes in' and I'm probably going to write it like that because I'm building tension for the reader at that point. Mostly I write for dialogue, and dialogue is what you read fastest when you're reading a screenplay. Description just slows it down..."

Aim toward page 17 to end your first act (including the teaser if you have one), page 30 to end Act Two, around 45 to end Act Three, and somewhere between 55 and 65 at the end of Act Four (57 to 60 pages is an average total length). Those are approximate guides, not rules, though. A filmed episode might run anywhere from 44 to 52 minutes (without commercials), depending on the outlet, but you won't know the actual length of your script until several drafts from now when a shooting script is read through by the cast and timed with a stopwatch. I gave you that page count only so you can check yourself. If you're way off — for example an hour script that's 30 pages or 90 — it's time to trouble-shoot. Here are some quick diagnostics:

IF YOU'RE RUNNING LONG:

- Are the speeches over-written, explanatory or redundant? Tighten the dialogue.
- Have you indulged in set decoration, directing on the page, or over-blown description? Take a sharp knife to these.
- Are certain acts long, though the script is the right length? Move the act breaks by enhancing a different cliffhanger or re-ordering scenes.
- Have you indulged in backstory or secondary characters or tangents? Return to your original outline and stick to a clean, clear telling.
- Have you engaged the scenes as close as possible to the conflict? Have you ended scenes immediately after the climax or goal? If you have written prologues or epilogues to your scenes, get rid of them.
- Is there too much story? If your outline was accurate, this shouldn't be a problem, but you might have fooled yourself in the outline by counting sequences of scenes as one beat. If so, you need to re-think the stories themselves, or delete an entire arc. This is major work, not editing (see the discussion of "second draft").

IF YOU'RE RUNNING SHORT:

- Have you fleshed out your scenes? A script is not merely an outline with dialogue. It requires re-imagining each dramatic moment as an experience. Make sure you've fully told your story, including reactions as well as actions.
- Do you have enough story? If your outline only seemed to be complete, but actually contained mostly a premise or the circumstances in which a story would occur, you'll need to go back to the outline stage and create more events, more real turns — more of a plot. Re-write the outline before you re-write the script in this case.

AT THE END OF IT ALL...

Sorry, there isn't an end, at least not anytime soon. This process will go on for as many more drafts as you can stand, and if your episode is produced, some writers revise all through post-production and only quit fixing things when they're forced to because the thing is on the air! In television, this obsessive tinkering is limited, fortunately, because shows get on the air very quickly.

If this is an assigned script, you probably have to deliver it to the head-writer now. But if you're ahead of schedule by a day or so, don't hand it in early. Take that day to let the script "cool," then re-read it with as much distance as you can muster and refine what you can, but deliver on time. TV schedules don't have much slack, and slackers don't get much work in TV.

If this is your own spec with no deadline, now is an opportunity for feedback. Have your draft read by everyone, not just other writers or your grandma who thinks everything you do is perfect. Sometimes an outside reader will ask what you need to hear: "Why would she do that?" "I don't get why they don't just make up." Or you might hear awful reactions: "Is this supposed to be a parody of *Friends*?" Don't be crushed by one stupid reader. On the other hand, the reader might be on to something. It's a gift to have the chance to re-consider.

If readers are too polite, or don't know how to give feedback, ask them three simple questions:

- Do you care about the people in the stories?
- Were you rooting for something to happen?
- What do you think this script is all about?

After all the input, I suggest setting the draft aside for a couple of weeks, if you can manage that. With enough distance, you might see what you need to change by yourself. You'll also see typos that your eyes glazed over no matter how well you spell-checked and proofread. My favorite was a student script for the series *Boston Public* innocently handed in with the "l" missing on the first page.

YOUR SECOND DRAFT

You need to understand the difference between revising and rewriting. The kind of editing you do every day — fixing spelling and punctuation, tightening lines, omitting a speech, clarifying an action, lopping off the heads or tails of overlong scenes — all those corrections are parts of normal writing. Rewriting is a whole other job.

A rewrite means re-thinking the structure and sometimes characters as well. You're still dealing with the same general story, but you want a fresh way to tell it. You can't do that by crossing out lines or replacing words. Go back to the drawing board.

Start by putting aside the script. I mean it. As long as you cling to the precious moments you've written you'll be tied to your first draft. Take a breath and let go. Maybe you'll be able to use many of the pages you've written; and certain scenes, even sequences, might survive intact. But when you begin a rewrite, everything is on the table or you'll turn into a pretzel trying to fit a structure around scenes that don't belong.

Depending on the notes you got from the producer or readers, your episode may require a new outline. Can you work with your existing outline as a reference to re-organize the beats, or do you have to start over? Either way, boldly get rid of what hasn't worked and add completely new elements, even a new arc, if necessary.

Then begin the second draft using the new outline, though, again, you might be able to keep much of your first draft. Now, I'm not saying to throw out the story the show bought (if indeed it was bought). On that point — being told to do a second draft on an assignment is terrific news. The alternate is being cut off after the first draft and having your script given to another writer. Don't imagine for a minute that anyone's first draft is shot exactly as first written, not even when the show-runner writes it himself! And if you're on assignment, the second draft generates a payment.

I had a funny experience with a rewrite. I'd handed in a first draft (this was actually a TV movie) and the network called for an in-person meeting at their office. That didn't bode well because if notes are minor they're often given on the phone or in a memo. So, in we went — the producer, a company executive and me — anticipating a high-level effort to save the project. As it happened, this particular network exec wasn't experienced, and she sat there going page by page through the script. Two hours. And at the end of it she'd asked for changes in five lines. Five lines! The producer was so steamed that he told my agent to bill the network for a full second draft, which amounted to something like a thousand dollars per word. Don't count on that kind of waste in episodes, though. Showrunners mean it when they want a rewrite.

If you're speculating, draft numbers make no sense. Every selling script is "First Draft," even if you've written this thing 11 times. To keep track for yourself, you could put the date of the draft in the lower right corner of the title page. Or you might run a header showing the revision dates of specific pages (some screenwriting programs have this application). But submit your script with no draft numbers or dates. And no colored pages — that's for production revisions after the shooting script. Remember, the sample you send to a producer is always shiny new, hot off your printer.

YOUR POLISH

Technically, a "polish" means what you'd think — a small revision, like polishing a surface, fine-tuning. Frequently the term is used for a dialogue polish where a writer goes through a script and sharpens the speeches. Polishes do not include re-structuring or creating new characters or story arcs.

Sometimes a cultural "wash" is called a dialogue polish, too. That occurs when a character's background is not familiar to the original writer and a second writer is brought in to make the character speak naturally. Usually that kind of polish is not credited.

For you, if you're working on a series, a polish may or may not appear in your contract, and if it does, the payment is slight. That shouldn't matter. If you're fortunate enough to be kept on an episode after your second draft, cling with your teeth and fingernails and polish anything including the boss's chair. Scripts keep changing, and the more you're willing to do, the more the final product will be yours. Of course, if you're on a staff, you'll be polishing other people's scripts routinely, sometimes because the original writer is busy with something larger. It's a normal stage in preparing a script for production.

As for your spec script: Polish until it gleams.

What's Next?

Do it again! If you're speculating, write another spec for a series that demonstrates you can work in a different genre. If you're writing on assignment, you'll have the thrill (really) of seeing your creation on screen. And if it's well received, you'll get another assignment in the future.

No matter how this script turns out, the best way to write better is to write more. If this is your first dramatic episode, you've taken a great leap. Just think how much you learned. And next time it will be easier. Just kidding. If it's easy, you're not stretching. So don't expect easy, but once you're comfortable with the basics, next time will be more fun.

Finally, when you have a few writing samples in your portfolio, you're ready for the next step: joining a staff.

Summary Points

In writing your own spec script, go through all the steps from outline to first draft, second draft, and polish.

An outline is a list of scenes or beats in the order they will occur in your script. It's the first professional step and generates a payment and "story by" credit if you're writing on assignment. You may create the A, B, and C stories separately and weave them together, watching that cliffhangers fall at the act breaks.

All teleplays are in normal screenplay format, written on standard screenwriting software, using the submissions option rather than as shooting scripts.

Rewriting a script is not the same as editing, and involves re-thinking structure or characters.

A polish is a smaller revision that refines dialogue and tightens scenes before presenting your script.

Ask for feedback on your finished script and be willing to re-write many times before giving it to a producer or agent as a writing sample.

Spotlight on Writing Your Pilot

In the beginning is the world. When you write a pilot script, you're the creator of a universe that includes places, people, churning and contradictory desires, threatening situations, even day jobs. And always at the core are secrets: mysteries so deep and intricate they will take 88 or 100 hours to discover. But most writers don't start with those specific revelations, or even with the cast. And unlike movies, particular arcs in which characters grow and change are not usually the creator's agenda on day one.

Many pilot writers begin with total mental immersion in a location where they will dwell virtually for years. David Simon, creator of HBO's searing and insightful urban drama, *The Wire*, insists his show is about Baltimore. Each season focuses on one aspect, such as the schools or the media, but he says the initial inspiration wasn't the closely perceived drug dealers and police, or the teenagers portrayed with heartbreaking realism, just: Baltimore.

For John Sacret Young, creator and show-runner of *China Beach* (who was also a writer-producer on *The West Wing*), the world he wanted to create was in the Sixties. But how does a writer focus such a broad time to fit a TV show? He said:

"When you think about the Sixties, what are the things that come to mind? Obviously, Civil Rights, Vietnam, the turmoil in the American family collective, and we asked what else was interesting. We came up with women's rights. What was women's role in society? What were their challenges and liberties? So we thought if we looked at the role of women, what would be an astonishing place to put the show? Someone later described it as being the women's sauna inside this big men's locker room.

"When we started to talk about it, started to do research, and started to interview, it became clear that they went to serve America in the Army. But what they found was enormously complicated in terms of the emotional shock to very young women with even less preparation. We wondered what they knew about the country and what you're going to see coming into a triage on a bad day. The good news was that they were trying to save and

157

John
Sacret
Young

help people. The bad news was that they were then embroiled in this conundrum, surrounded by this alien atmosphere. What an interesting intersection of forces. That excited us.

"Besides the nurses, there were other women there as reporters and with the Red Cross. In the case of the character K.C. — as a sort of capitalist, she was an independent contractor with a past that almost necessitated that she either die or escape. So the forces that were driving her were not dissimilar to the characters that, let's say, Henry James was writing about or Hemingway was writing about.

"We talked about who are the characters that interest us, and the time period, and the war. What time should we set it in the war? If our characters are there, what are the prospects for stories, what are the ways these characters will intersect and deal with each other and have stories to tell? Before I wrote the pilot we definitely did backgrounds on all of the characters and wrote up bios on them. We talked about stories, but they weren't laid out specifically, although, before the series was picked up, we did lay out possible episodes. I don't think we had any idea where the series would ever go."

For John Sacret Young, the pilot emanated from both a geographic and cultural setting. But sometimes the "world" is tied to a quest or special character rather than a place. No one would mistake *House* for a show about Chicago. Instead House's world is his diagnostic unit in his hospital; and within that, the internal landscape of House's need to overcome "a world of pain" (his own) propels the stories. And no one would mistake House's hospital for the one in *ER*, though it's also in Chicago. And *Grey's Anatomy*'s Seattle Grace Hospital is in a big American city too, though it claims a world of its own. Try this exercise yourself: How does the "world" of Grey's differ from both *House* and *ER*?

Damon Lindelof, co-creator of *Lost*, also began his world with a place: a mysterious island where a plane has crashed. But he advises that the starting point for most shows is usually not as challenging: "When you talk about television shows, there is a franchise element and the franchise is the world. A hospital, a law firm or a precinct — those are the easiest worlds for a television series. You know what kinds of stories inhabit those worlds. The harder worlds are a spaceship that is being pursued across the galaxy or you're on an island in the middle of nowhere that the audience knows you cannot leave.

6·34

INT. THE BEACH - NEAR DAWN

is no nonsense yet something to look at. The arc of the
coast the long leisurely dunes, the cobalt sea shuffling up
surf.

The two women walk back to Colleen's tent without words.
At last a

A wind blows and lifts the sand to their ankles and to their knees.
Like pinpricks. In one gust they have to turn their backs

n squint respit ---

BARBER: Do you ever get over it, does it ever get to better?

McM: I thought it would, I thought it had to.

BARBER: It can't get worse

McM: It does. But I saw you: you know in your heart you made
a difference. It's a good feeling. There's the loss and the
guilt that goes with feeling good or still there's the fact: you were
there. He had a mother, a sister, a girlfriend & you were there,
you were there
you gave him a home before he died so far from it.

& they can't find McMurphy's tent

McM: where is it? where's my tent
BARBER: Did we take a wrong turn at the last light?
McM: It's right here. I know it is ---

She takes two more steps & encounter a huge sand heap. somebody
should rake it, garbage men should clean it up! There's debris everywhere

McM realizes what it is --- The remains of her tent. The tent have been
hit, wasted. It's gone. everything in it.

McM: It can't be!
BARBER: Oh my God!
McM: in s down to the crevice. gets down on her knees amidst
the blow up. The pieces that lie & the grains of sand
CONT
2 pages on

Handwritten page from *China Beach*

"The question is who's going to be interacting with that world? That's what separates a good cop show from a bad cop show and a good medical show from a bad medical show. They both deal with the same patients, but the issue is: Who are the doctors who are tending to those patients? A feel-good show like *Grey's Anatomy* is a much different show from *ER*, but only because of the people. Otherwise it's exactly the same show as *ER*."

Okay, let's say you've fully moved into your new mental home — the world of your series. What's next? Not writing — not quite yet, though you should be jotting notes all along. Now you need to fully imagine what makes stories happen in your world. That's not limited to the pilot episode, but requires figuring out the "motor" of the show. Do people come in with cases to solve? If so, that doesn't necessarily mean a legal or crime case, or a disease. In a sense, a case could be a relationship issue, or coping with alien invaders or special powers that can change history (as in *Heroes*). As long as characters have long-range quests that incur conflict, and their stories present both internal and external jeopardy, you can discover the "springboards" for stories within your world. This potential for future stories is the essential that differentiates writing a pilot from writing anything else on screen.

Once you know how your show "works" within a rich world, your next step is probably to draw out the main cast. I use that phrase "draw out" as opposed to introduce or even create, because if your world is fully enough imagined, these people already live there. In fact, if you have a problem knowing the three or four or five people who your show is about, you should go back to step one and delve deeper into your world. That's not to say you'll know everyone in a large ensemble cast, or that characters you didn't see at first won't step out and greet you as you write. Actually, as a writer it's wonderful to be surprised like that. But beginners shouldn't tackle a big ensemble anyway. It's difficult enough to write a few people well!

Some writers do thorough bios of their characters at this point. Some sketch out moments, phrases or images that "pop" a character. I once wrote a pilot where I needed a way to tag a character (express her) in order to pitch the show. I saw her speeding into the outskirts of Los Angeles at dawn in a beat-up convertible, bare feet pressing the pedals to the metal while her butt danced on the car seat to the sound of "Mustang Sally." In another glimpse, close and tight, she took her time licking the remnants of Kentucky Fried Chicken off a paper wrapper while a motel proprietor banged on her door. Only one of those moments actually appeared in the script, but both helped me visualize her at an early stage.

Let's say you have your world, your springboards, and your main cast. Yes, you're creeping up on writing the thing. Remember that you must grab readers even before this pilot ever gets to viewers, so your first ten pages (or less) are critical. Don't lay back and wait for episode 88, or even 22 to reel in your audience with a revelation. Get a sense of anticipation started now.

What do you need to generate anticipation? Answer the basic dramatic questions: Do we care about (or are we intrigued by) your main character? What does the character want urgently? Why does she need it so desperately? Who and what opposes her? Are the chances of succeeding and failing nearly equal? Then you rev up the action until we expect her to reach the goal — at which point you twist it, pulling out the rug, so we discover this quest will have way more ramifications, to be continued in later episodes.

Of course, that's oversimplifying. The point is that in the early pages you need to set your series in motion by rooting us in at least one member of your main cast and establishing the series franchise. As for writing the world, I recommend that you don't write text to describe it. As vital as is creating the world for your series — so important that we began with it — it has to "breathe" through your script, not ever feel "made." That is, the world of your show *is* the show; it's where your people live. If you have to explain it, something's not alive here.

After all that, you're ready to plan your pilot as you would any ongoing episode of your show. Does it have four acts? Five? A teaser? Think about the grid and the discussion of structure in Chapters Three and Four. Since you're the creator of this show you get to make those choices (at least until some network tells you otherwise — but you should be so lucky as to have a network!). Then move right along to outline, first draft, and all the revising and polishing that follows.

Once upon a time, spec pilots were indulgences in a fantasy of running a series of your own. Now, agents and producers will read them as writing samples. And, yes, sometimes they even get made. Because of this opportunity, I asked my colleague, Georgia Jeffries, to speak to you about her experiences with pilot writing.

GUEST SPEAKER: GEORGIA JEFFRIES

Georgia Jeffries wrote and produced for *Cagney & Lacey* and was Supervising Producer of *China Beach*. She is on the faculty of the USC School of Cinematic Arts.

GJ: I've written eight drama pilots — the most enjoyable television writing I've ever done because of the opportunity each provided to define and explore a whole new world.

When I teach my pilot class, I tell the students that creating a series is a hybrid of short story writing and screenwriting. It is, ultimately, the creation of a novel on film. Just as Dickens wrote "episodes" of his novels in penny magazines week by week and month by month, so must the pilot writer conceive complex characters whose stories will have the potential to evolve over the long haul.

Right now (with due respect to Dickens once again) is "the best of times and the worst of times" to be a pilot writer. There are exceptionally imaginative pilot storylines that foster a higher bar for creative product. Yet it's also an extraordinarily competitive job market. There are indeed more buyers — pay and basic cable as well as the broadcast networks. But because of vertical integration, a number of those buyers are often owned by the same conglomerate. Seventy to eighty percent of all pilots ordered by the networks are being developed by their own auxiliary companies. If it's on ABC, it's fairly certain that it's going to be produced by Touchstone. So if the pilot writer doesn't have a deal at Touchstone, chances are s/he will not get a pick-up from ABC.

Stakes are higher than ever because of multi-million dollar production costs coupled with continuing losses at the broadcast networks. They're competing with each other to reclaim the audience they're losing to the Internet and video games. The amount of serialization this past season was an effort to hook in more viewers. But at least half of those pilots — several really excellent in quality — failed commercially.

I believe that means we need to target the audience in a new way with more "limited series." I remember the iconic *Twin Peaks* which made such a lasting impression. An agent of mine said that it should have been a mini-series spread over several seasons. And that is essentially what HBO and Showtime are doing with a number of their series today, ordering only 10 or 16 episodes at a time (with a long hiatus in between) instead of 22 or 24, the usual broadcast order. That translates into more time and freedom for the creative artist behind the show, and conversely more time for the audience to discover the show amidst such a plethora of choices. The more the marketplace expands and re-defines what it is a series can be, the more opportunity for more pilots to be written by new talent.

PD: When your students try to do pilots, what do you warn them about? What traps do you advise them to look out for?

GJ: My largest concern is that they come into the classroom trying to emulate only what they've already seen on TV. I encourage them to take creative risks. After they watch what's on the air and read a number of pilot scripts, they have to distance themselves, take a long leap off the cliff of their own psyche and think about what they would like to see. The only way to write effectively is to stop censoring themselves as to what is or is not possible.

PD: When a writer approaches writing a pilot what does she have to keep in mind that's different from writing an episodic script?

GJ: Thinking long term is the major difference. Our students are required to write synopses of ten episodes for the first season. They really should be thinking even farther ahead to what the 23rd episode is going to be for the second season.

How is a pilot different from writing in a series? Well, that's easy: the only voice they have to emulate is their own. But that's often the problem! They may not have discovered their own voices yet, and what they think is their voice may just be copying J. J. Abrams or Shonda Rhimes. Defining one's own unique voice requires an acutely observant eye and a kind of bold irreverence. It takes guts to be original in an industry that feeds on novelty but often fears true innovation.

PD: How do you deal with all the exposition students sometimes think they need to write in pilots: They have to explain the world, introduce all the main characters, start the stories running that will have long arcs?

GJ: One of my students had a real challenge with that this semester. She was writing a science fiction show and going into great detail about the planets and space stations, all of which distracted from the story instead of grounding it. The big instruction for her was to contemporize this faraway world. Come back from the future and put it into the present in a way the reader can understand.

She was best able to do this with witty dialogue that sounded like contemporaries talking at a coffee shop on campus. That was the key — making those characters speak in a vernacular that was identifiable. She also had to reduce the narrative text to the most essential and dramatically interesting description. That meant putting emphasis on the verbs and the nouns to keep a sense of dynamic action – both physical and emotional.

PD: When you create your own pilot, where do you start? Do you start with the world or the characters? What is the creative evolution for you?

GJ: I generally have started with the world.

PD: That's interesting for you because you're such a "character" person.

GJ: Yes, but for me place *is* character. The first broadcast pilot I wrote was about young female surgeons at Walter Reed Army Medical Center in Washington, D.C. So it was a very specific location — a military hospital full of returning vets. A later script, this one for pay cable, was also set in Washington, D.C. — but in a far more rarefied world of power and intrigue on the Beltway.

In this most recent pilot I've written, the characters were alive in my mind for awhile before I could put them on the page. That didn't happen until I decided to take them home to Illinois. I'm from the Midwest originally, but I've never written a pilot set in the Midwest. At last I had a place I wanted to take them.

PD: If someone wanted to write a pilot who didn't have the fortune to be in your class, or even in film school, what would you advise them?

GJ: First they should visit the Writers Guild Library on Third and Fairfax in Los Angeles because that has the richest collection of award-winning, critically acclaimed pilots in the world. Study a number of those pilots as well as later episodes in the series.

Also they should take heart that it's not beyond the realm of possibility that they could actually get their pilot on the air. This is a 21st-century phenomenon. It certainly was not a possibility when you and I were starting out. It wasn't even a possibility ten years ago, but the market is hungrier than ever for the next hit.

The FX show *It's Always Sunny in Philadelphia* began as a short script and a six-minute video submitted by a creative team not yet established in the business. Miracles do happen, but only if you've prepared by doing your best work.

PD: When you go into a pilot [like the one that dealt with racial politics in Mobile, Alabama], you have certain themes, certain subjects you want to explore, then how do you proceed? Did you do an outline? Did you think through a whole year of arcs? Or did you really just start with the premise?

GJ: I always did story treatments, of course, but was never required by any of the networks to do a bible of future episodes. I did that on my own, assembling a tremendous amount of research for myself. With each of my pilots I put together — and I'm not exaggerating — files that were three to four inches thick, all full of character and story ideas. I was constantly pulling out articles from magazines, recording something I heard on NPR. I never felt I could relax and assume I had enough story fodder to get to the magic 100th episode.

I remember some of the earliest direction I got on my first draft pilots was, "take us further in the opening story... bring us into the heightened drama earlier." My initial instinct was to hold back some of the mystery to surprise the audience later, but I learned that was a luxury I couldn't afford. I had to hook the executives first, while still keeping a number of tricks up my sleeve. That meant sometimes painting in more obvious colors than I would have liked (because I think the best storytelling is subtle and "between the lines").

I kept getting notes on my pilots to go bigger and broader earlier on so viewers would know exactly what was at stake. So I learned to push the characters to the emotional brink in that first episode.

When I guide my class through the pilot process, I tell them to create at least ten questions the viewer could agonize about at the end of the first episode — what's going to happen to this or that character or story point. If viewers think they know the answers, they're not going to bother to come back for the second episode. That also helps to determine the ten short synopses students have to come up with for future episodes.

PD: On the business side, what advice might you give a novice who wrote a pilot and found herself suddenly in business with a network.

GJ: One of the best pieces of advice I received at the very beginning of my career came from a friend who advised me to get an entertainment attorney to serve as part of my business team along with my agent. So even though the attorney commissions an additional 5% of any of my fees in addition to the 10% for the agent, I've kept that attorney for twenty years now. I want that extra advocate protecting my interests in case some of the executives, producers, directors or actors are represented by the same agency.

PD: Do you prefer writing a pilot to either a movie or an episode of a series?

GJ: Yes, no question, because I'm thinking long-term. I'm thinking 22 hours, not two hours.

PD: Even though a movie is just as original, this is much bigger.

GJ: And even more demanding. We know what it's like to live 14 hours a day with these characters, day after day, during seasons when you have a six-week hiatus if you're lucky. I could never approach a pilot half-heartedly. Creating any successful series demands a commitment of body and soul.

CHAPTER 5

IT'S WHO YOU KNOW: WORKING ON STAFF

Recently, a student on the verge of graduating asked me what was the single most important lesson I'd learned in writing for television. Her question started me thinking. Of course, I'd acquired writing skills, some insights into what works on screen, and a few experiences negotiating the system. But that's not what she meant. She was looking for career advice gleaned from what I might have done better.

I fast-forwarded through mistakes I'd made, like the time I turned down a staff position on a series because three better opportunities were around the corner. Well, one show wasn't picked up; on a second, the producer decided to write the pilot himself; and for job three, another writer was chosen. I found myself out of work as a writer for more than six months. Fortunately, I've had a "day job" teaching screenwriting at USC throughout my writing career, but it's not unusual for writers to be "between assignments" for months at a time. I'm telling you this at the start of the chapter on staff work where the pay is consistent and you may feel lulled into a sense of security. Here's my advice: Get yourself some other survival resource, whether that's an alternate writing venue (like journalism or educational videos), or a non-writing job, or a partner who helps carry expenses. But was that the most important lesson I wanted to pass on to the student?

I also thought about scripts I might have written better. When you see your work on screen, sometimes you're grateful — really — to the actors and directors who bring a moment to life. But once in a while you cringe, "I did not write that clunky line... did I?" Or, "Does this seem as slow to you as it does to me? Why didn't I tighten that beat? No, it was the director's fault... or was it my fault?" But all that's really fleeting.

The more I considered what mattered in building a writing career I came to a single lesson: Make friends. No doubt, you've heard the line "it's who you know, not what you know;" or, put another way, "this town is all about relationships." Those glib sayings fit certain agents, managers, and producers. But I suggest you think about it somewhat differently as a writer.

Especially on TV series staffs, the act of creating is not private, though you certainly bring your unique talents. Writers tend to want to work with other writers who enable them to do their own best work. That often means choosing collaborators who make them comfortable enough to take creative risks, and who can be trusted to deliver quality dialogue or story twists or humor or tales of life. Much of this rests on what's on the page. But no producer-writer has the time to comb every writing sample. Producers hire whom they know.

Now, that doesn't mean you have to party with powerful people or suck up to their families. It means forming networks of professional trust. You do that through good work followed by staying in touch. Students just out of film school often form workshops that meet at each other's apartments, not only for continuing feedback on writing, and commiseration, but also for the connections. One of my writing students formed an alliance with a producing student who wanted to be an agent. On graduating, the junior agent got a job as, well, a junior agent, and brought along the writer as a first client. In time, they rose together.

If you're not in film school, you might make similar connections at seminars, workshops, and extension classes open to the public. Or maybe you'll land a beginning assignment on a small show. The people in the cubicles next to you aren't always going to be in those cubicles. Someone's going to move on to a better series, someone's going to become a producer, someone's going to be asked to recommend a writer, maybe with qualifications just like yours. Join professional groups, and when you're eligible, become active in the Writers Guild. Even if you're shy or a hermit (or so focused on the characters you're creating you don't want to be bothered with actual humans), push yourself out of your shell. That's the one thing I wish I'd done more, and I offer it to you as the career lesson I learned.

If it wasn't for my history with one particular network executive I wouldn't have been able to tell a story that meant a lot to me. A teenage friend of my daughter was visiting one day and mentioned, all too casually, that her mother had been diagnosed with breast cancer. The girl blew it off as if it didn't affect her. I realized she was in deep denial, utterly unprepared to face the reality of the upcoming surgery. Thinking about her, it occurred to me that dramas had been done about breast cancer — and the last thing I wanted to do was a disease-of-the-week movie — but no one had dealt with this serious subject from the daughter's point of view. What interested me was not the illness but the relationship and how such an event would affect a teenager's sense of what it means to be a woman, and what would happen if she lost her mother.

Had I set out to write a script, or even a treatment, or even a pitch, and asked my agent to arrange meetings with potential producers, followed by waiting for their responses, followed by scheduling network meetings, and re-scheduling them after they're postponed, followed by who-knows-how-many network pitches, followed by who-knows-how-long-I'd-wait for an answer that might be no ... half a year might go by before I could write this, if ever.

Instead, I picked up the phone. I had some credits at CBS — four were on series and a couple of others on original dramas — and a year earlier I'd shared a table with one of the CBS Vice Presidents. We were at the ceremony for the prestigious Humanitas Prize that gives awards for writing in film and television, and I was a finalist for an original drama that she'd greenlighted. When I didn't win, she leaned over and whispered something like "let's try again," or "let's do something else." I don't think I actually heard her words over the applause for my competitor.

But that was enough of a "relationship" for her to take my phone call. I did a minimal pitch, like "let's do something about breast cancer but from the teenage daughter's point of view." She said "Sure. Who do you want to produce?" I chose a company I'd worked with before because I liked their attitude of respecting the script and I believed I could trust the taste of a particular producer there. Also, I knew they'd be approved because they were a frequent vendor. The network V.P said fine. One quick call to the producer's office, and the deal was done. A year later, that project, "Between Mother and Daughter," did win the Humanitas Prize. My point isn't about winning awards, of course. I'm showing you how wheels turn based on relationships — not personal ones, but through mutual respect.

At other times, I've lost out on being considered for staffs of shows because I wasn't part of a social circle — the show-runners simply didn't know me. I understand how frustrated you may feel on the outside looking in. So in the spirit of learning from my mistakes, here's a tale of:

THE STAFF FROM HELL

(Cue howling wolves and lightning)

Anyone who has been on staff has a war story. That's because the proximity of staff writing resembles a trench during a battle. You make close buddies, or have to watch your back, or both. When I entered my own staff hell, I already had a number of produced credits and had spent time on staffs before, though they were either outside the mainstream or short-lived because the series were quickly cancelled. So this was my first experience on a staff of a major network show, and I made every mistake in the book — only there wasn't any book at the time. I wish I'd had this book because I might have avoided:

MISTAKE 1: DON'T SEPARATE FROM THE STAFF.
Since the series was new, it was allotted a floor of empty offices on a studio lot. The show-runner walked the whole staff over and let each of us claim the office we wanted. I thought the quality of my writing was what mattered so I grabbed the quietest spot waaaay off in a distant corner. Meanwhile, the savvy guys nabbed offices that hugged the show-runner's. Every time he walked out of his office he saw them, and they'd be at hand for quick rewrites — the staff members he'd come to rely on. And they'd be first to overhear gossip — actors in or out of favor, network pressures, production or story glitches — and nudge their drafts accordingly.

This principle of staying in the mix infuses all the situations below, though it applies mostly to beginning staffers. At higher echelons, producer-writers can't be in the office all the time because they're on the set or away on location shoots. And on many shows "creative consultants" aren't around at all unless they're called. But these lessons are meant for you.

MISTAKE 2: DON'T MIX PERSONAL AND WORK ISSUES.
Every staff becomes a family, dysfunctional or mellow. Now imagine your family members locked in one room together all day, every day for

six months. Got the picture? A degree of intimacy is unavoidable at the writing table when the staff is delving the feelings and motives of characters, pulling from their own experiences. "When a guy stood me up, this is what I did…" That sort of insight can inform the realness of storytelling — a good thing.

But honesty can rise awfully quickly to "tmi" (too much information). You'll know you slipped over the edge between confessions in group therapy and story beats by the discomfort in the room or the head writer saying "let's move on." Remember, this is collaboration on shared character arcs that involves "catching the voice" of existing characters. One day, if you're the series creator it may also be a more personal expression; now, you're on a team.

Even if you're cool at the writer's table, watch out to maintain "friendly professionalism" at lunch, at the water cooler, everywhere at work. The other writers may be competing with you. On the staff-from-hell, I stopped by the office of my "new friend," whom I'll call Mr. Horns. Like me, he was a lower-level staffer trying to get a toe-hold on the career ladder. Two tiny pink booties from his baby daughter hung from his desk lamp.

I related immediately — I also had a young child. Ruefully, he said he left in the morning before she was awake and came home after she was asleep and was too busy writing on the weekend to spend time with her. "I'll see her in six months when we're on hiatus," he shrugged. I commiserated and confided that juggling my schedule was an issue. He shook his head — his wife didn't work, so she took care of everything at home. "You're not going to be able to do this job," he said flatly, as I noticed the protrusions on the sides of his head. And he was sure to relay my problem to the boss.

MISTAKE 3: DON'T HAVE OTHER PLANS.

Unfortunately, Mr. Horns was partly right. Working on a series staff consumes most of your time and all your energy. It's great for people who have few outside obligations, but balancing a home life is tricky. I did work on one show where the entire staff had kids, and it was so well-organized that we almost always arrived at 10 and left at five. The Supervising Producer had the clout to negotiate a deal to arrive at 8:30 so she could leave at four, most days, and be around when her kids came home from school. That's rare, though.

This is not about women's issues or family versus career. When you agree to join a series staff, your life has to change. You can't take much of a lunch break with friends. Chances are you're catching lunch in the studio commissary or at your desk. You may have only an hour between the morning staff meetings and an afternoon screening, or between casting and dailies, or between a quick, urgent script polish and breaking a story for the next episode. If you drive off the lot to lunch, you'll be late for your afternoon meeting. Fuhgeddabout it. As for your other screenplays, your novel, dating, or camping out in the desert — hey, that's what hiatus is for.

MISTAKE 4: DON'T WORK AT HOME INSTEAD.

Each staff member writes individual episodes in addition to work-shopping everyone else's scripts and re-writing other people's drafts. In a full season, you can usually count on two episodes, but depending on the size of the staff, how much the boss likes your work, and how clever you are at pitching stories, you might write more.

Maybe you're used to working in bedroom slippers at 4:00 AM, or blasting a CD in your private room, or shutting your door and hovering over the computer in silence for hours, then going to the gym before returning to your computer. Sorry, folks, none of that's likely on staff. Personally, I find it difficult to concentrate in a public office off a noisy corridor with interruptions every half hour, having to break for screenings and meetings. But some writers tune out the world so well they can write in the office all day. And headphones may help.

On the staff from the netherworld I wanted to prove myself by bringing in a wonderful draft of the first episode assigned to me, and deliver it ahead of schedule, certainly within two weeks. So I asked Mr. Horns if he thought it would be okay to write at home. "Absolutely" he grinned widely. "Do whatever it takes to write what you want to write. Just go. And if it takes three weeks, that's cool too. Don't waste your time coming in." I asked the show-runner for permission, and he shrugged "Sure," though he was busy with something else.

So I went home. For two weeks. Let me tell you, in that two weeks the script slated to run before mine killed off the character I needed to twist my story, a pivotal location was ruled out by the network, two actors in the cast were having an affair, and an intern took over my office because "no one was in it." By the time I brought in my draft, still warm from copying, it was out of touch with the series. And so was I.

Learn from my experience: Stay connected, even if you get virtually nothing written all day and have to work all night at home.

MISTAKE 5: DON'T BE PRECIOUS ABOUT YOUR SCRIPT.

You become attached, of course. Look how wonderful your script is: The shape of a certain scene builds to a climax then twists unexpectedly and turns the story just in time; a precise detail reveals passion felt but hidden; in a nuance of character, the backstory is deftly sensed; a phrase came so perfectly as if the character was writing instead of you. It's everything a writer would want from a script, or so you believe as you type "Fade Out." So it's difficult to bring your script to the table, no matter how supportive the staff, and no matter how often you've been through the process.

But the day arrives when copies of your script have been distributed to the staff, and everyone is assembling for the meeting at which it will be discussed. I said discussed, not shredded. Let's not be paranoid. Somehow, you'll need to distance yourself from it now. Try to think what's good for the show, not what bolsters your ego. It really doesn't matter how hard you worked, or how you arrived at the reasoning under a speech or action, or how much you don't want to lose a certain moment.

If the consensus of the staff — or simply the opinion of the head writer/ show-runner — is that something isn't clear or doesn't tell the story well or is not credible or steps on something in a different episode, or any other criticism, I advise you not to argue. Of course, you may clarify your intention, but then let it go. If you're a good enough writer to be on the staff you're skilled enough to re-write and come up with a revised draft that's even better than this.

If you don't, someone else will.

MISTAKE 6: DON'T "DIS" THE CULTURE OF THE STAFF.

Skilled professional writers fill the staffs of television shows, but that's a little like saying most human families consist of people — it's a minimum requirement but doesn't tell much about what goes on. Each staff develops a kind of culture, just as families do. This comes from shared interests, experiences, memories, and (in the best cases) shared goals. If you think you and your dog begin to seem alike after awhile, consider a room full of writers melding their minds to tell stories about the same characters.

Often the show-runner sets the tone — formal, laid back, brooding, artistic, intellectual, homespun, sex-tinged, political, romantic, drugged-out, pious… and so forth. Sometimes the culture fits the nature of the series, but not always. In the case of the staff-from-hell, the prevailing ethos had nothing to do with the subject of the series. It was blatant misogyny.

Every staff meeting began the same way: A half hour of sports talk, football, basketball or baseball, recapping the plays from a game in detail, arguing over which man is better. And there I sat, the only woman in the room, irrelevant because I didn't know about guys doing things with balls.

Even when the sports-talk gave way to writing, the sense of the room remained. And one day, when we were working on an outline for an important episode, and it was time for a break, the entire staff (except me) convened to the men's room, where they stayed for 20 minutes, finishing the outline.

I wracked my mind to figure out how to function with this staff since watching sports and shooting hoops in the parking lot seemed more important than anything I could write. The frustration mounted until one day I erupted, "Are you finished with the male bonding yet?" Mr. Horns couldn't contain his smile that I'd finally sunk myself, so my future episodes would be his; he'd get the promotion, the raise, the credits and acclaim — or so he calculated. If I'd been wiser and more confident, I wouldn't have tried to join on their terms, but might have discovered other interests in common with at least one of the staff and created an ally. "Dissing" the culture of the show — putting it down — alienated me further and made it more difficult to work.

Think about high school. Everyone is in cliques and you're the new kid who just transferred. How do you begin fitting in? Probably you start with one interest, and someone else interested in it; a first friend. An important lesson.

MISTAKE 7: DON'T WORK ON A SERIES THAT'S WRONG FOR YOU.

The staff from down below was probably a wrong fit, no matter what I'd done. Lots of TV series are out there and even though you (understandably) need to start somewhere, misery is not an essential rung on the ladder. You need references as well as good work to move ahead. A show that you have to omit from your resume can hurt you more than having had no job at all. When you apply for your next staff, the new producer will certainly phone the former one, and may ask the other writers how it was to work with you.

I stayed through my entire contracted season with this show, but in retrospect it would have been better to leave sooner and get on with my writing and career. I'm not advising you to quit when the going gets rough; if the quality of the show is worth it, and you can write well despite bad vibes, stay with it and amass those credits. But if the quality of your writing is suffering, go ahead and bail after speaking with the show-runner, especially if you can negotiate a non-damaging reference from him. With all you've learned, you can go on to another, better staff. You're not alone. Almost every TV writer has had a difficult experience at least once, and most omit the rubble of their histories from their resumes. You'll survive it, too.

THE GOOD STAFF

Emmy Magazine, the publication of the Academy of Television Arts and Sciences, asked in 2004, "What does it take to make a creative ensemble run smoothly?" J.J. Abrams, Executive Producer of *Alias* answered, "The key is having collaborative, smart writers who keep the room running. Whether it's the official show-runner or someone else saying, 'We have to get past this and keep going.' It's crucial to get to the act breaks and the end quickly, so you can reverse and make it better. You need people who share the same vision and are collaborative and mutually respectful."

Abrams continued, "You want to make sure the show isn't repetitive, but you want to keep doing certain reveals. How do you keep doing that so that the show isn't contrived? A show like *Alias* can be preposterous — how do you keep it real? As a viewer, I'd be furious if I invested in a show that ultimately went nowhere."

For Abrams, the best thing about working on a staff is "being in the trenches with people you admire, respect, and who bring to the group ideas that make you smile. That's fantastic. When things are working, you celebrate with them, and you despair with them when things don't work. Whether you're celebrating or commiserating, you're doing it together."

A SLICE OF LIFE

For a well-run staff, let's peek in on John Wells, who heads *ER*, *The West Wing*, and many other shows.

Picture a long dark wood conference table dominating a conference room. Ten chairs surround the table for four senior writers, four staff writers, one full-time researcher, and Mr. Wells. At the back of the room, more chairs and a few couches for full-time physicians on the staff, and production personnel, as needed. All chairs face a monitor where dailies are screened.

The walls are hung with large whiteboards covered with plot points and story breakdowns for the 12 episodes to be completed for the season. On a sideboard, colored markers list ideas for possible scenes under the headings of Big, Serious, Humorous, and Other.

The staff begins laying out the season the first week in June. Working as a group for six weeks, they come up with the entire season's episodes — ideas for them and specific storylines, and the group "pounds them out." That means the team figures out all the major turning points of the stories, where the act breaks fall, and how many episodes an arc may cover, structuring the episodes.

Then an individual writer is assigned to go off and do a story treatment. (I discussed outlines and treatments in Chapter Four.) When that writer returns, he gets notes from the staff. The writer does a revision. Another notes session. Then he's sent off to write the script. When the script comes in, there's a notes session. He does a second draft. If that works, the episode is ready to film. In all, the process for one script takes about eight weeks.

On a visit to *ER* in an early season, *Written By*, the magazine of the Writers Guild, described the scene on a day a first draft has come in, so this is the first notes session on the finished script. The writers file out of their offices and head for the conference room, each holding a copy of the script. Wells is in position at the head of the table, and the room is full. Coffees are brought, but this staff gets right to business going page by page through every beat of the script.

In this episode, a teenager has cystic fibrosis and his mother is afraid her son will die. The twist is that the son doesn't want to be saved, which puts Dr. Ross in an awkward position between mother, son, and his Hippocratic oath. Someone asks about the kid's girlfriend, another about Ross' choice whether or not to save the kid. A debate breaks out over whether the writer is showing traits of Ross that the audience has already seen. While the staff throws out suggestions, the writer is busy taking notes.

However, I recommend you use a tape recorder. This experienced writer was able to get what he needed, but you might not. Three problems: First, you're not likely to be quick enough to catch every point, or distinguish what's worth noting among contradictory remarks. Second, under pressure your handwriting may be illegible. Third, by keeping your head in your notepad, you're absent from the discussion, and constantly behind. Unless the show-runner objects, tape the session so you can pay attention in the room, and deal with exactly what was said later, when you

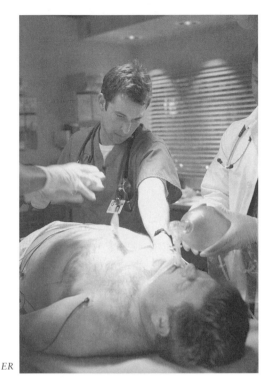

ER

can concentrate. Of course you'll also be writing directly on the script when suggestions relate to specific lines.

Back at the meeting, Wells says the story is almost there, but it's missing a pivotal action that will define the emotional rhythm for the sequence. That propels a debate about another character's developing depression. Then Wells cues a new discussion about comic relief scenes. And on the meeting goes for four more hours as they move from scene to scene to the end of the script.

This kind of meeting happens again every Monday, Wednesday and Friday afternoon. But don't misunderstand; it's not all about logistics and group-think. Writing on a staff still emanates from each writer's art. As Wells told *Written By*:

> Writers have a responsibility, and it's sort of a particular responsibility that all artists share. You have to find a way to return yourself to that place from which you work, and not allow it to ... float off of it into this pop-referential world in which we're only writing about or talking about things that we've seen or know from television and movies.
>
> I think that you, as a writer, you fight that and at whatever point you lose it, you're in big trouble. And your work suffers mightily from it, and then you'll have to find some way, if you're going to write again, to get back to it. And that's beyond all the dealings with success and all of those things which have their own problems, which you certainly don't want to complain about because you don't want it to go away but, artistically, it has an impact on what you're doing. And that balance is very difficult to strike.
>
> I look at writing as a craft and as a gift. As a craft you have to work on it all of the time, and as a gift you have to protect it. And one of the things you do to protect it is to make certain that your world doesn't become too insular. And, particularly, that your points of reference don't become too insular,

because then you find yourself writing exactly the same things because you have nothing new to say about the subject. That's when shows become uninteresting to people, because they feel that they've already heard what you've had to say, and they're not interested in hearing it again. So there's a constant need to be looking. Not to see your name again on another show or anything like that, but just creatively, to protect that place from which you write.

THE STAFF LADDER

John Wells stands at a pinnacle of success shared by very few creators of hour series including Dick Wolf with his *Law & Order* brand; David E. Kelly, who at one time ran *The Practice, Ally McBeal,* and *Boston Public* at the same time; and Steven Bochco, who has consistently had a series on the air longer than any other producer of drama, from *Hill Street Blues* through *NYPD Blue* to many other shows in between.

Each show-runner was a writer first, and though the top rung involves as much skill in management as writing, the entire television ladder is built on writing titles. This differs from theatrical movies where creative power resides in the director, and financiers can buy their way to a credit or even an empire as film producers.

Beginning at the bottom, here's every step:

1. FREELANCE WRITER

A freelancer is responsible only for writing a script and is not on the staff. As an outside writer, you won't participate in story meetings or screenings or have an office at the show, or share in any of the inner workings of the series. You might not even meet the staff except for the producer who hires you and whoever supervises your episode.

But you do have an opportunity to demonstrate your skill and talent. This teleplay — especially if you receive sole screen credit — can lead to a staff offer on this series or open doors at other shows. If it wins any acclaim, and a buzz begins about you, this one break could leverage a career. (See Chapter Six for more about how to break in.)

Minimum compensation for a primetime network series under the Writers Guild Basic Agreement is more than $30,000 for "Story plus Teleplay." (All figures are approximate because the W.G.A. schedule of minimums is revised periodically.) For comparison, that's around the same as a two-hour theatrical screenplay for a movie whose budget is under $5 million. Since networks license two runs of any episode, and successful series usually re-run, you will soon receive approximately the same initial payment a second time in residuals. Later, you'll amass more residuals if your episode re-runs in syndication, and that can continue for many years, though the amount declines to pennies after a while. On a series that continues to syndication, you might see well over $60,000 for a single hour you've written as a beginning freelancer.

But not all freelancing is network, and not all contracts guarantee the full ride. Network rates apply to ABC, CBS, NBC and FBC (Fox); HBO and ShowTime also pay at network levels, as do some other cable channels. But if you write for smaller cable outlets, prices dip to around $20,000 for "Story plus Teleplay." On cable, residuals are also calculated differently.

And you might not be allowed to write the episode to its finished draft. Inexperienced writers are usually offered a "step" deal with "cutoffs." That means you are given a chance to write the outline ("story"), and if it doesn't work, or it seems that you would not be capable of a quality teleplay, the deal goes no further — you are cut off. Someone else (often a staff member) takes over the project and writes the script from your outline, or even writes a new outline.

In those cases your credit will be arbitrated by the Writers Guild; you might keep credit for the story if it remains essentially what you wrote; or you might share credit on the story if more than 50% of what you wrote is in the final script; or you might lose credit altogether if the new writer had to start over and changed more than 50%. If someone else wrote the script, of course, you'll have no credit on the teleplay even if the underlying story was yours.

The next cut-off comes after the first draft. If the head writer/show-runner believes you failed to catch the voices of the characters, or didn't convey the sense of the show, or the writing is just not excellent (for example flat or expository dialogue, unfocused scenes, lack of tension), the script will be given to a staff writer or another freelancer. Just as happened with the "story by" credit, the teleplay credit will be arbitrated and the second writer might be awarded some or all the screen credit, depending on how much he changes.

In a step deal, you are paid separately for each stage. Using network rates, the story alone is around $12,000, the first draft is around $20,000, and the second draft is the balance of whatever has been negotiated. You'll notice this adds to more than the "story plus teleplay" contract, and that's intentional. It's a kind of reward if a writer is asked to go to the next step of the project (if "the option is picked up") though the contract did not guarantee continuing.

As with the "story plus teleplay" model, you'll receive residuals for network re-runs and syndication in proportion to what you've actually done (when you're cut off after the story, clearly you don't get the full residual for the episode).

If freelance assignments were abundant as they once were in television, freelancing could be a fulfilling lifestyle for a writer because you could do well on a few assignments a year, exploring various genres that interest you, and have time to write features, novels, or have a personal life. But today, most series are written by the staff.

Before I describe the staff ladder, here's one more note on freelance assignments: Many are rewrites rather than original scripts. For example, an agent sends your sample scripts to a producer who likes your writing and invites you in. You go to the meeting and pitch episode ideas (stories), but the producer might not be listening for something to buy. Instead he's hearing your insights into the show and what you bring to the creative party. If you impress him, he may give you a story he has already developed that needs to be re-thought from the outline up, or a teleplay that needs to be rewritten though the story basically works, or even a pretty good teleplay that just needs a "dialogue polish" (that means revising the lines but not touching the structure). Say yes. Think of it as dues.

Back when I was freelancing, that happened at a western series called *Paradise*. I didn't know anything about the Northwest in the 1900s, though I'd watched the show and liked the characters enough to generate ideas. I had an agent and some produced credits by then, so setting up a meeting wasn't difficult, but I knew stories alone wouldn't be enough. I spent days researching the era to ferret tales from their world. Often, I've discovered vignettes and unexpected characters from research, and I've found that those gems of reality breathe life into storytelling. So armed with well-honed pitches and smart on the history, I went in.

But one after another, the pitches fell, sometimes before I completed the log line. Companies don't want to risk hearing a story that's at all similar to anything in the works. Thus I came to the end of everything I'd brought and gathered my notes to leave, when the producer reached behind him and took a script off a shelf. It was a finished draft by a good writer who hadn't been able to render one of the guest cast convincingly. Since they liked my writing and I'd brought fresh textures that fit their show (thanks to my research), the producer thought I'd understand the script's potential, and gave it to me to rewrite. Though I ultimately shared screen credit with the original writer, my next episode for them was my own.

2. STAFF WRITER

A staff writer is sometimes called a "baby writer," someone who's never been on a staff before. Think of it as a year of post-graduate education, with big differences: unlike film school, you are paid instead of paying, the work you do is measured by professional standards, it's seen in the real world, and you get no social promotions — you're up or out by the end of the season. For students from top film schools, being taught by credited industry professionals is not a novelty. But for other recent grads, this might be a first opportunity to be mentored by working writers.

Let your expectations be to learn, grow, form relationships, and write every assignment exactly as needed. If you're given one scene to tighten, don't think you'll grease any wheels by re-structuring the entire script, or rewriting scenes on both sides unless the boss says okay. Depending on the size of the staff, during a season you might be given one script to write, especially if a senior writer is available to "supervise." That means the senior writer will advise you at every stage; but that person is also standing by to write the script if you can't. No one has time to wait while you figure it out. If the staff is small, and you're on top of your craft, you might even write two episodes that are credited to you.

Staff writers receive regular salaries according to Writers Guild minimums. A beginning staff writer on a primetime network show is paid around $3,000 per week ($12,000 per month). But your contract might be limited to 20 weeks (or less), with an "option" to renew you for the rest of the season. Off network, some beginning salaries fall as low as $750 per week. And if you write a script the fees will be credited against your salary, so you won't see additional payments until you go to the next step:

3. STORY EDITOR / EXECUTIVE STORY EDITOR

Once you get past freelancers and staff writers it's tricky to guess what any job title means on a particular show because those ranks may be honorary. You see, as a writer advances in a series, his agent negotiates a new title every season. "Story Editor" is for people who are beyond staff writer, but how far beyond depends on the size of the staff and the show-runner's style. For example, a story editor may be a virtual beginner, or one of several seasoned writers on a staff where everyone except the executive producer is a story editor, or the puzzling title "executive story editor" may even indicate the head writer.

In any case, story editor doesn't mean someone who sits and edits stories all day. Like all the other rungs on the ladder, it indicates a writer who does all the stages of an episode from breaking stories, through outlines, through first drafts, and re-writes. Generally, a story editor would expect to write two original episodes in a season, and might be asked to polish or re-dialogue scenes in other people's scripts.

If you're first trying to break in and your pitch meeting is scheduled with a story editor, though, see if you can change to someone higher. A story editor usually doesn't have the power to hire anyone, and, worse, he wouldn't have much personal incentive to make your pitch sound usable when he relays it to the show-runner. On the other hand, if the story editor is a buddy who recommends you, that might have some weight, if the boss trusts him. In a way, we're back again to whom you know.

Story Editors are salaried employees on contract for a defined number of weeks, just like staff writers. They're paid more, though — in the vicinity of $6,000 per week (depending on the length of their contracts), and that's boosted by payments for writing. The minimums under "freelancing" apply to anyone above staff writer, so if you're receiving approximately $24,000 per month as a salary, and you are also assigned an outline ("story") for an episode at the same time, you'd earn around $12,000 on top of the salary, for a total of something like $36,000 that month.

Now, before you're carried away with visions of paying off your student loans, I warn you: You'll only see a fraction. Your agent takes 10%, federal, state and local taxes may add to 40% or more, guild dues are around 3%, and you'll have other mandatory reductions (disability, social security, and so forth). If you have an attorney, he'll take 5%, and if you also have a manager (though you don't need both an agent and a manager at this level), that might be another 15%. All of that comes out of the gross (off the top) before you see a dime. In fact, you won't even see the original check. That goes to your agency which takes out its share and mails you an agency check. And remember, shows get cancelled; writers are frequently out of work for months at a time. As they used to say on a cop show, "be careful out there."

4. PRODUCER

If you watch screen credits before or after a show, you'll see lots of names called producer or co-producer, but they don't all do the same job. Some are like line producers on theatrical movies, dealing with equipment, schedules, budgets, crew personnel. Others are writers who have risen to the producer title but have nothing to do with physical production. Their job is to write and re-write, much like a story editor. And some are hybrids — mainly writers, though they interact with production (especially casting, and in creative sessions with the director and editor) and have a presence on the set.

Typically, producers are invested in forming the season and are responsible for the quality of the episodes, along with the show-runner. So if an episode needs to shoot tomorrow and a script has last-minute problems (no matter who wrote it), a producer may be the one up all night re-writing, though the credit would likely remain with the original writer. Not taking screen credit is one of the courtesies that higher level staff members traditionally give lower staffers and freelancers.

Producers on a set are also expected to re-write on the spot if a scene isn't working or the director or actors have a problem with a speech or action. Sometimes this involves staying out with the crew past midnight in the freezing rain. Offsetting the long hours is not only the satisfaction of having influence over the shape of the series, but, frankly, good money.

Producers normally are not salaried in the same way as story editors. They may have "points" (a partial ownership expressed as a percent of profits), and producing fees for episodes that air. This results in a bookkeeping oddity in which producers might work all summer without compensation to put a show on the air in the fall, but then pull in hefty sums (possibly in the $20,000 range) each week an episode airs.

At this level, the studio may begin looking at you to create an original series while you continue up to:

5. SUPERVISING PRODUCER
The distance from story editor to producer to supervising producer is in increments of responsibility, but all are writers. Some Supervising Producers actually run the writing staff, or even virtually run the show, while others spend the entire season writing and re-writing episodes like everyone else.

If you're breaking in, you're likely to pitch to someone with this title. Though your deal will need approval from the executive producer, this office usually has the power to give you an assignment and guide your script.

6. CREATIVE CONSULTANT
Now here's a mystifying title. On theatrical features it might refer to

the person a movie is about, or the original writer who was totally re-written, a famous writer who polished the final draft, an expert specialist, the financier's nephew, or the director's yoga teacher. On TV series it's a specific job, though the status depends on the situation. Normally, the title goes to a highly regarded writer who comments on drafts of scripts but is not expected to keep regular hours in the office. This person may or may not actually write any episodes or attend meetings.

At one time I was working on a show where the neighboring bungalow housed an action series that seemed to be staffed solely by four executive producers. They were all good writers in their thirties who had been writer-producers on other shows, now promoted to the top title. Writing their series was no problem, but as for managing it, each of the four was lost. Any visitor could quickly figure out what was going on — in the shadows was a semi-retired "*eminence gris*" with the obscure title "Creative Consultant." His credits were so eminent indeed that he didn't want to be known for this little action show, and anyway all the executive producer titles were taken. I think he educated the "executive producers" as quickly as he could and got out of there, but when I knew that staff, the Creative Consultant was actually the show-runner.

7. EXECUTIVE PRODUCER / SHOW-RUNNER

Executive Producers come in all sizes, and it's not unusual for title promotions to create a glut at the top of a series that's been around for years. Most of those executive producers are (as you've guessed by now) simply writers. But two other categories share this title, and you want to know who's who when you go to a show, especially if you're making a first contact.

Some shows have two tracks at the very top — one is the executive producer in charge of physical production: technology, crew, schedules, location planning, construction, equipment, and so forth. The other executive producer is the head writer, in charge of content, which means all artistic aspects of creating and executing the scripts, including directing, editing and casting. These two people work as a team, a useful division of labor on some shows. Occasionally you'll also see an Executive Producer credit for a star with the clout to be called The Ultra-Grand Exalted Poobah, but don't expect that person in the writers' room.

Among all the executive producers, only one is the show-runner. Often, that's the person who created the series from its original conception, and may have written the pilot, though that's not always the case. For example, on *ER*, the pilot was written by Michael Chrichton, who continues to receive screen credit as an Executive Producer, though he doesn't work at the show. A bevy of other Executive Producer names also appear in the credits. But only one — John Wells — makes the key decisions and runs every aspect of the show.

Steven Bochco and David Milch, two "guest speakers" in this book, are creators and show-runners, though they interpret their roles slightly differently. Mr. Bochco is clearly at the top of *NYPD Blue* and his other shows, but no longer writes episodes, himself. Mr. Milch, on the other hand, regards himself as a writer first, and writes or rewrites many of his show's episodes, including the pilot for *Deadwood*.

If I could bless your early career I'd say: Be part of a staff where the show-runner is a great writer, because you'll want to honor that experience in your craft anywhere you work ever after.

Summary Points

Episodes of television series are created by writing staffs which collaborate under show-runners. Staffs may range from a few writer-producers to many writers, divided into levels.

If you join a staff, you will write your own episodes as well as participate in breaking stories and contributing to the work of other writers.

Freelance assignments are often audition scripts for writers who are not on staff.

Staff writer is the entry level on a show, and is an opportunity to learn from more experienced staff members.

Story editors are a step up the ladder. They re-write scripts and write their own episodes.

Producers and supervising producers are senior writers who also may run the writers' room.

The executive producer title may refer to the creator of the show or the show-runner, or might just be one of many senior writers on staff. It might also be a production title. The show-runner is a writer at the top of the ladder, and is in charge of all aspects of the series.

The traditional ladder has become flexible in certain venues which seek young talent or different perspectives.

Spotlight on Blogging the Shows
Heroes, Friday Night Lights, Grey's Anatomy

Don't even begin your spec until you've passed four hurdles: (1) Read this book (duh, you're already here). (2) Watch a marathon of episodes of the show you're speculating until you're so close you know how it smells. (3) Read sample scripts from the show — as many as you can find — taking note of the structure. And here's the focus of this spotlight: (4) Troll the show's websites.

Every successful television series has an official site, usually sponsored by its network. So just by googling the network you can make your way to the name of the show. Alternately, if you google the show's name, the network site will probably be first. Occasionally you can download episodes. For example, NBC was briefly streaming the entire past season of *Friday Night Lights* to attract a larger audience after the network airing. Add to that bulletin boards, fanzines, individual websites ranging from the show's creators to bit players, summaries of every episode, gossip, biographies, and links to books and merchandise. On that last point, it's unlikely you'll write a better episode while wearing a cap and t-shirt with the show's logo, but hey, whatever spins your wheels.

The location you want will have interviews with the writers, and that may take some searching because most sites tend to feature the cast, assuming (probably correctly) that fans are after the actors. The best writers' sites are interactive in which writers or show-runners respond to intelligent questions about the writing process. Some are blogs or blog-like; that is, they may be edited, but these seem to provide the most direct insight into the personal experience of writing a particular episode or planning a story arc. Interviews with the producers, especially by fellow writers rather than celebrity journalists, are nearly as helpful. In the very best, you not only peek into a particular writers room, but also gain insight into the art and craft of writing for television.

It would take a whole book to survey all the excellent internet resources, but I'll sample a few interesting ones for you. The producers of *Heroes* run an illustrated comic-book style site called *9th Wonders*, in addition to the official NBC website. Early in the show's first season, Damon Lindelof (Executive Producer of *Lost*) interviewed Tim Kring, Executive Producer of *Heroes*. Here is Lindelof's question and Kring's answer:

DL: "How does it feel to be leaving the relative safety of a self-contained crime drama (Jordan finds body, Jordan solves murder) to enter the fun world of serialization, in which many of the questions you pose will not be answered for many, many episodes? You had always wanted to take Jordan more in this direction, but were forced to abandon it by the network powers that be. Is it sweet that the same network is now embracing stories with much longer arcs?"

TK: "It's very exciting to challenge myself in a new way after being confined by a 'closed-ended' type of storytelling. Having had a long career though, I've gotten used to trying to reinvent myself over and over again. The strange thing is that I find myself coming full circle sometimes. When I first started writing TV movies, I was known as the 'horror' guy, then the 'thriller' guy, then the 'teen comedy' guy, etc. But in reality, having just written a new episode of *Heroes*, the muscles used in facing a blank page are remarkably similar no matter what genre you're in. I still struggle over crafting a scene one line at a time. And I still look for truth and reality in every emotion. Where it is really a different animal is in the writers' room — the breaking of the stories. It has to be much more diligently planned out because every beat of the story has a domino effect. Pulling one thread can really make the whole house of cards come crashing down.

"It is certainly 'interesting' (read 'sweet') that the network is now embracing the very type of storytelling that was off limits less than two years ago."

In another interview on *9th Wonders*, writer-producer Jesse Alexander expanded on the importance of character as the ultimate driver in storytelling and his delight in being able to expand across episodes:

"Having done serialized, genre-y shows before — on networks — I'm quite familiar with all the ways they can go wrong. Tim Kring based *Heroes* all around CHARACTER. It's not about people waiting to be told answers to a mystery. Or discovering how convoluted their world, and family relationships, truly are. *Heroes* is all about ordinary people dealing with something extraordinary that has happened to them — and figuring out how to deal with it. We're not stuck in an endless cycle of plot reveals. We're telling thrilling character stories where our people are actually making the plot. We will never run out of stories for this show. Not to say that the show won't change — certainly as more people develop abilities, and more people learn of these abilities — the world our *Heroes* live in will get ever more complex, and rich."

Alexander went on to describe how the show is written: "Our process at *Heroes* is very team oriented. Many shows have one writer cranking out an episode in solitude. From my experiences on serialized shows — I know that rarely works. And even when it does — you get very behind in getting the work done. And when you get behind — and the deadlines hammer you — story suffers. Our team of writers — or League of Heroic Scribblers, as I like to call them — finds strength in numbers.

"We all get together in the room, come up with story, and the scenes for every episode — and then we *all* write scenes for that episode. This enables us to get the scripts written in three days instead of three weeks. And it means all of us know exactly what's going on in every episode.

"There is always one writer who has their name on the script who is in charge of bringing all the scenes together, and shepherding the script through production. But every writer on the show has written bits of the episode. It's a much more honest approach to the way TV is written, and is the only way to write a serialized show like *Alias, Lost,* or *Heroes.* We're all loving the process. Loving the work."

For a different tone, check out *The Crafty TV and Screenwriting Blog* which carries discussions with writers from various shows and aims at information on how to write for screen. In the January 7, 2007 blog, Bridget Carpenter, a writer on *Friday Night Lights* had this exchange:

Crafty TV: "FNL seems to have a more fluid structure than a traditional hour drama. There's a main or 'A' story, which belongs to Coach, but instead of having a secondary B and a tertiary C story that take up the rest of the episode, we get a weave of stories, where each of the characters seem to have their own stories that run in parallel. Y'know, like in life, but more interesting. Do you feel that's true?"

Bridget Carpenter: "That is indeed true. In fact we never, or almost never, talk about stories in terms of A/B/C. It always seems that we have an innate 'room understanding' of the weight of each character's story in each distinct episode. We'll pay more attention to Smash for a few episodes when we get into his taking steroids, the pressure that he's feeling to excel, his drive to make 'the list'— and as a result, another character's story for that episode/episodes may recede temporarily. We do tend to go back to Coach and his family more often, because he's the character that links pretty much everyone else in town."

Crafty TV: "There's usually a football game, but it can come at the beginning of the episode or the end of one. Is there any sense of 'the following things have to happen in every episode'?"

Bridget Carpenter: "It also can come in the middle! That was something that excited all of us from the beginning — that when we have a game, it should serve the story of the episode — it doesn't have to cap it. That said, a football game has a natural energy and drive that often makes its way into Acts 4 and 5.

"As we break episodes, we ask ourselves, is there a football game in this episode? If there is, then we talk about when we want it to be and how it's helping to tell the stories of the characters within the game."

Compared to Carpenter's clear logic, want to sample some really candid tales of life in the writing trenches? Then check out the *Grey Matter* website by the writing staff of *Grey's Anatomy*. Through blogs, each episode's writer reflects on the work soon after it airs. Among all the interesting revelations, I found producer-writer Krista Vernoff's insights especially valuable for you, as you can see from her description of writing her first episode (which aired in May, 2005):

"Okay, here's what I remember: I remember that we all met, this bedraggled group of writers, for the most part all coming from other recently cancelled shows. I myself had come from a sweet little show called *Wonderfalls* that Fox killed after airing only three episodes.

"There was, of course, Shonda who had never been in a writer's room before and who lurked outside the door, brooding and disturbed like maybe we were all vampires who would eat her soul if she stepped foot inside.

"And then there was me. WHO WOULD NOT SHUT UP.

"I swear to you, I got this amazing case of verbal diarrhea and I just KEPT TALKING.

"It was the nerves. And the fact that I'd been unemployed for four months and had had way too much time on my hands. And the nerves. Did I mention the nerves? And did I mention how Shonda, who had finally made her way inside the room, kept looking at me like if I didn't shut up soon she was going to leave and never come back?

"And still, I KEPT TALKING...

"It was truly an appalling, humiliating, mortifying day in my career. Okay, week. And so, when I got assigned 'If Tomorrow Never Comes,' I felt like I had a lot to prove. Like if the script didn't make up for the compulsive talking, I might not get to come back for season two. The theme was procrastination, which I know a thing or two about and we spent a week talking about the stories in the writers room and then I went away to write....

"Believe it or not, we actually do think about what kind of message we put into the world. And the message I wanted to give was not, 'Hey it's okay to put off going to see a doctor for two years 'cause it all turns out alright in the end.' George needed Annie to die so that he could actually knock on Meredith's door and at least try to tell her how he was feeling. And I needed Annie to die so I could say all that stuff at the end about seizing the day already. 'Cause it's time. 'Cause life is short and you never know when it's up."

Krista Vernoff certainly did survive to the second season, and she explained how the show works in a blog in January, 2007:

"At the end of season two, we spent about five weeks discussing season three — really planning out all the arcs for the whole season. Then we went on a five-week hiatus and when we came back, we started breaking story (which is what we call outlining episodes). As we break story, we usually veer from what we had planned either a little or a whole, whole lot. Because sometimes things that work in theory do not work in execution and sometimes things that we think are BRILLIANT by 7 pm on a Friday seem absurd by 9 am on Monday. It's not a perfect process, it's not a linear process, it's a creative process. And that process sometimes involves Shonda sitting up in bed at 3 am having had an epiphany that completely destroys all of our plans but ultimately works out really well for the season. Or sometimes, we read a script and think it isn't working and sit and try to brainstorm ways to make it work and we come up with major story points that way.

"For example, last season, Izzie having given up a baby for adoption was never discussed in the writers' room. I read the script and felt like it was missing a personal connection and I went to Shonda and the writer of the episode and said 'What if Izzie had a baby she gave up for adoption' and they liked it so we put it into the script and put the script out and the writing staff was as surprised as [the actress] was because sometimes we get so far behind and so tired we forget to even put out a memo saying, hey, by the way, Izzie gave a baby up for adoption.

"In some ways, with some characters, it's exactly as we planned. With others it's vastly different. But to give you an example of how and why things change, I will tell you that when we planned the season we had not planned to bring Izzie back to work nearly as soon as we did. But what happened is this: We were watching the early episodes and what we found was that we desperately missed having Izzie at the hospital, hanging with the interns. She has such a unique spirit, such a unique energy, and the interns felt (to us) out of balance without her. Tony and Joan and Zoanne [staff writers] wrote SIX DRAFTS of an Izzie arc for episode five this year ('Oh, the Guilt') — and none of them were working. And they are terrific writers and so what we realized is that the reason the stories didn't work, is because we were tired of having Izzie out of the hospital, separate from her friends.

"So three days before that episode was set to shoot we had to completely re-break and rewrite it. It's the one where Izzie goes to the hospital to clean out her locker and ends up seeing the Denny Duquette M and M and then hangs out all day and sees Cristina doing a running whip stitch and knows she wants to come back to work. Can you imagine how much work it was to integrate Izzie into that episode that late in the game?

"Again, our writers are rock stars. 'Cause the thing is, when we pulled that story thread, it wasn't just that episode that unraveled. There was an episode set to start prep three days later, there was an episode in script stage, an episode in outline stage and an episode on the board in the writers' room. ALL of those episodes were affected by that decision. It was a MOUNTAIN of work — many, many 12, 13, 14-hour days. But it was worth it because it was the right call."

By now you realize how intense a staff commitment can be. Then imagine the emotional commitment to take a personal story you love about a dying father of one of the cast, planned for a single episode, and expand it to two shows — re-writing under deadline pressure in a single day. Krista Vernoff described her experience:

"I wrote this episode as one hour. But we shot it and it came in at 61 minutes and we only get 43 minutes per hour and so we were faced with the choice of either cutting 18 minutes — which really would have just destroyed the episode — or shooting four more days and making it a two-parter. It hurt. It was painful and laborious and I was terrified that the decision to go two hours would compromise the episode creatively and it really was such a beautiful episode at 61 minutes.

"We took the story back the writer's room. We break each episode as six acts. So our task was to take six acts and make them twelve. We made twelve columns on the dry erase boards and put act one on act one and put what had been act six on act twelve. Then we put all the scenes we had already shot on the board — and we talked about what we could add. We knew we needed approximately 20 scenes and 20 pages of new material. We watched the 61-minute version — the whole staff — and then talked about which storylines could use fleshing out.

"The other thing worth noting is that we had one day to re-break the scenes, and then I had one day (the next day) to write them. We were here till 11 pm that night but by the time we went home we had added twenty new scenes. Did I mention how much the writing staff rocks? I have to say, some of the new scenes are some of my favorite scenes in the episode. Anyway, we did what we had to do, and I think that in the end, we made it work."

That quick tour of websites for *Heroes*, *Friday Night Lights* and *Grey's Anatomy* gives only a hint of the riches available for every show. But now that you're beguiled, I need to warn you: Visit, don't live there. Your writing must come from your experiences in actual life. Get up and get away from the computer. Yes, your spec script for a show should be well-informed by what they usually do. But if you're only bringing what they usually do, why do they need you? So, after you've immersed yourself in the minds behind a show, put them aside. This is about you, and in the next chapter you'll move on to how you can break in.

How To Break In

I want to tell you a fairy tale that really happened, or so I've been told.

Once upon a time — actually the mid 1980s — a young woman fell in love, not with a man but a television series whose main character seemed just like her. Each week at 9 p.m. on the day of her show, she would sit on her couch facing the screen, wouldn't answer her phone or flip a channel. Often, she found herself thinking about the motives and dilemmas of the characters and talking to her friends about stories that might happen. She noticed the speech patterns of each character, how conflicts were set up and resolved, and how the plots were interwoven. And then she made the leap: I could write this.

Gamely, she sat at her electric typewriter, knocked out a 60-page "spec" and mailed it to the show. A "spec" is a speculated script — no one asked her to write it, no one's going to pay, but it would be her ticket to ride. Except that the script was returned unread with a form letter stating that they don't accept unsolicited manuscripts. But she was in love, so she tried again.

Script two — somewhat better than the first simply because it wasn't her first — went off to the show. And back it came. Now, this woman had no film school degree, no relatives in the business, no screen credits, no agent. And where she lived no one else had a clue how to break in either. But she was in love.

So here came script three. By now she'd read books on screenwriting and researched the series to find hints where the stories were heading. She aimed this third script at what she thought was a gap in the series, and she included a short cover letter that showed she had something unique. So she sold this one, right?

No. But this time the envelope held something amazing: a note if she was ever in Los Angeles, come visit the office. You know how fast she bought that air ticket.

Luck, fate, or curiosity, who knows, she managed to get an appointment. And what did she have in her hands? Ah, you thought it was script four. Nope, she got smart. She brought pitches, short summaries of 10 stories that were perfect for the series — twice as many as writers normally bring to pitch meetings. And she told those stories with wit and insight in five minutes each. So she sold one!

Just kidding. She sold nothing but left with an armful of sample scripts, a log of what they had in development, and suggestions for areas of interest. The producer said he'd be willing to hear her pitch again.

Next time, she finally heard the winning sentence, "have your representatives call business affairs." Does that mean she sold a script or was invited onto the staff? No way. But she'd nabbed an assignment to write an outline, which you know from the previous chapter is the first paid writing step. The producer's assistant showed her their "beat sheet" style, and she managed a workable story that — hooray! — was sent to first draft ... to be written by someone else. She was too inexperienced to write, though she would receive "story by" credit. With that, she re-located to Los Angeles to watch closely as the episode developed.

And then she pitched another episode. It was good. They let her write the first draft. It wasn't so good. But she learned as the script was revised, moving through the writing staff, production, and post-production. She pitched, outlined, and wrote another episode — better. She made allies among the writing team. And finally, when the series was renewed for the next year, she was invited onto the staff.

And she rose through all the writing ranks, staff writer, story editor, producer, supervising producer. And three years later, in the last season of the series, she became the executive producer, running the show she loved. The End.

Within that fairy tale lie tips for breaking in, which I'll detail below. In fact, every writer who has broken into drama series can tell you a war story, and you can take cues from each. Here's mine:

Writing for screen never occurred to me, growing up in New York City, but I'd always written — poetry, stories, plays, journalism — and by the time I graduated from college at 20 I'd won some prizes and published in small magazines. Mostly my adolescent journalism idealized about the potentials of television if characters could reflect the diversity of our population, the true experiences of women, and the realities of urban life. (That was before HBO and the other cable channels, not to mention the better network shows, broke the old network mold and won awards for doing just that.) Based on my articles, I was hired as program director for an experimental public TV station in Los Angeles. So I arrived, with one suitcase and a winter coat that would be useless, 3,000 miles away from anyone I knew. A few months later, the station went broke.

But I'd met people and someone tipped me that MCA-Universal was searching for a young woman in feature film development because they'd never had a woman executive. In my three years at MCA, I saw predictable names always attached to movies while scripts by less known writers (even ones with agents) never made it to the executive floors, and even when a movie was greenlit, years passed from script to exhibition, during which time the original writer was replaced (and his replacement was replaced). But a few floors down in the television department and the units who made series, scripts were on the air in months, the writer's credit intact.

So I set out for a TV career. By this time I'd written three spec features, having learned the craft from the pros. My first job was an uncredited dialogue polish on a TV movie, a typical beginner's job. That happens when an established writer has completed all contracted drafts, and a new writer revises lines though her name would not appear on screen. In this case the young characters didn't sound real, so I spent two weeks rewriting for a flat fee.

That job got me my first agent because the producer needed to negotiate with someone, so he made a few referrals. Hey, if a producer wants to hire you that's a sure shot to an agent. I went with one who was beginning, like me, and grew with the agency for years.

Now I was ready to try writing episodes. But how? I found a fresh angle: Watching episodes of *Trapper John, M.D.*, I felt one of the main cast was being ignored. I knew Madge Sinclair was a wonderful actress, having once seen her on stage, and I took a chance the series might be obligated to her after years on the air. So I asked my agent to arrange a pitch. As a kid with no experience, I didn't have a clue about A, B, C stories or the four-act structure, so I had to be taught by the producer. But the episode was made. Madge brought my lines to life. And later that year she won an Emmy for her performance in the first episode I ever wrote.

I didn't stay with this series. I freelanced at several others, and it was a while before I was on a staff, but that first break was a kick.

It all comes down to these rules:

WRITE WHAT YOU LOVE.

This is not self-indulgence; it's the way to write well. What separates you from everyone else trying to break in? For our fairy-tale heroine, passionate identification with the main character in the series, understanding the struggles and feelings that protagonist would face, gave her stories the force of reality. You might find your break-in angle from experience in a field like medicine, law, or police work, absorption in a genre like sci fi, or even in your family background. Your passion will lead you to authentic stories.

So when you choose a show to spec, pick one you watch often. Sounds obvious, but I've encountered would-be writers who think they're playing the system by speculating shows they would never watch, thinking they're easy to break into. Doesn't happen that way. First, all shows want to hire the most gifted writers they can attract, not reluctant pragmatists. Second, never write down — it hurts you as an artist and damages your reputation. Third, it's not going to succeed. It's obvious if you don't really have a feel for the show. And finally, what you are creating in a spec is a showpiece, not an actual episode, and this brings me to the next point:

DON'T SPEC THE SERIES YOU PLAN TO PITCH.

Okay, that's opposite the lesson in the fairy tale. A few series will read specs for their own show, but most won't, and you don't want them to. Think about it — the producers know their show's minefields. Outsiders wouldn't know the producer is going to scream if he hears one more pitch about the dog, or another swimming pool corpse, or a romance between two actors who (you couldn't know) had a fight yesterday. But producers on a different show will be able to see your script for the great writing it is without the encumbrances. So go ahead and speculate for a series you know well — then develop pitches for a different show within the same genre, or of a comparable quality. For example, at one time the producers of *ER* would read a script from *NYPD Blue* to judge a writer's ability.

And ability is what you're demonstrating — talent plus skill. So choose to study and write for the highest quality series that interests you. Look for one that's been on long enough to be recognized and maybe won some writing awards. (You can find a list of award-winning series through the Writers Guild of America and the Academy of Television Arts and Sciences, both listed among resources at the end of the book.) You'll sharpen your screenwriting; and the show's multi-faceted characters may pump up your dialogue.

Quality of writing is the immutable rule. And that brings me back to our fairy tale, and the next principle:

ASK THE RIGHT QUESTIONS ABOUT A SERIES.

Notice what the woman considered when she first tried the show: the motives and dilemmas of the characters, stories that might happen to them, speech patterns of each character, how conflicts were set up and resolved and how the plots were interwoven. All these can be discovered in the episodes. Once you delve into the underlying motives by asking why the characters behave as they do, you'll uncover the roots of future stories and also subtext that will color the way you write these characters. It is this more subtle layer of characterization that producers want to see in a writing sample because it suggests a source for further writing, as opposed to flat characters or "types" pushed around to serve a plot.

What stories might happen to the characters? Don't answer by using plot lines already set in the show. Those story arcs will be complete before your script is done, and big changes that turn the series are made by executive decision, not by freelancers. Instead, ask what urges or issues come from the characters at a point of stasis — that is, when they behave normally, rather than guessing how the narrative will evolve over the year. Or come up with an angle of your own for the main cast. For example, if you speculate a *Six Feet Under* (an HBO series set in a funeral home) and you're a carpenter, how about a problem for one of the main cast involving how coffins are built.

Ideally, every character's dialogue is specific and expresses background, education, attitude, intelligence, and personality. Listen well, and ask yourself how Tony Soprano's choices of words and his phrasing differs from Dr. Melfi's on *The Sopranos*, or how President Bartlet's differs from CJ's on *The West Wing*. A critical hurdle for an outside writer is to catch the "voices." You may begin with the actors, but don't let that fool you. The differences are on the page.

Conflicts and plot structures are somewhat determined by the hour format and, in network television, by act breaks, as you saw in Chapter Three, but don't let that hang you up. Do what it takes to keep readers turning pages. Production companies and agents will read only a few pages and if they're not hooked, the script gets tossed. The tension has to stay high and the reader needs to be surprised often — not by a gimmick but by a turn in the story that is true to these people. Be unpredictable within the world of the show. For example, in a story about breast cancer, give the disease to a guy because men can get it, too. Be fresh, creative, unexpected.

You see, it's all about good writing, the same qualities you'd apply to writing a feature or other dramas. That's not to say you shouldn't ask about the shows you're speculating or pitching. Do your research. Unlike our woman of the 1980s, you have the Internet. Most series have Web sites, and many have fan sites, too. The official site will assure you basics like spelling the characters' names and a history of the series. Some include statements by the producers with hints to their taste or sources of inspiration. Watch out for the fan sites because they might not be accurate, but the best include summaries, and some list every episode that's been aired, which will save you from writing or pitching what's been done.

The right questions are always about stories and characters, not special effects, costumes, budgets, casting, gossip or marketing gimmicks, so stay focused.

HAVE THE RIGHT TOOLS.

Our lady of the 1980s toiled on an electric typewriter; no one does that any more. For your computer you must have — must have — a professional screenwriting program. The Writers Computer Store (in the resource list) will advise you of your options; if in doubt, "Final Draft" is popular. Each series adopts specific software which their writers must use, but for speculating, any program that creates a standard screenplay form is fine. As you can see in the sample in Chapter Three, the hour drama looks the same as a feature screenplay (though sitcoms are formatted differently). To be considered at all, your scripts must appear perfect and professional.

HAVE REPRESENTATION.

Easier said than done. Our heroine was out in the cold, sending scripts that were returned unread until her extreme tenacity caught a producer's attention. You could try that, but it took her years in easier times, and she got lucky. So let's talk about agents — why you need them, how to get one, and what to do if you can't.

TV series give the illusion of being so accessible, even friendly, that fans sometimes imagine they can join in. From the outside, series writing seems easier than it is, and television appears less formidable than features, so shows would be inundated with amateur scripts if they didn't have filters. Also, production companies won't risk a lawsuit from a stranger who might claim a show stole his story. That's why companies rarely read scripts that arrive "over the transom" (unsolicited and unrepresented).

You need an agent because that's who gets you read, knows where the jobs are, and puts you in the room. Without, it's difficult to know which show is looking for new writers (or at least, willing to consider one). The agency also negotiates your deal, generates your contract, and collects your pay, deducting its 10%.

While feature film companies may buy original screenplays, television runs on assignments. The agent may know of an opportunity on a staff, or that an open episode is looking for a writer with a particular background, viewpoint or style. The agent sends over samples from several clients who meet the criteria. After reading the samples, the producer may invite you in for a meeting. Or, if you have an idea for an episode, the agent messengers over your writing samples, and if the producer likes your work enough, he might invite you in to pitch.

But a lot of good those systems do you if you don't have an agent anyway. Here's what you need in your writing portfolio before you begin your agent search:

• At least one polished full-length original screenplay that showcases your distinct voice.
• At least one hour-long TV drama script in a genre similar to your target.
• At least one more TV drama in a different "franchise" that demonstrates another tone.
• Original stories ready to pitch to series.

Now you're ready to begin. A long list of agents is available from the Hollywood Directory (see resources) and the Writers Guild. The Guild asterisks the ones willing to consider new writers but don't take those asterisks too seriously. Some "open" agencies turn out to be filled; others who didn't offer may nevertheless be interested in a client with something they want.

How do you make your way through all those names? Try to identify those who represent the kind of writing you do. Some agencies aim mainly at Hollywood features, indie productions, or sitcoms, so check if their client list includes writers with credits in television drama. You'll also have to choose between the "packaging" and "boutique" agencies. Big packaging agencies supply all the talent — actors, directors, producers, as well as writers. That can be a powerful asset if you're included in a package led by experienced show-runners. On the other hand, a boutique will give you the personal attention a new writer needs.

Begin on the phone. If you don't have personal referrals, cold call each likely agency. Don't ask for an agent but focus on whoever answers or one of the assistants and say you're looking for representation for writing dramatic TV series. You may extract the names of agents who specialize in this or the new guy in the agency who's building his list. Get the names spelled. Out of 100 calls, 10 may be interested. Okay, you only need one.

Next step is a one-page letter to a specific agent emphasizing your strengths — screenwriting awards, a film school degree, well-reviewed plays, published fiction or journalism. If you don't have those, hook the reader with some specialty like having crime stories to tell from your years as a cop. Move on quickly to what's in your portfolio, for example spec scripts for *House* and *Friday Night Lights*, plus an original pilot and a feature. Your aim is to be invited to send one script.

Now comes the wait. You can probably call once every couple of weeks to remind the assistant; just don't bug people. Meanwhile, your letter is at other agencies you've contacted, and in six to eight weeks someone may ask to see your writing.

Even though you're aiming at episodic series, the first script the agent may want is an original. This is to separate your talent from the style of the series you're speculating. Later, when the agent is ready to judge your skill in series writing, the spec episodes will be useful.

Let's say you've jumped through those hoops and you're meeting with agents. Good agents are looking for clients with the talent and perseverance to grow, as interested in where you'll be in five years as whether they can place you on a staff this season. In fact, an agent who only wants a quick sale is likely to drop you if you don't make him money in the first few months. You deserve better.

You're building a relationship, you hope, so you want someone who understands your goals, can guide you to a show where you start building a career, and has the clout to push open that door. The choice is personal

— the hungry young agent, the empathetic one, or the seasoned vet with a long client list? High class problems, of course.

What if you don't get a bite? Next stop is managers. The main difference is agencies are regulated by the state and have agreements with the guilds which define how much they can charge and their responsibilities. Managers are unregulated, so watch out. Professional management companies function very much like agencies except they charge 15% of your earnings or more, compared with 10%. Justifying the bigger bite, managers may cover more than agents, sometimes all of an artist's business life.

For you, a manager may be available when agents are out of reach, and they can open most of the same doors. They're not listed with the guilds, but you'll find managers in the creative directory. So take the same steps: call, send a letter, send a script, and interview as with an agent.

If you zero-out with managers too, entertainment attorneys sometimes have connections to producers and may pass along your work or make an introduction. If you retain an attorney for this, the customary charge is 5% of all your screen work in lieu of an hourly rate.

Still too tough? Here are some end-runs around the representation problem.

- Get a job on the show. Any job. Production assistant or secretary are fine. The point isn't a career in photo-copying but relationships with the writers. Once they know you, they won't be able to avoid reading your work. And when you're around the series, you learn the inside tips.
- Go to film school for a screenwriting degree. The best schools promote their graduating students to the industry, and friends you meet there help each other.
- Write for an actor. Many actors have small production companies to find them material. You might get into a show by writing a compelling role for one of the less-served cast who will fight for your script. You'll need to figure how to get the script through to him or her, but it's not impossible.
- Start with new and alternative outlets. Apart from network and national cable primetime programming, dramatic writing jobs may be available off-network, in niche cable outlets, in off-hours, on public television, and on the Internet. Those markets don't tend to work with agents anyway (not enough money), so you apply directly to the producers where your enthusiasm may be welcome.

BE IN LOS ANGELES.

Our heroine flew to an L.A. motel the minute she thought a producer would see her. She was lucky he kept the appointment. But a show-runner juggles delivery deadlines, last minute re-writes, and emergencies on the set, so appointments are re-scheduled once, twice, three times. How long can you sit in that motel?

Some people re-locate and work a day-job while poring over the "trades." You know Hollywood is crowded with would-be writers, actors, and directors who followed a dream and were still working as waiters — literally and metaphorically — a decade later. But as a writer you can work wherever you are, so don't leave home until your portfolio is strong, you have a bite, or you're coming to film school. The woman in our tale moved after her first assignment. Then she glued herself to the production, and that led to her next assignment.

Whether you move sooner or later, you do need to live in L.A. to write series television. A few mainstream American shows are now based in other cities — New York, Miami, Vancouver, Toronto. But most staffs are on the studio lots. As you read in Chapter Three, TV writers work collaboratively, so there's no way to avoid the palm trees.

THE SECRET OF SUCCESS

My USC students sometimes ask how likely it is they'll make it — what are their chances of breaking in? The first year or two out of school are usually rough, but I've discovered which ones succeed five years later. They're not necessarily the most gifted, the brightest or the best connected, though talent, smarts, and relationships do help. No, the ones who succeed have a single trait in common: they didn't give up.

Tales from my recent MFA graduates reflect 21st-century realities both better and worse than I'd experienced a decade earlier. Worse is that freelance assignments are tighter. Now shows depend on staff writers for most episodes, so freelance gigs are really auditions for staff.

But so much is better, more open. Okay, each show has fewer freelance episodes, but the number of series has multiplied in a world with 400 channels (counting cable) which do original programming. When I was first breaking in, I had to pitch to guys (yes, guys only), an old guard who held a lid on traditional network formats and the kinds of plot-driven stories that had proved reliable. Too many of their shows seemed alike — mind-numbing for a creative person. Some of them are still around, but in an era when shows compete with the Internet and new venues to attract viewers, those show-runners are becoming dinosaurs.

Among new trends:

- Shows that prefer non-episodic samples (features or even stage plays) in an effort to identify original talent, along with TV specs;
- Potentials to pilot original series or use a spec pilot as a sample (see Chapter Two);
- Hybrid forms including dramedy, reality/drama, and music/drama;
- On cable, no more four-act structure; five acts in syndication;
- Blends of techniques — animation with live action, for example;
- Content that includes non-traditional lifestyles, cutting-edge issues, honest relationships, gutsy language, and fantasy;
- Computer-assisted imagery which enables locations and effects formerly impossible.

In Chapter Seven, you'll find re-prints of two articles I published in the Los Angeles Times and an update. The first article interviewed MFA students from my USC episodic drama class six months after they graduated. I interviewed them again three years later. And the update asks where they are six years after graduation. These are today's stories from the trenches of breaking in.

Take Brian and Kelly. On graduating, they each had feature screenplays written in school, and episodes for *ER*, *NYPD Blue*, and *X-Files*. But no agent signed them immediately, and both took day-jobs. Brian hooked up with a young independent director and worked without pay for a year writing *But I'm A Cheerleader*, a satire about a girl sent to a camp to "cure" her of being a lesbian, whereupon she falls in love with another girl. The indie film was made on a shoestring but garnered Brian notice in *Variety* as a writer to watch. Meanwhile, Kelly was hired to write a script for a French actress.

A year later, they were both still at day jobs, frustrated with director-driven features, trying to break into TV, and they decided to team up. *Cheerleader* got them in a door at the WB, an off-network that hires young writers with limited credits. Here, they pitched an original series — not an episode — and actually got an assignment to write the pilot (something unimaginable in the past). It wasn't picked up. But by now the

WB execs knew the team and recommended them to *Smallville*, on their network. From here, their story is traditional — they wrote an episode, joined the staff, and now they've risen within the show. They tell me they're happy.

So, in a way, we've come full circle from our fairy tale. It is all possible. You *can* break in.

Summary Points

To break into writing for television, you first need a solid understanding of how TV drama series differs from other kinds of writing.

Second, choose one high-quality show to learn well. Fully grasp the "voices" of all characters, as well as the kinds of stories the show tells and its structure.

Once you've learned your target show, write a spec script, but do not speculate an episode of the same show you intend to pitch. You will probably need spec scripts from several shows in different genres.

Once your spec script is polished, try to get an agent or manager who will expose your work to producers. Ideally, you'll get meetings after your scripts are read.

Working on a show in any capacity, including writer's assistant, researcher, or secretary, may help you make contacts who will read your script.

It takes years for most new writers to break in, and the key is to generate many scripts that keep you growing as a writer – and don't give up.

GUEST SPEAKER: DAMON LINDELOF

Damon Lindelof is co-creator and executive producer of *Lost*. Previously, he produced and wrote other series including *Crossing Jordan*.

PD: *Lost* crosses usual genres — it's not sci-fi, not action adventure, not a family drama, not a character-driven drama following somebody's quest, and yet it's all those things. As one of the co-creators, from the beginning what was it you set out to do?

DL: *Lost* is a product of not really having enough time to think about something. At the end of the day it couldn't have been developed in any other way but the way it was developed, in sort of a glorious chaos. Normally the pilot season starts in the summer when studios buy ideas from writers, and then the writers go off and write outlines and then drafts and usually before Christmas the networks and studios get those drafts and they come back after Christmas and in January the networks start announcing the pickups of their shows.

But three years ago at the end of January when all the pilots were already being picked up, Lloyd Braun, President of ABC, said he wanted to do a show about people stranded on an island. JJ Abrams and I said independently (because we hadn't met yet), well, there's no place for the series to go. It's not a dramatic show. How do you do *Survivor*, the drama? That's a game show. They run obstacle courses and vote each other off the island. The drama there stems from the fact that every week someone is not going to be back next week. It's not about survival. Every once in a while someone will try to start a fire or catch a fish but the audience doesn't want to see people catching fish. Still, Lloyd was passionate about it. He said please do your best.

PD: Why do you suppose he was so passionate?

DL: He had a vision; he wanted something different. At the time ABC was struggling with launching new series. They had crapped out of new dramas for several years; they were the number four network. And the police dramas, or medical dramas or legal dramas — you get those every year. But this was a different setting. The showman in him said there was nothing like this on television.

This liberated us to create what we wanted. I called JJ, though I thought it was the worst idea ever — I didn't think it was a TV show. But I said to him if you had to do it as a series it would require certain elements such as a massive cast, and it would have to be a huge ensemble piece and you'd have to know nothing about anybody. Maybe you could dramatize their past by having flashbacks of them prior to the crash. So you'd be doing two shows — one that took place after the crash and another show that took place before the crash. We didn't know how we would make that work. And I said it has to be really weird. It has to be like an episode of *The Twilight Zone* every week. There have to be twists and turns and an external source of conflict that would send the characters into conflict with each other.

It needed to be a mystery show. It is that franchise: every week the audience watching has to think "I'm watching this show because I require the answer to mysteries." What is that plane that Kate is playing with? Why does she want that case so bad? What is the secret Locke whispered to Walt? Those are answers on a shorter term basis. But the answer to the fundamental questions like "What is that thing moving the trees; what is it about this island that drew them here?" will be in play perennially. It mirrors our daily lives because we all live our lives in this sort of über-mystery: What does it all mean? What am I supposed to do? If *Lost* was going to be anything, it needed this idea of mystery. It turned out JJ had come up with the same ideas before we met.

I saw this show opening up with the guy lying in the middle of the jungle and this dog comes up to him. The guy's got a scratch on his face and we have no idea what's happening. The guy sits up and reaches into his pocket and pulls out a little bottle of alcohol, and then he hears a noise. The dog runs off and he follows the dog, and we come upon the crash with this guy. This is much different from a show where you're on a plane with 15 different people and then there's turbulence. Here, you know nothing. You don't know who he is and suddenly he starts to help people. You realize he's got some medical expertise. So you, the audience, are playing along at home. You're figuring it out. That ended up being shot for shot what the pilot opening was.

We didn't start actually writing until three or four weeks later. We generated an outline based on the foundation of let's populate this island with really awesome characters who have pasts they don't want to talk about and make it a redemption metaphor. The characters all made mistakes off the island and now the island gives them the opportunity to evolve as people. In the early episodes viewers thought it was literally purgatory; that theme was so rich: I was a bad person, now I'm trying to be a better person. Characters were saying things like "Why can't we all start over?" Also the viewing audience is so savvy that they're looking for twists. At the time *Lost* premiered much of the zeitgeist was *The Sixth Sense*: it was a popular fictional device that characters didn't know they were dead. We certainly played with that expectation. Then when we started killing off characters it disproved that theory because you can't be deader than dead.

The show was a happy accident based on fear. The fear was: It shouldn't be a TV show, so any idea you have can be justified. When one of the guys who had been in a wheelchair could walk around again, there was concern whether that was a sci-fi idea. Is it too weird? Our response to the Powers-That-Be was we have to do stuff like this; it's the only way we can maintain it as a TV show. It was tremendously liberating.

PD: That's interesting that the opening of the pilot came to you fully imagined. Is that how you work as a writer?

DL: Ideas often come to me as an image system — that picture of a guy waking up in the middle of nowhere. At first the title of the series was "Nowhere," so I had the idea of being nowhere and coming at it through a single character who was going to portal us in, who we'd begun to care about. And then we'd gradually introduce other characters through him.

PD: Now you and Carlton Cuse have been running the show together, and JJ hasn't been around since the beginning of season one. You also have a staff of writers. How do you work with the writers?

DL: I can illustrate with season three. We finished writing the finale of season two at the very end of April last year. We had already made some changes in our staff so we had our season-three writers raring to go. Without a single day off, we finished season two and immediately started working on season three.

We do this thing we call mini-camp with all the writers — around nine people altogether. For three weeks we sit and talk blue sky — here are ideas we have for the next season. Here are the extant mysteries we're going to solve. Some of the ideas are vague at first but they become mandates, like we're going to discover how Locke got in the wheelchair. We've known how, but the question was when are we going to tell that story? When is the right time emotionally for him? We also were inheriting a lot of story from the end of season two so we knew the first sweep was going to deal with Jack, Kate and Sawyer in captivity with the Others. Conversations had been going on for years but now we were going to tell those stories: who are the Others, what do they want, what is their relationship to the island, why do they want Jack, Kate and Sawyer?

For the first week it's all very story driven. By the end of episode six we will know this is why they kidnapped Jack because they want him to perform this surgery. And then Jack is going to pull an end-around and free Kate and Sawyer. What do we need to do within those six episodes to get to that point? What's going to make Jack make that decision? Oh, I know: What if he sees Kate and Sawyer sleep together? That should happen in episode six, and that will trigger... So all that sort of stuff is starting to come together and then you say here's what's going to happen in the finale. We know what's going to happen but the question is when are we going to reveal it to the audience and how?

So by the end of mini-camp we have our design. We were in Hawaii but we worked every day. We'd wake up, go into a conference room, work for four hours and jet over to the set and hang out with the actors and look at the locations on Oahu that we hadn't used yet that we want to write to. It was an incredibly intense week, and then we worked for two more weeks with the writers while we filmed the two-hour finale, and then it was on the air. At that point in the season you're right up against it. Once we locked the finale, that was the end of that three-week period and everybody took a month off, which was the first time I'd had off since the inception of the pilot.

When we came back in July we were ready to hit the ground running. The entire writing staff sits in the room and we talk about each story beat by beat. We talk through what the scenes are and occasionally even rough out dialogue. During this period anybody in the room can say "Hey what if we did this?" Ultimately I'm the one who says I love it or let's move on. But the stories are gang-broken.

Then once we're done finishing the story, which is a three or four-day process, putting it up on the board, the writer of that episode peels off and begins to generate the outline. Then the room starts on the next episode. We do the episodes one at a time. There are procedural shows that can do several at a time. But because of the serialized nature of our show, everyone needs to know exactly what preceded their episode.

For me, since I'm the producer, I don't get to excuse myself and go write the script. I write the scripts nocturnally, and then I'm back in the room the next day. What happens is by the time you get to the fifth episode, you have five episodes in the pipeline. At any one time, one episode is being broken, one is being outlined, one is being scripted, one is being shot.

PD: For anyone who is not on your staff it sounds impossible to spec an episode of *Lost*.

DL: Unless they come up with a concept episode. We do have episodes that are not beholden to over-arcing serialization. One example was the Rose and Bernard episode, where we learn about their past. Now that story you could spec out. But the B story in that episode was questioning Henry down in the hatch. Someone outside the show wouldn't know about that.

PD: If someone wanted to spec an episode of *Lost* anyway just as a sample, what would you advise them to look for?

DL: *Lost* is actually a simple equation that is difficult to execute. The hardest part is figuring out what is happening on the island in any week. Most weeks we start with something like: we have an emotional story to tell about Kate. Once you know that story, you go and break out the flashbacks. You figure out how that ends. That's sort of the easy part because you're not restricted by any of the normal boundaries of storytelling. You can have EXTERIOR: HOTEL ROOM, and any of the things you can do on any other kind of show. The tricky part is what to do with that on this island. If you know the flashback is that Kate made this choice in the flashback, what can be happening on the island to thematically illuminate that again?

If you want to write a spec *Lost*, pick a character that you like the most, tell a story about them from any point in their lives that really solidifies a trait of theirs. Then design a story on the island that gives them a choice. If they made the wrong choice in the past, now they make the right choice. Sometimes the metaphor seems vague until it's right in your face and you go, oh, that's what this was about.

LIFE AFTER FILM SCHOOL: CAUTIONARY TALES AND SUCCESS STORIES

For the past decade I've followed one group of M.F.A. students who happened to take my class in writing episodic TV drama. I witnessed their early (and continuing!) struggles as their careers blossomed. First interviewed for *The Los Angeles Times* just months after they received their graduate degrees from the School of Cinema-Television at USC, I interviewed them again for *The Times* three years later, and finally four years after that for this book.

Together, the three sessions form case histories that hint at what to expect as you begin to write for television. Most of all, I hope their stories give you hope: When the industry appears impenetrable, they remind you that you're not alone. When the doors nudge open, they tell you what they did to walk through. And if they succeeded, maybe you can, too!

THE CLASS OF '97

(The following article appeared in *The Los Angeles Times*, Feb. 8, 1998)

Reunion. Six months after graduating from USC's School of Cinema-TV, eight students from my advanced television writing seminar meet again in our former classroom. Reunions are bittersweet. Now we gather at night, the comforting predictability of school assignments and the company of hundreds of others taking the plunge into the industry with them, all gone. A few are thrilled to have professional assignments. Others, still mailing samples they wrote in school, trying to get agents, claim they're not jealous. Right.

I've taught students like them for a decade, holding out the prospect that hour-long episodic drama in shows like *ER, NYPD Blue, Homicide, Law & Order, X-Files,* and others offer opportunities for the most incisive, challenging writing they'll find anywhere. Now the industry is dotted with stars of previous classes — not just mine but from other USC professors. It's a hot time for new TV writers.

The graduates gathered tonight understand the power they'd wield in television and feel responsible for what they give the public, quick to put down gender and ethnic stereotypes and relationships that don't seem real. It's an attitude not typical of earlier generations. Credit for it goes to the trailblazing series they've studied, and to living in a multi-cultural America very different from what was reflected in earlier decades of TV.

Drew Landis and Julia Rosen became writing partners at USC Brought to the U.S. from South Korea by his minister father during the Amerasian adoptions in the 1970s, Drew worked in politics in Washington before entering the Graduate Screenwriting Program. Julia grew up in Los Angeles and made films that won festival competitions. Together, they speculated scripts for *ER, NYPD Blue, Early Edition, Party of Five, Frasier,* a drama pilot, and two features before graduating. That portfolio got them signed by The Artists Agency, a TV-movie deal, and a possible position on a new series. Credit all those sample scripts, and their certainty about television.

Drew: "An agent asked at one of our first meetings why we want to write for television. It's because when I watch I love the connection to the continuing characters, and having experienced that, I want to translate it every week."

Julia: "For me, it's that feature films nowadays are comedies or spectacles. But you go anywhere in the United States and everybody is watching *ER* and they know all about those characters. The way to reach people and talk about real subjects and get to people's hearts is television."

Wendy West wanted to write TV since she was a child. "I found an old diary, pink, with bunnies. I was excited to see what I did as a child. But when I opened it, I found pages and pages of 'Today on *Alice,* Flo said kiss my grits' — whatever was on TV each day."

Her *X-Files* spec won her a staff writer position on an upcoming WB series, but it hasn't been as she'd imagined. "I feel a little left out. My first script was not exactly what the show is. Working in the real world, you need to be a chameleon. That doesn't mean losing your voice but you have to adapt to the style of the show you're writing. So much of film school is spent trying to find your voice so it seems counterintuitive to think you should lose it somewhat. But only somewhat. I guess we're waiting to see the stamp of a Wendy West script, but you can bet on someone falling in love or at least tripping over her own heart."

Still hopeful, Wendy tells the group, "A good day is like our class for eight hours. One of the reasons I went into television is I like collaboration, knowing people are there to help you get through the outline. You're not alone the way you are with a feature."

That yearning for community echoes among them, all single, in their 20s. Gib Wallis wrote and performed plays off Broadway and on London's fringe before film school. Now he works as an actor while looking for a writing agent. He chose television because: "With features if they want somebody to rewrite you, how much of the original vision is left? With a TV show, even if you're the youngest and you're re-written, they have to see you at lunch. You have writers working with writers so they understand."

That's his dream. But it's a hard fit to the past months. "Right before graduation I sent out 50 query letters and to my surprise I got six meetings and I thought I'd hit the jackpot with people wanting to read my *ER* sample. They said give us several weeks. But every time I called I got this response of now is not a good time. Finally they wanted to hear back from me in July; only the TV staffing season ended in June. I told them I'd hoped they would have read it in time, and they said, oh, we're glad we got your script but there's no way we're going to read it because we're staffing right now. We're trying to get jobs for the people we already signed. I felt there was this little window and I wasn't able to get into it quite soon enough."

Eric Trueheart graduated in English Literature from Harvard, but is equally frustrated since finishing his MFA. He wrote five spec scripts but "It's extraordinarily difficult to get people to read. I've had a lot of time to think about what it means to be a writer." While at USC, Eric was mentored by Glen Morgan and James Wong, then on *X-Files*, now Executive Producers on *Millennium*. "They were great letting me look in on the process. But they're so busy they haven't read anything even though I wrote a *Millennium*."

With television hard to crack, some graduates accepted jobs rewriting features, like Kelly Souders. Having grown up on a ranch in Missouri, she wrote fiction before entering the Graduate Screenwriting Program, where her feature thesis won highest honors. Kelly discovered "Without the episodic TV class the feature would have been a real struggle. I had to take someone else's character in someone else's story and put the structure together, and I learned that in episodic."

She's emphatic: "The quality is in television. I can't tell you how many times I came out of a theater and said I'm never going to a movie again. These big action things have no characters. It's like marketing people put the film together. And then you watch *NYPD Blue* and *ER* and it's the best writing I've seen."

They long for believable characters and more of the spectrum of people in the real world. Wendy describes *Homicide* as "amazing" in its depth of internal issues among African American characters. "The scenes between Andre Braugher and James Earl Jones were riveting — how Pembleton was conflicted over covering up to protect a black hero." Other students point to episodes on *ER* when Benton coped with the illness of his mother — how refreshing to see African American women written with dignity. They're aware the main cast includes Latinos in *Law & Order* and *Chicago Hope*, and Asian and Native Americans on *Star Trek:Voyager*.

Michelle Takahashi, now analyzing scripts for a production company, wrote an *X-Files* spec that sprang from a Japanese Shinto ritual. "I tried *X-Files* because they do cross-cultural stories like the Guatamalan vampire goat, and the Chinese occult. I tried the same subject for features but it's a hard sell. Agents told me not to do a mainstream feature where the main character is a minority. But on *X-Files* Mulder and Scully take you into different cultures."

Wendy agrees, "We have role models in TV we don't have in features. It's great to see women doctors sticking their hands into someone's body to save his life. It's not just this season. Believable women go back to Cagney and Lacey who had real relationships — they weren't just cops, or sex objects. Back then it was a big deal that women wrote that series. Probably they had to fight for it to be truthful."

Not everybody is into the fight, at least, not right away. I see Brian Peterson around campus, no longer in jeans, wearing a tie. He took a job at the School until he has more scripts. "After graduating, you really have to figure out who you are again." Heads around the table nod, understanding as Brian continues, "We were all zombies in the last month of school. We all felt so much was riding on our feature thesis, and we were supposed to start off the block with a big bang. I sent out my query letters and went home to Montana and regrouped. It turned out my feature wasn't useful for television. A couple of agents called me back and said I loved your *ER*, it was great. And I said so? And they said so? So, where are your other TV scripts?"

It's easier to return to the ideals of writing than cope with waiting. They retell moments from shows we studied like Dr. Greene losing a patient in childbirth on *ER*, a controversial issue in *The Practice*, gutsy innovations on *EZ Streets*, true relationships on *My So Called Life*. Michelle admires "series that cut askew, subversive like the episodes of *X-Files* and *Millenium* that laugh at themselves." Gib likes "shows to experiment with the narrative. Some of that is in *Ally McBeal*, interweaving her fantasies in a way that's provocative." Brian wants "a world I can see come to life like *Twin Peaks* that created its own world."

Revisiting friends. Shared goals. Tonight it's easier to get fired up about politicians who want to censor their art than deal with getting assignments that compromise it.

Eric argues, "In one of Bob Dole's anti-TV campaigns, he complained about *NYPD Blue*, saying the last good cop show was *Dragnet*. *Dragnet* was a cartoon. If people want cartoonish versions of morality spelled out, they're welcome to it. But the realistic dramas are supremely moral because they're grappling with issues everyone is trying to grapple with, struggling to come up with moral answers to them."

Kelly: "Television gives people a clear moral choice: the on and off button. I don't watch certain shows, but it doesn't mean they shouldn't be on. There are shows I could never be interested in because they don't have enough honest reality. To me, that dishonesty is as damaging as violence."

Julia: "*NYPD Blue* and *ER* challenge people in ways people who watch shows like *Touched by an Angel* wouldn't want to be challenged. Those people know they're not going to leave with a sick feeling. They want the issues simpler, but for emotions to still be there. There's room for that."

Eric challenges Kelly: "If you were offered a job, could you write for one of those "angel" shows?"

Left to right:
Kelly Souders,
Brian Peterson

Left to right:
Julia Swift,
Andrew Landis,
Kelly Souders

Left to right:
Wendy West,
Gib Wallis,
Julia Swift

Left to right:
Eric Trueheart,
Wendy West,
Gib Wallis,
Julia Swift

Kelly: "I don't think so. I'd be pushing away my experience. Though they say 'never say no' to your first job."

Ah, jobs. That punctures the debate. I lead the conversation back to school. Looking back, what counts?

Drew: "Me and Julia finding each other."

Julia: "We're able to have an extended version of our class all the time. You learn the questions. Do you have the act breaks? Where do your moments come in? Whose scene is this? What's the arc of your character? You go through them, one by one, and make changes until wow, this works. Before, I wrote from my heart but had no idea how to make it powerful. When we graduated, we turned to each other and said 'Thank God.'"

Kelly: "For the rest of your life when you're sitting at a computer you'll be hearing your teachers in your head. You hope what they're saying to you will help you work."

The eight former students turn to me as if I have one more lesson, some secret I know. I do know that five years from now those who refuse to give up will have "made it," as generations before them did. They'll do it by writing unpaid script after script until the craft comes naturally, by learning nuts and bolts on shows they'll one day leave off their resumes, and finally by not losing sight of the great writing they studied on television today. Beyond craft, they've come of age in a "golden era" of television dramas. They'll stand on the shoulders of those giants.

THREE YEARS LATER: THE TV STUDENTS OF '97

(The following article appeared in *The Los Angeles Times*, July 5, 2000)

Three years after graduating, they meet again. They had been MFA students in my class, a few months out of school and mostly out of work, when *The Times* first ran a feature on them. Since then, six other classes have come and gone through my course in writing episodic television drama at the USC School of Cinema-Television, each with its own angst and triumphs.

Now seven of the former students meet in my backyard on a sunny afternoon to talk about what happens when *Variety* (the entertainment trade daily) names you one of "The Ten Writers to Watch," and exactly how much unemployment pays; how exhilarated you feel rising to co-producer of a TV series, and how you find out your show is cancelled; how to avoid letting producers know you're pregnant, and being single with no time to date; how a chance meeting can luck into a break, and yet old friends are what keeps you going.

While they were in school, I predicted that any of them who wanted a TV writing career enough, who didn't give up, would have it within a few years. Now, let's see.

Brian Peterson went home to Montana after graduating then returned to a job in the Dean's Office by day, while sending out his scripts by night. The next fall, director Jaime Babbit, who had an idea for a movie, *But I'm a Cheerleader*, made an offer. Some offer: write a screenplay for no pay.

But Peterson sparked to the subject: "a cheerleader whose parents send her off to rehab because they suspect she's a lesbian, but she discovers she really is gay, and at rehab she falls in love."

Peterson says, "I spent a whole year re-writing it for nothing, and then it finally got shot. It was the kind of thing you dream about: you see these hot pink signs that say "Cheerleader," and you say, 'Oh my God, that's mine.'"

While the film was screening at festivals, *Variety* named Peterson one of the "Ten Writers to Watch." Despite that, "every time *Variety* mentioned *Cheerleader* they said Jaime wrote and directed it. People who don't know better have this love affair with writer-directors."

Peterson concluded, "After that experience, Kelly and I started pitching pilots for TV."

That's Kelly Souders, whose thesis script, "My Slut Mom," was optioned by a producer soon after we last met. But Souders asserts, "Every meeting I had on it was about toning it down. I'm not going to tone it down."

For about a year she co-wrote another feature with an actress, but that hasn't been produced either. So she was also looking towards TV, and they remembered an idea they'd had at USC, and their agent got them meetings.

"Everybody we've met in television has been fantastic, 180 degrees from features," Souders says. The team sold their pilot, and "we'd love to be in the situation to hire everybody at the table," Souders offers, to a round of cheers.

In the time from their 20s to pushing-30, from being outsiders to working in the industry, Souders says, "You start getting protective of what kind of work you want to do. It's easier on your self image," to which Peterson quips, "But not always on your checkbook."

Everyone groans with understanding, even Wendy West, who was the first on a series staff. West laughs that she was also first to discover that unemployment pays $230 per week, when that series was cancelled. But a producer she'd met there invited her onto yet another show... which didn't make it on the air either.

"The way we found out was we opened up the paper and it said we were being suspended. Meanwhile, our sets were being built. In fact, there was a delivery of lumber that day."

But she had made more relationships. So, when one of the producers moved on to the *Law & Order* spinoff, *Special Victims Unit*, he brought West along. Now in her second year on the show, she was promoted to story editor, and this coming year she will be a co-producer.

West: "It's wonderful, exciting, fantastic. [Executive Producer] Dick Wolf is so smart and talented; it's not an accident he is where he is. His notes catch exactly the little things you know don't really work, but you tell yourself, well, nobody will pick up on this. Then he sticks his finger in it, and you say, all right, all right."

West looks warmly over at Andrew Landis and Julia Rosen. "Last year Drew and Julia were on the lot so it was more fun because we could get lunch."

Landis and Rosen teamed up before they left school, and armed with sample scripts for five different series, they garnered an agent before anyone else, and they won contests. Rosen observes, "Producers need something that says other people think you're good."

They nabbed their first real job on *Hercules*, "by going in and pitching something outrageous," Rosen says. Landis adds, "They have people on staff who are going to write the show, so you can only bring something that's yours."

Between *Hercules* and the staff of the short-lived series *D.C.*, Rosen married Andrew Swift, a producer on *True Hollywood Stories*, and became pregnant.

The only one of the group who is not single, Rosen confides, "I hid my pregnancy while we were working on *D.C.* People think if you have a newborn you're not going to work, and that's not true for me. In order to be a good mother I have to be a happy mother." As it happened, *D.C.* was cancelled before the baby was born, and the team found themselves out of work, anyway.

Everyone at the table has done temp work while waiting for the next writing job, but Peterson warns, "People don't see you as a sexy writer if you have a day job."

Michelle Takahashi admits she works for a construction company. Then she smiles, "Next month everybody is getting laid off." While she was in school she thought about a feature set in Japan, and at her job, she says, "I think about it almost every day." She saved her money, and now she'll finally have time to write the script, she says.

Takahashi's three years are typical of hopeful writers, if such a thing as "typical" exists in a volatile industry.

On the other extreme, Eric Trueheart, far from his Harvard literature degree, is writing an animated feature, *Guy Futomaki: Ninja Temp*, which he sold to Fox. "It's the story of a trained Ninja. His clan has been destroyed and he's forced to come to America where he can only survive by doing temp work."

Truehcart's route to the sale was "Hollywood," in the worst sense. "I had a so-called agent who wouldn't sign me, but he mentioned "Guy" to a studio executive. So we go over, and there's this 24-year-old development guy in an expensive shirt. I told him, you know, it's animated. He said, 'We're thinking live action.' I said, 'We're thinking like *The Simpsons, Beavis and Butthead*.' He didn't get it, but he started pitching it around town without us, when he didn't have any rights to it."

Trueheart shakes his head, "It was classic Hollywood. It's not that these guys are evil. They're just driven and oblivious."

Ultimately, Trueheart made his deal with Fox, but his success on the fringe began doing web work at the company run by Steve Oedekerk (writer of mainstream comedies like *Nutty Professor II*). There, Trueheart made a friend who occasionally asked him to write for their Internet shows. Trueheart worked on *Thumb Wars* and *Thumbtanic*, for which he also appeared as a thumb.

With an edgy reputation growing, he landed a staff writing job on Nickelodeon's new animated series, *Invader Zim*, which Trueheart describes as "torqued," while "Guy" is developed.

"It's the first time getting a steady paycheck for writing. It's a weird experience."

Now immersed in Hollywood, they speak of staying in touch with what's real. Landis and Peterson are training to run in the Chicago Marathon to benefit Aids Project Los Angeles. And Landis, who was brought to the U.S. from South Korea during the Amerasian adoptions of the 1970s, wishes he saw more faces on television who look like the friends everyone here has, people of diverse backgrounds.

So, it turns out, three years after graduating, my prediction came true: those who went for it succeeded in beginning their careers. Now they ask: what will they do with their new-found status; what really matters?

Seven Years After Graduating

The class re-convened in my backyard in August, 2004. Kelly Souders had gotten married. Julia Swift showed us photos of her "baby," now grown into a beautiful little boy about to enter kindergarten. Now everyone present was drawing at least a partial income from writing and several had been able to quit their day jobs. We began by passing the tape recorder around the table, each writer bringing us up to date since we last met. As enthusiastic as I'd known them as students, though wiser, they offer their experiences to you:

ERIC TRUEHEART
Three years ago I was going into animation, which was a great education working on a staff. I worked with talented people that the network didn't really seem to like and they spent a lot of time telling us how to write jokes and stuff. There were only three writers on the whole show including me and a comic book writer who didn't know much about structure but was really funny. Actually, I learned a lot about comedy sitting on that show. You spend time crafting a joke but sometimes a scream can just be really funny. Then it was cancelled so I was fired.

I started working on features with a friend from USC but people don't know if they can produce it. I've also been working on my own comedy

Left to right:
Kelly Souders,
Brian Peterson,
Pam Douglas

Kelly Souders
(at head of table)

Left to right:
Gib Wallis,
Julia Swift,
Andrew Landis,
Kelly Souders

Left to right:
Eric Trueheart,
Wendy West,
Gib Wallis

show out of a warehouse that's been the pick of the week in *L.A. Weekly* — *The Ministry of Unknown Science* — and we do these elaborate shows that are part-live, part-video.

We were repped by CAA [Creative Artists Agency] for about a year but we discovered they had certain ideas how to promote our show that were different from the way we had envisioned it. So in the process we learned that what an agent can really do is step in at the last minute and help, especially when you have someone who repped *Survivor* and they're repping our sketch comedy show. At first, the agent didn't want to invite network people to our show, but one of our friends had connections, and now we're speaking to both Sci-Fi Channel and Spike Network who want to do something with us.

Then there's just the constant therapy and self-evaluation that all creative people must do. I thought I was going to graduate and be all set, trained to do this stuff. I've been trained — it's like dental school. I still think hour long drama is great but I haven't had the chance to do anything in it yet. And I've had a lot of trouble finding how I sell myself in the industry, but it's been like Zen. Now I'm in on another animated show. I've sort of fallen into animation but it doesn't pay nearly so well and it's not Guild.

[In other words, the production company is not a signatory to the WGA Minimum Basic Agreement, which means that writers have no protections on payments or working conditions and do not receive Guild benefits such as health and pension.]

WENDY WEST
I've been working in hour long drama, thanks to Pam, God bless her. I worked on some interesting shows that got cancelled, a medical show and a crime show. One was called *Gideon's Crossing* and the other, *Line of Fire*. I never wrote crime in your class but that seems to be what I do. If there's not a dead body I feel like something's missing now. I think it's interesting because you encouraged us to write from our heart and the business is just about writing what sells. I'm working on this *Law & Order* on the beach; it's like *Lethal Weapon*. It takes place in Hawaii. I knew this guy from last year's show and I got a meeting on the current show and it was between me and another person and he helped me get it. So I owe him — a lot.

GIB WALLIS

Around three years ago the Mark Taper Forum was doing this thing, and I got tapped to do artistic response to the events of 9/11. I wrote a one-act play and that was cool because I always loved theater. It was a 65-seat theater and there were people sitting in the aisle. Then enough people began requesting short plays and longer plays for different things. Now I'm working on a farce with original songs and it'll be up in October.

Since I still have a day job, it's been an interesting challenge to keep being inspired. When you're in film school, you have great people around you to talk about story and character but when you go out, there are a lot of people who want to talk about selling things or setting things up. I'm a member of a playwrights' group called Playwrights Six and, for me, to meet with people regularly to talk about the art — that was my favorite part of film school.

JULIA SWIFT AND ANDREW (DREW) LANDIS
JULIA

We've been together for six years, longer than that, eight years? We did a pilot with Regency and the WB based on a weird part of my life and that was very interesting and fun. When you write a pilot you have the flexibility and the salary, which is great. But writing my own life was very difficult because I had this strange life growing up that I've always tried to hide. We were at a meet-and-greet at CBS and the executive pushed me to [talk about more ideas]. So I told him about growing up in a mob family, half in Vegas and half in L.A.

The story was about the year I went to college. My father turned my grandfather into the FBI and took off. I watch *The Sopranos* and it pisses me off because Tony is tough at work and nice at home, which is just wrong. It was interesting because we would be on the phone with network executives and the characters name is Maia, but they would call her Julia. They brought on Carlton Cuse as a producer and we loved him, and he said to Drew, "Your assignment is to go home and get Julia drunk and ask her questions about her family." And we did! We got pages of stories that would blow you away. We gave it to Regency, and they loved the stories. But it ended up being too "complicated." The emotions weren't all on the surface and Carlton and the Studio wanted it to be more complicated, and the network wanted it more on the surface. So that was interesting, learning whose advice to take.

Then, later, our executive, who became the head of drama at UPN, was interested in bringing the project back. But Regency said no, they wouldn't make enough money from UPN. You have to be very aware what studio you're at when you're doing a pilot because certain studios only work with certain networks. The UPN executive made a deal with us to have a blind pilot and then she left, and then the president left, so the development season passed and they brought in some people who didn't make the deal with us.

Before that, we'd written a play, and we made a deal to make that into a TV movie, which never happened, but we learned to be very careful about what rights to give up. So now we're pitching a new pilot, more drama, and we have a studio that wants to go out with us, but the executive called us and he might be moving, so who knows? As long as you keep those relationships you can move with them, but it's difficult.

PAM
What makes your partnership work?

DREW
Being able to communicate honestly five or 10 times a day. It's better than working alone, to get someone else's eyes to see what I don't.

JULIA
It's also really nice to have another pair of ears after talking to executives and trying to figure out what they mean.

DREW
Having a strong partnership puts everything in perspective.

BRIAN PETERSON AND KELLY SOUDERS
KELLY
Three years ago was right before *Smallville* so I was writing grants for the Science Center and I didn't have a car.

BRIAN
We'd partnered up and were working on these pilots. I'd taken a job transcribing EcoChallenge tapes. Then in one year we got a pilot with Fox and were on staff on *Smallville*. It was interesting because which do you take — the pilot or the staff — and we really debated that. Luckily, we got an exclusion [on the *Smallville* contract which would have required exclusivity] partly because we hadn't turned in the pilot yet. It's kind of been a two- year second draft.

PAM

So even after your writing credit on *But I'm a Cheerleader* you didn't get work?

BRIAN

No. That was an unfortunate career move because I needed to go into meetings with ideas. I got a couple of rewrites but then we had to start over in TV. It's great, though, because we learned as much in working in TV as we learned in film school.

KELLY

In your class we really learned to write a scene, the shape of it, when to come in, and that we use everyday.

BRIAN

The work-shopping we did in class, learning what notes to take and what not to take, was great.

PAM

Day to day, what do you do on *Smallville*?

KELLY

Right now, we're rewriting other writers, dealing with production, writing our own scripts, dealing with the scheduling. People in the room tend to either be really good at story or really good at character. For us, we make a great team, but it's funny because our strengths and weaknesses are similar. For us, the story is always a weak point and, over the last three years on the show, we've really learned a lot.

BRIAN

Being on a staff we have such a great group of mentors, you have a built-in support group, we know about each other's lives.

KELLY

It makes a big difference because we landed on a show where the people above us are really smart. We'd been working together for years but on our own time so it was more relaxed and we weren't depending on each other to pay our bills. Suddenly to have that switch in 24 hours was a struggle, our first couple of days on that show. The end of the first day, Brian was ready to lop off my head and, at the end of the second, I was ready to lop off his. Now, after work we'll go to dinner or to a play so we're able to separate the friendship from the work relationship.

BRIAN
It's like marriage, deciding everyday you'll be together.

KELLY
But it's an arranged marriage because we never really agreed to be partners. We met for one pitch together and then we were suddenly there.

PAM
A question for the entire table: If you could talk to your own young self at USC, what advice would you give?

ERIC
Get a day job because it takes forever to earn a living, but there will be breaks. A job will be a financial and psychological safety net. It gives you that freedom to figure out what you're doing without having your life depend on it.

KELLY
Wendy gave me a magnet, "If you're going through hell, keep going." For me, I think this is a longevity race. If you can keep at it and hang in there, then do it.

BRIAN
Have samples in a lot of different genres because people like to read different shows. Keep updating, keep going. Just as soon as someone says there's an opportunity, you can't wait a week or two weeks, you have to give them a script.

DREW
You really have to network a lot more than we're comfortable with. You really have to force yourself when you're done with your writing to meet people. Your agent can only do so much, and a lot of the jobs come from what you hear.

ERIC
Get a job on a show as an assistant. Just get in that environment, there are so many stories you hear of a writer's assistant pitching an idea and the show using it.

KELLY
There are two freelance episodes we have a year and we give them to the assistants.

GIB

At film school we heard a lot about people not selling pilots unless they have been on a staff. Wrong, wrong, wrong, wrong, wrong. I have several friends who've sold pilots, even if they haven't gotten them on the air. I had a pilot idea and I've been pitching it and just finished the script, but I've heard of people getting more success with pilots than with staff jobs.

PAM

You're right. Seven or eight years ago when you were in school it was rare for people to sell pilots if they had never worked on a show. In the intervening years, beginning writers have gotten interest in their pilots even if they've never had any television experience, and producers are willing to read pilots as samples. That's part of how the business is changing.

WENDY

My advice: Keep writing. The business has changed; they want to know what's out of the box. It wasn't that way when we were getting out of school. I got a job off a short story — it's crazy. Everyone on *Six Feet Under* — Alan Ball hired almost no one with television experience. Also, it's important to be in a writing group. I think those people who didn't stay in a group just fell out of writing. It's really hard to get yourself pumped up, but having a place where you have to produce every week or two weeks is valuable.

JULIA

We were taught in school to write what we love and we came out thinking we're going to write what we love but have some action in there. You can write a genre that's not your dream genre but infuse that with you and the marketplace will respond because it has that bit of whatever makes you different.

DREW

[I recommend] the contest route. If you win a contest, it gives them a reason to meet with you.

ERIC

I'm sure everyone's scoping out the new young thing. But the agencies are very conscious of money and reliable people so, sure, you've got a 23-year-old with the hot pilot, but if it's not picked up then they're dead. There's always the network mentality that they want the next hot thing but they always need the people who have the experience to get the job done.

JULIA

Because of vertical integration, the networks own the studios and the studios own the networks, so small places with creative executive producers are gone. The networks have their development component so you have very few people choosing shows. I think that financial model has to change, and the only way it's going to change is if people get tired of seeing the same thing over and over.

WENDY

One of the things that I'm constantly reminded of is that this town is run on passion, which is great. But when we send out scripts, people are so afraid that they're going to choose something that they'll get fired over, or that the advertisers are going to pull the show. You have to wind through so many obstacles until you get to the final piece and then that's pushed to the middle ground.

JULIA

I think that as this generation raised on HBO grows, then something has to change because they won't want to go back to that middle ground.

BRIAN

As you mature into the industry, you realize the venues that are appropriate for your work. Every major studio wants their Emmys and Oscars so they will support producers like Alan Ball. So there is a chance to be an artist, but you really have to focus on it.

GUEST SPEAKER: RON MOORE

Ron Moore is Creator and Executive Producer of *Battlestar Galactica*, and was a producer-writer on *Roswell*, *Carnivale*, and *Star Trek: The Next Generation*.

PD: I'd like to bring you back to the "big bang" of this show because you not only run it, you created it. What was going on for you creatively that led to this show?

RM: I had been approached by the studio, Universal, to come up with a take on *Battlestar Galactica*. There had been a few attempts over the years and they'd all gone by the wayside. I wasn't sure I wanted to do it because I'd done ten years at *Star Trek*, and it was enough already with space opera. But I went out and got the original pilot. I'd seen it on the air in the '70s but when I watched it again I was struck by the dark premise at the heart: an apocalyptic attack destroyed humanity. The show was about the survivors and the Cylons chasing them forever. I thought that was a really interesting format because the core was this disturbing notion of death and being lost in the cosmos.

Typically, TV shies away from that. And in the original show you can see they were having trouble squaring that as well, because what they did was, yes, we were attacked, but now let's go to the casino planet, trying to be escapist and fun like *Star Wars* and elements of *Star Trek*. So I thought, what if you took the premise and really did the show and asked yourself in those circumstances what would happen to real people? If you took normal, screwed-up people who just happened to be the ones that made it, what would that show be like?

PD: In creating *Galactica*, did you start with characters, or did you start with story, or world?

RM: I knew I wanted to maintain the premise: the show was about the survivors who were on this last battleship. Then I decided the old show was about a family. I looked at the family tree and decided to make some changes. The daughter in the old show didn't serve any purpose so I just lost her. Then I made Starbuck a woman immediately, and decided she's the surrogate daughter to the father figure. The father figure of Adama had no counterpart, neither a mother nor any counterpart in the civilian world. I didn't want it to be just a military show. Okay, the premise was that the remnants of human civilization were in these fleets. So how do they govern themselves? Are they going to try to maintain their democracy as they move forward? Is the president to be a real player in this show, unlike the old one? And I decided that should be a woman, and that sort of completes the family, and that's who the show is really about.

The other character that interested me was Baltar. The human race in the original was not only attacked and destroyed; they were also betrayed. Baltar betrayed them to their enemies. But then I tried to figure out, why would he do that? There's no reason I could fathom that anybody would do that, so I came to the conclusion that he does it inadvertently as part of his weaknesses. He is, in many ways, the most human character of them all in his capacity to rationalize and always look for a way that it's not his fault. He doesn't mean to do anything evil but somehow always ends up doing amoral or even evil things.

Those are the general parameters I thought that show was about and how I was going to translate it to this show.

PD: Was there a character who you initially identified with or who you wanted to build as the core of the show, or do you see it as more of an ensemble drama?

RM: I saw it as an ensemble, a cast of characters who were from different strata of society. There were Adama and Laura at the top, but I also wanted to establish characters like Chief and Callie — people doing the hard work at the bottom of the food chain who are not usually covered in these kinds of shows.

PD: After the pilot, other voices came in from other writers on your staff, and characters developed in ways maybe you didn't foresee at the very beginning. How do you deal with evolving from your premise to making a show that has very long legs? What were the big creative turns from a writing point of view, and did they surprise you?

RM: The way I typically work is to set out targets to write to. For instance, up to the end of the first season in the show bible, I'd sketched out what the show was about. At the end of the first season Laura Roslyn would be in jail and Adama would institute a coup against her. I knew that was a good place to end season one with a cliffhanger. I kind of knew what the arc would be to get us there.

PD: And you knew that from the inception?

RM: From the time we were considering the series. The mini-series was its own development, but when we started considering the series, I said, okay, this is what the arc of the first season will be. In that first season, when we were writing and breaking the stories in the room, I like a lot of freedom to play around, and it turned out we didn't take the path that I set out from the get go. However, we still tacked toward the same target. As Laura became president and had to shoulder the burdens of the entire human civilization, I wanted to see that character change — a presumable "liberal Democrat" becomes hawkish and much tougher and much more concerned with security and very tight-fisted and starts cracking down on people, taking away liberties and freedoms in the name of security. It's interesting that Adama, the military guy, would go, hey this isn't what I swore to defend.

But during the first season we started doing stories that touched on a religious idea. Laura was having a connection to prophecy and her cancer was having her take this drug that was giving her visions, and I started to be much more interested in the religious aspects of the show. And then we realized that actually we could get to the same place. The storyline of the fleet rebellion never panned out — it didn't give us much. But the stories about her becoming religious were very rich. If Adama thinks she's a religious fanatic and she's doing things based on faith or what she thinks God is telling her, that's enough of a reason for him to move against her.

In general, I like a process in the writing room where you're free to re-invent stuff. You have an idea what the show is and play around with it a lot, and when the writer goes off to write the teleplay, I say "Surprise me." I want to be surprised on reading it. I want to learn things about the characters I didn't know. Take a left turn when I thought you were going right. That makes it fun for me to read.

PD: How large is your writing staff?

RM (counting names on his fingers): Seven.

PD: Do you sit around a table and break each show into beats according to the arc you set out for the whole season then send them off to outline...

RM: Usually the writing staff will break it while I'm off doing something else.

PD: You're not in the room.

RM: Sometimes I am, for a big story. But at this point in the series I'm not. They will break the initial idea. Then I'll go in the room and they'll pitch it to me and play around with

it. Maybe we'll have to re-break it to get it to a place where I'm happy with it. Then they go to outline, which is mostly a sales document for the network.

PD: Does SciFi Channel have to sign off on each episode?

RM: They have to sign off on all the outlines and scripts. All the networks want to put their two cents in. Our story breaks are kind of general. When I was at *Star Trek* I was schooled in detailed breaks. We sat there for hours and days and we broke every scene down almost to dialogue, and sometimes pieces of dialogue went up on those boards. It was tedious and took forever. And now after doing that for so long, I have a more instinctive feel for how it works. I can generally speak about what the shape of the episode is, the shape of the beats. Then the writers go off and write the teleplay. I prefer to do more changes in teleplay. The outline is just kind of a sketch.

PD: Do you do the final polish on everything?

RM: I used to. I did that definitely for all the first season and most of the second, but now I do less of that. The staff is getting the voice of the show so I say "Okay, bring something more to the party," because I don't know that my voice every week is necessarily the most interesting and effective way to tell the story. And also I just get tired.

PD: Speaking to students or would-be writers out there who might try to spec an episode for this show, what would you tell them to write?

RM: It's a hard one to spec. You'd have to spec it in full knowledge that it's not going to fit into any of the continuing stories. They'd have to give me an episode that's a one-off that has nothing to do with this giant arc. To me the show is most effective when it's telling more than one story, cross-cutting between the ups and downs of various characters. You want the show to not be neatly resolved. The show is at its best when it's not a morality play: so it's not obvious by the end of the show that the right thing to do was X. Sometimes I want to arrive at the end of the show and not be sure whether X was right or wrong. The best ones, to me, are where you get to a place in a scene or an act and you suddenly say I'm not quite sure who I'm supposed to be rooting for here. What do I feel about this? I think raising the question is much more interesting than provoking a reaction.

PD: If you did read an outside script, what elements would you look for in terms of story or voice or character?

RM: I don't like reading specs for this show. I'd rather see something original — a movie, even a play. I look for really interesting characters more than plot or even grasp of narrative structure. I can teach you that, and the writing staff can teach you that. You can sit in the room with my staff and break a three-act structure...

PD: Are you using three-act structure?

RM: No, I was talking in a general sense. We're four and a tease. But what I mean is I can give you a structure that will get us there. But characters — that's really hard. It's what an old boss of mine, Ira Behr used to call finger-tip stuff — those little touches of character and life, the things that make this an interesting person. If you know how to do that you're a writer; if not, you're not. With a structure, you can bang out a plot, getting a guy from here to there and catch the bad guy, but the characters are dead. Those aren't good scripts.

PD: Finally, is there anything you'd like to say to the hopeful writers out there and the people in film schools?

RM: Two things: One is the apocryphal story I was told when I started on staff on *Star Trek*. Someone told me about Heifitz, the great concert violinist, standing in the wings ready to go on at Carnegie Hall. This young kid comes up to him and says "Please, please will you listen to me play the violin?" "No, kid, I don't have time." "Please, please thirty seconds. I just don't know if I have it, do I have it? Will you just listen to me?" The kid plays. And Heifitz says "No," and goes on stage and performs. The kid leaves and never plays again. He has a whole career, a family, and many years later he runs into Heifitz at a charity, and says, "You don't remember me, but when I was a kid I came up to you and asked if I had it. Now I'm successful and I'm happy but I have to ask how could you do that? How could you listen to me play for thirty seconds when I was just this young kid and tell me I had no talent?" And Heifitz says, "That's what I tell everybody because it's the kind of business where if you can be discouraged, it will discourage you."

The other piece of advice comes from when I was on a panel of TV writers and they were asking what we would tell young writers. Harlan Ellison, the great science fiction writer, was sitting next to me. He grabbed the microphone and leaned forward and said "Don't be a whore." That pretty much summarizes it.

In the Future:
Mobisodes, Webisodes, eTV, ITV, Lions, Tigers and Bears — Oh My!

An image of blue lights from televisions all over the world opened the first chapter — people watching in their living rooms, sharing an experience with millions of strangers who also care about Meredith or Starbuck or Jack or Bill, the "friends" who will visit at the same time next week. Well, the blue lights are still on — even more of them — but from multiple TVs, DVDs, cell phones and computer screens watched privately in separate spaces.

In his 1967 book, *The Medium Is the Massage*, Marshall McLuhan envisioned a world where people were connected not just by what they watched but because they were watching it together — a modern "electronic hearth" that replaced the neighborhood front porch. His idea of television — especially primetime storytelling — as the heart of a "global village" still resonates.

But subscriptions to TiVo jumped from 3.5 million in 2003 to 6.5 million in 2004; and by 2009, at least 49% of American households are expected to have some form of personal choice in what they watch and when. McLuhan's vocabulary has morphed into phrases like "time shifting" and "appointment viewing." Todd Leavitt, President of the Academy of Television Arts and Sciences told the *L.A. Times*, "[TiVo] has fundamentally changed the way we use television. 'Must-see TV' goes out the window; the water cooler show goes out the window. You create your own schedule."

Beyond choosing when they watch, people are choosing how they watch, and directly influencing what they watch. Ron Moore, who runs *Battlestar Galactica,* said, "It's going to just become 'media,' and it will stop having distinctions that no longer mean anything. TV and computers are going to become the same thing. You're just going to have a box or boxes at your

disposal, and you'll put everything on this box ranging from
blogs to what we know today
as TV shows and movies.

"I think there's more freedom
and more opportunity, and it's
exciting that in a lot of ways
there are so many styles of
material to do. Getting away
from the tyranny of the time
slot, that it's an hour episode
which means that with commercials you have 41 minutes and
32 seconds each week, which is
crazy. It would be nice to not
have to worry about that.

"I also think fracturing the
audience into various niches is a good thing. When broadcasting meant
broad broadcasting when only the big three existed, they had to appeal
to a gigantic swath of audience. To hold those huge numbers they had to
make the stuff that had the most common denominators. Now, when you
break it up into smaller chunks, *Galactica* and shows like *The Shield* can
appeal to specific audiences. Critics say it's the golden age of TV because
of the quality of the shows, but I don't think any of them could have
survived in the three-network era. Now the high quality shows can sustain
themselves with dedicated fans who are interested in their particular kind
of material."

But even a network show like ABC's *Lost* that aims for a wide audience
simultaneously plays to its internet viewers. Show-runner Damon Lindelof
noted: "We have to keep our eye on the mothership at all times and the
best ideas will always end up on the show. But we have constructed very
elaborate backstories to explain things, and those ideas would never end up
on the show because they don't really mean anything to our characters.

"If Jack and Kate were to learn the origin of the numbers, most people
wouldn't really care. So we decided let's give the fans who really care
about the origin of the numbers the answer. It's a sci-fi-ish technobabbly
thing and you can tell that on the internet. So we constructed this internet
experience of a girl who investigated the Dharma initiative and had the

The Sopranos

payoff be another Dharma film in which it was explained. But we could never tell that on the show or your head would spin.

"It's not an alternate universe. It's more like having a compendium besides a text that gives you a deeper understanding. Other mythology-based shows like *X-Files* and *Star Trek* also have a 'canon.' For us, we say we generated this and it is part of the *Lost* universe."

Showtime's *The L Word* went further. Brenna Hajek, who "interactivized" that series, told *Written By* in May, 2005: "Interactivity and enhancements can deepen the connection between an audience and a story. Shows can be enhanced in a number of ways, from little extras like providing additional facts, all the way to full-blown alternative storylines and imaginative new characters.

"The episode itself would remain unchanged, respecting viewers' desire for a completely linear experience. Viewers opting in for enhancements receive additional content without distracting from the storyline. During certain key decision points, the show is paused and a question is raised about the action taken by the character in response to a scene. The viewer is then shown a 90-second video clip of the character in question doing sort of a modern-day soliloquy explaining why she reacted the way she did.

"Once the viewer experiences this additional insight, it's her turn. Using her remote, she chooses what she would do in that same situation. After answering several of these personality questions, we are able to loosely match the person with the personality type of one of the characters on the show and at the end of the episode, viewers are treated to another piece of exclusive video in which the character to whom they're matched addresses them directly, giving a little personality profile."

Despite the audience input, Hajek observed, "Writers are storytellers. Interactivity should be considered just another storytelling tool in a writer's repertoire."

Terry Borst, who writes the monthly "Alt.screen" column for *Written By*, sees the evolvement of eTV (enhanced TV) and ITV (interactive TV) as both a future opportunity for writers and a source of success for shows right now. "The resurgent interest behind dramatic scripted programming is due not only to great writing but also to the ease in which viewers can interact with each other on the internet, quickly creating show loyalty and spreading the word to others. As that interactivity carries over to a one-screen television format, the chance to extend and expand the world of a show further increases."

Whether or not viewers (or writers) want all those enhancements and interactivity, they're here to stay because advertisers are pushing. Allison Dollar, CEO of the Interactive Television Alliance (ITA), the trade association devoted to accelerating the deployment of interactive television, thinks it may impact the way television is written.

"'Mass market' describes the old relationship between advertising and programming. ITV changes the cadence and timing, particularly on episodics because you're not going to require the same peaks and valleys for your spots. Some very successful writers are aware of that and they're working with advertisers right from the start. Reality programming, like *American Idol* or *Project Runway*, has the advertiser connection already, but it's going to be permeating more serious dramas because when the business model is exploded then you don't have the ad time being bought and sold in the same way. The money either comes from consumers or it comes from advertisers. You'll probably see more of a return to traditional sponsorship where advertisers are book-ending the shows and, yes, product placement.

"The simplest way is advertainment where the product stars like in BMW films. I think we're going to see more hybrid business models where something's not built into the storyline but into the story structure so that advertisers feel they can support a particular show, for example, that driving a certain kind of car is part of core characterization as in movies like *Batman* or *James Bond*."

Up to now, we've spoken about extensions of dramas as we know them. But what if you let go of the tether? What are the opportunities for writers if an existing series, or even an existing network, is not the basis? I spoke to Frank Chindamo, president of Fun Little Movies, which runs on channel 19 between CNN and MTV — but that's not a channel on your television; it's on Microsoft and SmartVideo which plays world-wide on computers and cell phones. I asked if he sees mobisodes and webisodes as an opportunity for people trying to break into the business.

Frank
Chindamo

FC: "It's absolutely the easiest way to break in because it's an area where you can generate the product. If you're a writer and you have any connection to show business — I mean even a friend who has production equipment — you are able to produce your own idea."

PD: From a writing point of view, how do the dramatic elements change when the story is only minutes long?

FC: "The way I look at storytelling for the small screen that has a short attention span is exactly the same as when we look at storytelling for television: story, story, story and character, character, character. The more compelling your story is and the more compelling your characters, the better show you're going to have.

"We tend more towards soap opera in terms of drama. The hooks are every one to three minutes, preferably immediately. We try to hook the viewer to come back to watch the next one to three minutes, and the next and the next and the next. You could develop one long sequential story or separate stand-alone episodes. But no matter how you do it, you have to hook people in.

"When we're watching television we're devoting 30 or 60 minutes to it. But on the very small screen of the internet or mobile phone, people are asked to devote no more than three to five minutes of their attention.

"One of the most important things for a writer to understand about this process is that the bigger the screen, the more subtle you can be. The smaller the screen, the more outrageous, the more compelling, the more quirky you need to be. Stories that would be completely off the wall for a television series have played tremendously well on a small screen.

"On the other hand, Fox launched their multi-multi-multi-million dollar campaign for their series *24* on cell phones. Those turned out to be such a colossal flop that they actually set back for six months to a year the whole mobisode industry. That's because it was all hype, and the story was not compelling. They gave you a quick bit of story and then more hype and then a quick bit of story and more hype.

"Two types of entities are involved in mobisodes. One is the kind of company that produces videos that cost millions of dollars to make, like Fox or Sony. Their plan is to produce mobisodes or webisodes that wrap around a TV show or movie and send people toward the big ticket item. But if you're an independent company, you have the freedom to produce the original content and hope that it will either be a hit on mobisodes or webisodes, or graduate into television or movies."

PD: Looking to the future, what do you think the opportunities will be for people coming out of film schools with screenwriting degrees, or people trying to break in?

FC: "Becoming a TV drama writer is extremely difficult because at the end of the day somebody's going to have to devote millions of dollars to your writing in order to get it on a television network. But with this, someone has to devote thousands of dollars to your writing to get it made. The opportunities here are much more plentiful. Whether you're going to get anything done really relies on you, your writing, and your independent network — other writers, filmmakers

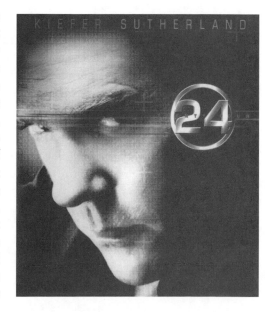

and that sort of thing. If you can create that independent scenario you have a much better chance of having your work get made. And the only way your work will be seen is if it's made. With mobisodes, your fate rests in your own hands."

So where does that leave writers like you? If you've read this book because you hope to create a series of your own, special opportunities lie in narrowly defined new markets. But for all good writers, opportunities abound. A spec script that has guts and passion and the skill to deliver them professionally will always be useful. And storytellers will be as valued in the coming age as we've been throughout history. Actually, we may be needed even more to define and link cultures that have fractured.

No matter what the delivery system — networks, premium cable, basic cable, syndication, cell phones, internet — the creative process starts with you. Barbara Hall, Creator of *Joan of Arcadia*, said in *Variety*, "We don't pull any punches about the nature of human existence. We go through stages where cynicism is the trend. I'm skeptical but not cynical. It's about the intention. That's the best way to start and it all evolves from that place. I think we need something that celebrates humanity more and the resiliency of the human spirit."

Paul Wolff, who was Supervising Producer of *Life Goes On*, an ABC drama about a family whose son has Down Syndrome, said "I was able to put in what I cared about. Television is so immediate, you get immediate response. Millions and millions of people see it in one night. If you touched somebody you knew it, and you knew that what you were hoping for happened. On *Life Goes On* we had a core audience of people who had Down Syndrome in their family, and they watched us every week. We used to get floods of phone calls. I was very moved by the parents.

"It's very rare that you're able to do it," Wolff continued, "TV is a business like anything else and you have to do what the network expects. You can't start off saying, 'I'm going to send a message' because it won't come out well. You really have to concentrate on becoming a craftsperson so that when it's time you can write something with a message very well that's also entertaining."

But *Life Goes On* existed in a different era of network ownership under a company called Cap Cities, and Wolff commented "Tom Murphy [Cap Cities' president] had a heart. The pilot of *Life Goes On* wasn't the kind most people would put on. But he still held that old-world belief that the network should give something back to the community. It was wonderful for him because the show was a hit too."

I asked what advice he'd give a beginner who wants to write for television now. "I would give the same advice to any writer, which is to get the stars out of your eyes and don't think about the money. You have to write from your heart, write what matters to you. To be a real writer you have to write beyond the fame, the success. You have to be a writer first."

Ask any writer and you'll hear the same: It starts with you. So now that you've learned what's special about hour drama series, and how TV development works, and what it takes to work on staff, how a script is crafted, and how to approach writing your own episode, and you've even heard how to break in, and what the future holds — all that adds up to just one moment: when you sit down and start to write. And now that time has come. It's your turn.

APPENDIX 1
RESOURCES FOR YOU

Writers Guild of America, West
7000 West Third Street
Los Angeles, CA 90048
(323) 951-4000

Intellectual Property Registry: www.wga.org
323-782-4500
Office is open 9:30 AM to 5:30 PM Monday through Friday
Drop-off is available 24 hours outside the Guild

James R. Webb Memorial Library
(323) 782-4544
Located on the first floor of the WGA
Open to the public to read scripts and view shows
10 AM to 5 PM, Monday through Friday, and Thursday to 8 PM
(closed the last Friday of each month)

Writers Guild of America, East
555 W. 57th Street
New York, N.Y. 10019
(212) 767-7800
(WGA East does not have a script library)

Writers Guilds affiliated with the WGA are located in many countries, for example The Writers Guild of Great Britain and the Writers Guild of New Zealand.

Museum of Television and Radio (West)
465 N. Beverly Drive
Beverly Hills, CA 90210
(310) 786-1000
Reading and viewing is free and open to the public
Noon to 5 PM, Wednesday through Sunday

Museum of Television and Radio (East)
25 W. 52nd Street
New York, N.Y.
(212) 621-6600
$10 admission. Screenings and seminars.
Noon to 6 PM, Tuesday through Sunday

Academy of Television Arts and Sciences
5220 Lankershim Blvd.
North Hollywood, CA 91601
(818) 754-2800
(The television academy does not have a script library)

APPENDIX 2
PERMISSIONS

Thank you for permission to use interviews, excerpts, and images:

Interviews and comments

Steven Bochco, June 8, 2004
Frank Chindamo, January 7, 2007
Allison Dollar, July 9, 2004
Ann Donahue, December 19, 2006
Georgia Jeffries, April 21, 2004
Andrew Landis, August 7, 2004
Damon Lindelof, January 11, 2007
David Milch, May 25, 2004
Ron Moore, December 19, 2006
Brian Peterson, August 7, 2004
Melissa Rosenberg, January 4, 2007
Kelly Souders, August 7, 2004
Julia Swift, August 7, 2004
Eric Trueheart, August 7, 2004
Gib Wallis, August 7, 2004
John Wells, September 10, 2004
Wendy West, August 7, 2004
Paul Wolff, September 1, 2004
John Sacret Young, July 10, 2004

Excerpts of outlines and scripts

Handwritten page from *China Beach* pilot, courtesy of John Sacret Young

NYPD Blue segments courtesy of Steven Bochco: Act One, "Simone Says," and Act One, "Hearts and Souls"

Outline fragment from *ER*, "Love's Labor Lost" written by Lance Gentile © 1995 Warner Bros. Entertainment. Used by Permission. All Rights Reserved.

Images

Individual headshots courtesy of: Steven Bochco, Frank Chindamo, Ann Donahue, Georgia Jeffries, Damon Lindelof, David Milch, Ron Moore, Melissa Rosenberg, John Wells, John Sacret Young

Frames from: *Deadwood* and *Sopranos*, courtesy of HBO.

Photo of *ER* © 2004 Warner Bros. All Rights Reserved.

Photo of *The West Wing* © 2004 Warner Bros. All Rights Reserved.

Snapshots in my backyard on August 7, 2004, courtesy of

Andrew Landis, Brian Peterson, Kelly Souders, Julia Swift,

Eric Trueheart, Gib Wallis, Wendy West

APPENDIX 3
SOURCES

Chapter One

Dick Wolf regarding franchises and brands — *Entertainment Weekly*, June 11, 2004

Comments about serials in "Don't Touch That Dial," article by Bill Carter, *The New York Times*, Oct. 29, 2006

Comments by Shonda Rhimes in "Grey's Anatomy" article in *Los Angeles Magazine*, Sept., 2005

Comments on *Sleeper Cell* in television review by Lynn Smith in *Los Angeles Times*, Dec. 9, 2006

Chapter Two

Josh Schwartz, *The O.C.* — *The New York Times*, March 22, 2004

Ron Cowan and Daniel Lipman regarding *Queer as Folk* — *Written By*, May, 2004

Chapter Three

J.J. Abrams regarding *Alias* — *Emmy*, Issue No. 2, 2004

The visit to the *ER* staff and John Wells' comments —

"A Week in the Life of a Showrunner" by Lisa Chambers in *Written By*, February, 1997

Spotlight on Writing Procedurals

Comments by Carol Mendelsohn and Ann Donahue in "The Women of *CSI*" article by Susan LaTempa, *Written By*, Oct. 2002

Comments by Ann Donahue from interview Dec. 19, 2006

Spotlight on Writing Your Pilot

John Sacret Young from interview July 10, 2004

Damon Lindelof from interview Jan. 11, 2007
Interview with Georgia Jeffries, Nov. 29, 2006

Chapter Five

"Hearing Voices" by Pamela Douglas is reprinted from *The Journal* of the Writers Guild, November, 1995
Aaron Sorkin's remarks were to an audience at the Writers Guild Theatre for the Writers Guild Foundation, May 27, 2004

Spotlight on Blogging the Shows

Excerpt from interview with Tim Kring about *Heroes* is from *9th Wonders* website.

Excerpt of interview with Bridget Carpenter about *Friday Night Lights* is from *The Crafty TV and Screenwriting Blog.*

Comments by Krista Vernoff about *Grey's Anatomy* are from the *Grey Matter* blog.

Chapter Seven

"TV Writers" article by Pamela Douglas was originally printed in the *Los Angeles Times*, Feb. 8, 1998
"Class Come to Order" article by Pamela Douglas was originally printed in the *Los Angeles Times*, July 5, 2000

In the Future

Todd Leavitt on TiVo — *Los Angeles Times, Sunday Calendar*, Sept. 5, 2004
Ron Moore from interview, Dec. 19, 2006
Damon Lindelof from interview, Jan. 11, 2007
Brenna Hajek regarding *The L Word*, and observations by Terry Borst about "eTV" in "Alt.screen" column by Terry Borst in *Written By*, May 2005
Allison Dollar from interview July 9, 2004
Frank Chindamo on mobisodes from interview Jan. 7, 2007
Barbara Hall, *Joan of Arcadia* — *Daily Variety*, June 17, 2004
Paul Wolff from interview, Sept. 1, 2004

Glossary

A – B – C STORIES. Parallel plots within an episode. Stories are denoted by letters (A, B, C, D…). Often each story follows the dramatic arc of one of the continuing cast.

ABOVE-THE-LINE. Production elements at the top of a budget breakdown, usually: producers, directors, writers, and sometimes composer or star. Crew positions are "below-the-line."

ACT. A dramatic unit made of a number of scenes. Network TV hours usually have four acts that build to cliffhangers before commercial breaks, though some have five or six acts. Cable shows which do not have breaks may structure episodes into three or four theoretical acts.

ACTION. In a script, the description below a slug line that tells what is occurring on screen. Also see **DESCRIPTION**.

AGENT. Someone who represents talent. A literary agent advances career opportunities for writers who are signed to him and usually negotiates his clients' deals. Agents are licensed by the state, and receive 10% commissions.

ANTAGONIST. A character whose goal opposes the protagonist's goal. Though sometimes considered the "villain," in quality drama the best opponent is a "worthy antagonist."

ANTHOLOGY. A show whose installments are free-standing and do not have continuing casts, such as *Twilight Zone*.

ARC. The progression of a character from one condition to a different dramatic state. Example: A character who is cold in the beginning loves someone in the end.

A.T.A.S. Academy of Television Arts and Sciences. Membership organization for all fields of television. Produces the Emmy Awards, among other activities.

ATTACHED. Talent (for example, an actor) is "attached" when that person commits to participating in a proposed show.

BACK NINE. The remaining nine episodes in a traditional 22-week season after the first thirteen are finished. Even if a series is given a full-season order, the **GREEN-LIGHT** to produce the back nine may depend on how well the first thirteen perform.

BACK STORY. History before the action on screen, usually incidents or relationships that shaped a character.

BACK-UP SCRIPTS. Extra episodes beyond the pilot that a network orders to assess a show's potential when it is not given a slot on the air, sometimes called back-up pilots.

BACK DOOR PILOT. A two-hour movie that suggests potential for a series.

BEAT. 1. A scene or step of the story; 2. A pause in dialogue or action.

BEAT SHEET. Also see **OUTLINE**. A list of events (turning points) in the story, often detailed in numbered scenes, though sometimes more generally in sequences or even summaries of entire acts.

BIBLE. A guide to the series, especially for writers and directors joining a show. Includes character biographies, rules for the world of the show, summaries of past episodes, and sometimes what the producers are seeking in tone, style or stories.

BREAKING A STORY. Finding the major turning points (and often act breaks) in a story before writing a detailed outline.

CLIFFHANGER. A suspenseful ending; frequently jeopardy or raised stakes at the act break and end of the season.

CLOSURE. In episodic drama, a story that is complete (arrives at its goal or conclusion) at the end of the hour.

COLD OPENING. See **TEASER**.

CONTINUING CAST. Main characters that return each week and "drive" the core stories in the series.

CREATIVE CONSULTANT. An experienced writer-producer who may oversee, re-write or write episodes, but might not be a full-time member of the staff.

DAILIES. Unedited scenes screened after each day of production.

DEVELOPMENT. The process of bringing a project from concept to production; also the period when a writer works with producers to refine a script through all revision steps.

DESCRIPTION. The actions, images and sounds on screen, excluding dialogue. See **ACTION**.

DIALOGUE. Everything the characters say that may include expressions (i.e., sighs) and pauses as well as words.

DRAMEDY. A hybrid of drama and comedy.

ELEMENT. Significant talent, such as a producer, director or actors that may be attached to a project to enhance its clout.

EPISODE. In dramatic television, a one-hour increment of the season; that week's group of stories. Also an installment of a continuing story-line.

EXECUTIVE PRODUCER. The top writer-producer on a TV series, often responsible for supervising both creative and business aspects of the show, overseeing the cast, crew and writing staff. See also **SHOW-RUNNER**.

EXT. Abbreviation for Exterior, used in **SLUG LINES**.

FIRST DRAFT. A script written by the writer before responding to notes from a producer. All **SPEC SCRIPTS** and all drafts before submission are "first drafts," no matter how many times the writer has privately made revisions.

FORMAT. 1. A proposal for a series that may include characterizations, genre, **SPRINGBOARDS** for stories, and suggestions for episodes or a **PILOT**. 2. The structure of a story, which may involve a **FRANCHISE**. 3. The printed style of a script, usually set by screenwriting software.

FRANCHISE. Storytelling categories that generate dramatic situations, such as medical, legal, or detective work. Successful series may also franchise their **FORMAT**, as in *C.S.I.*

FREELANCE WRITER. A writer who is not on staff and receives an assignment for an episode.

GREEN LIGHT. Approval for a script to proceed to production.

GUEST CAST. Actors not in the continuing cast who may appear in a limited number of episodes.

HIATUS. The break between seasons when the entire staff is on vacation.

HOOK. An early action or situation that grabs an audience's attention; also an opening of a pitch.

IN THE CAN. An episode that's ready to air.

INT. Abbreviation for Interior, used in slug lines.

LEGS. A series with legs is capable of generating numerous stories for episodes.

LOCKED. When a producer has approved the final version of an outline or script, it is locked.

LOG LINE. A one sentence summary of a story; occasionally might be two or three sentences. It quickly conveys the **PREMISE** and the dramatic **ARC** or **PLOT**.

LONG NARRATIVE. Stories that have the depth and range to continue for years, especially in serials.

MANAGER. Similar to **AGENT**, except that managers are not licensed and may represent their clients in areas beyond immediate assignments. Managers typically charge 15%, compared with a 10% commission for agents.

M.B.A. Minimum Basic Agreement, the agreement between the Writers Guild of America and signatories (production entities) that specifies minimum pay, health and pension, and other contractual issues.

OUTLINE. A list of every scene that will appear in the script, in order, beginning with number 1 in each act. Each outline "beat" is like a log line for that scene. However, some shows use outlines that are less specific. An outline is the first paid step in development. Also called **STEP OUTLINE**. See **BEAT SHEET**.

OVERNIGHTS. Quick national ratings that give a preliminary account of how many people watched a show.

PACKAGE. A commitment from actors or a director to **ATTACH** themselves to a show in the effort to make a network or cable deal; also all of the **ELEMENTS** needed to move a **FORMAT** (proposal) forward, which may include a pilot script and **SHOW-RUNNER**. Some packaging agencies want to represent all **ABOVE-THE-LINE** personnel.

PICK-UP. A decision by a network or cable outlet to air (or renew) a series.

PILOT. Prototype for a series; usually the first episode.

PITCH. Telling a story to a potential buyer; a sales presentation.

PLOT. The dramatic structure of a story; how a story is executed from premise to resolution.

PLOT POINT. A strong "reversal," or turning point in the story. Plot points may coincide with **CLIFFHANGERS** and **ACT BREAKS**.

POLISH. A minor revision in a script, usually tightening scenes and refining dialogue, or cutting a shooting draft for production.

PREMISE. The inciting question or problem at the beginning; answers "what if?" or "why?"

PREMISE PILOT. Propels a series by placing the main character in a new situation or beginning a quest from which future stories will spring.

PROCEDURALS. Clue-driven series that solve puzzles or mysteries and close at the end of each episode. Examples include *CSI* and *House*.

PRODUCER. Most TV producers are writers whose titles have improved because of experience and credits. Producers may supervise and re-write other writers. This differs from a line producer who is responsible for physical production.

PRODUCTION. Actually shooting the show, when cameras roll. Sometimes a series described as "in production" includes both pre-production (writing, casting, set-building), and post-production (editing, music, effects).

PROLOGUE. See **TEASER**.

PROTAGONIST. The character who drives the action and makes key dramatic decisions; the person the audience roots for.

RESIDUALS. Additional payments to writers and other talent when a show re-runs.

REWRITE. A significant revision of a script that may include re-structuring and creating new characters and scenes.

SCENE. The smallest dramatic building block, usually a step of the action, or a beat, with complete dramatic structure. In production, it is sometimes defined as the action in a single time and place.

SCENE HEADING. See **SLUG LINE.**

SEASON. A television season encompasses the months a show airs. Though the traditional network season runs September to May, cable and other outlets have different schedules.

SECOND DRAFT. A script that has been re-written after receiving notes from a producer.

SERIAL. A series whose stories continue across many episodes in which the main cast develops over time.

SHOOTING SCRIPT. The final draft which goes into production.

SHORT ORDER. A **PICK-UP** that commits to airing less than a full season, sometimes only a few episodes of a new show.

SHOW-RUNNER. The top **EXECUTIVE PRODUCER** in charge of a series, the one who determines the course of a show and supervises all aspects.

SLUG LINE. Some screenwriting software uses the term **SCENE HEADING.** In a script, **INT.** or **EXT.** is followed by the location of a scene, and time.

SPEC SCRIPT. A speculated screenplay written as a sample or in the hope of being sold. Beginners may write a spec of an existing series to demonstrate their skill.

SPRINGBOARD. A situation in a show that provokes action; aspects of a **FRANCHISE** that provide premises for episodes. Example: In a medical drama, the arrival of a new patient creates a springboard for a story.

STAFF WRITER. The first rung in the ladder of a writing staff, usually a beginner; also called "baby writer."

STEP DEAL. A writing contract which provides "cut offs" after each step of writing. For example, if a writer's outline doesn't work for the show, he may be cut off, not hired to proceed to the first draft.

STORY EDITOR. A member of a series writing staff above **STAFF WRITER** and below **PRODUCER** who writes and re-writes episodes.

SUPERVISING PRODUCER. A high-level writer-producer who may run the writing room.

SYNDICATION. The system of selling television series as packages to groups of stations and foreign markets after a network run is complete, usually requiring at least 88 episodes. A lucrative process that follows a show's first-run broadcast.

TEASER. Also called **PROLOGUE** and **COLD OPENING**. Dramatic material before titles that may or may not be related to the story in the episode which follows, but often does provide a **HOOK** or inciting incident.

TELEPLAY. Screenplay written for television.

TRADES. Daily newspapers that cover the entertainment industry, mainly *Variety* and *The Hollywood Reporter*.

TREATMENT. A narrative of the film, technically the entire script in prose without dialogue, but often abridged to a short summary.

WRITERS GUILD OF AMERICA. The professional union that represents screenwriters. It has two branches, West (in Los Angeles) and East (in New York), as well as affiliates in other countries.

ABOUT THE AUTHOR

Pamela Douglas is an award-winning screenwriter with numerous credits in television drama. She was honored with the Humanitas Prize for *Between Mother and Daughter* (CBS), an hour drama which also won nomination for a Writers Guild Award in 1996.

She received an Emmy nomination and an NAACP Image Award for writing *Different Worlds,* an hour drama on CBS. Twice, her shows won awards from American Women in Radio and Television — her original drama, *Sexual Considerations*, and her episode of the series *A Year in the Life* (NBC).

As a developer, she wrote the pilot, bible, and 13 episodes of the acclaimed PBS series *Ghostwriter*. Additional series credits include *Star Trek: the Next Generation*, *Frank's Place*, *Paradise*, *Trapper John, M.D.*, and many others.

She has been a member of the Board of Directors of the Writers Guild of America.

At the University of Southern California, she is an Associate Professor in the School of Cinematic Arts, where she teaches screenwriting.

Ms. Douglas is available for consulting and seminars.
Contact: *pamdouglaswords@aol.com*

ELEPHANT BUCKS
AN INSIDE GUIDE TO WRITING FOR TV SITCOMS

SHELDON BULL

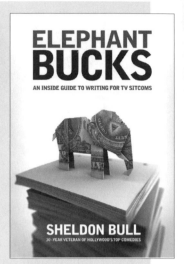

Elephant Bucks is the really big money you can earn by writing successfully for a television sitcom. But there's more to writing a hit series than hard-earned cash; there's the enormous satisfaction of seeing your best work come to life and entertain millions of viewers.

Sheldon Bull, who has written over 300 sitcom episodes, provides this comprehensive guide so that you can write that killer spec sitcom script and launch your career as a TV sitcom writer. You will learn detailed inside information on how to:

- Choose the right series to spec.
- Pick the right story.
- Write the scripts in a step-by-step method that will get you work.
- Use those scripts to get your big break in Hollywood.
- Handle TV pitch meetings, freelance writing assignments, staff work, agents, executives, and stars.

"I was fortunate enough to have directed many scripts that I knew were wonderful, but I didn't always know why they were wonderful. After reading Sheldon's book, I now realize so much more about the techniques involved in telling a good story. This book taught me a lot about the art of comedy script writing."
> – Jay Sandrich, Emmy® Award-Winning Director,
> *The Cosby Show, The Mary Tyler Moore Show*

"A comprehensive, well-thought-out guide for beginning writers. It would be a pleasure to read any spec script that used these guidelines. I only wish this had been around when I started!" – Susan Beavers, Co-Executive Producer, *Two and a Half Men*

"Sheldon Bull is not only the funniest man on two feet, but one of the most brilliant when it comes to explaining how to be funny, and how to organize your creative ideas into the sitcom form. This is the clearest, best, and only book that tells writers how to write for and break into the fabulous world of TV sitcoms step by step."
> – Blake Snyder, Author, *Save the Cat! The Last Book on Screenwriting You'll Ever Need*

SHELDON BULL has been earning Elephant Bucks as a professional television sitcom writer, producer, and director for 30 years. His career has included writing for *M*A*S*H*; developing, writing, and producing the hit CBS sitcom *Newhart*, starring Bob Newhart; writing and producing the hit ABC sitcom *Coach*; and producing, writing, and directing the hit ABC sitcom *Sabrina - The Teenage Witch*.

$24.95 · 280 PAGES · ORDER NUMBER 68RLS · ISBN: 1932907270

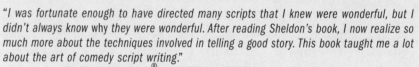

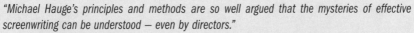

SAVE THE CAT!™ GOES TO THE MOVIES

THE SCREENWRITER'S GUIDE TO EVERY STORY EVER TOLD

BLAKE SNYDER

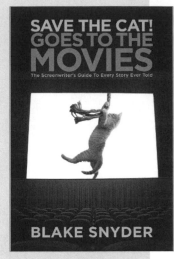

In the long-awaited sequel to his surprise bestseller, *Save the Cat!*, author and screenwriter Blake Snyder returns to form in a fast-paced follow-up that proves why his is the most talked-about approach to screenwriting in years. In the perfect companion piece to his first book, Snyder delivers even more insider's information gleaned from a 20-year track record as "one of Hollywood's most successful spec screenwriters," giving you the clues to write *your* movie.

Designed for screenwriters, novelists, and movie fans, this book gives readers the key breakdowns of the 50 most instructional movies from the past 30 years. From *M*A*S*H* to *Crash*, from *Alien* to *Saw*, from *10* to *Eternal Sunshine of the Spotless Mind*, Snyder reveals how screenwriters who came before you tackled the same challenges you are facing with the film you want to write — or the one you are currently working on.

Writing a "rom-com"? Check out the "Buddy Love" chapter for a "beat for beat" dissection of *When Harry Met Sally...* plus references to 10 other great romantic comedies that will make your story sing.

Want to execute a great mystery? Go to the "Whydunit" section and learn about the "dark turn" that's essential to the heroes of *All the President's Men*, *Blade Runner*, *Fargo* and hip noir *Brick* — and see why ALL good stories, whether a Hollywood blockbuster or a Sundance award winner, follow the same rules of structure outlined in Snyder's breakthrough method.

If you want to sell your script and create a movie that pleases most audiences most of the time, the odds increase if you reference Snyder's checklists and see what makes 50 films tick. After all, both executives and audiences respond to the same elements good writers seek to master. They want to know the type of story they signed on for, and whether it's structured in a way that satisfies everyone. It's what they're looking for. And now, it's what you can deliver.

BLAKE SNYDER, besides selling million-dollar scripts to both Disney and Spielberg, is still "one of Hollywood's most successful spec screenwriters," having made another spec sale in 2006. An in-demand scriptcoach and seminar and workshop leader, Snyder provides information for writers through his website, *www.blakesnyder.com*.

$24.95 · 270 PAGES · ORDER NUMBER 75RLS · ISBN: 1932907351

THE WRITER'S JOURNEY
3RD EDITION

MYTHIC STRUCTURE FOR WRITERS

CHRISTOPHER VOGLER

BEST SELLER
OVER 170,000 COPIES SOLD!

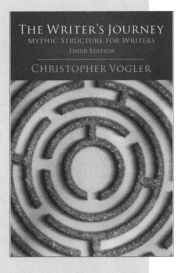

See why this book has become an international best seller and a true classic. *The Writer's Journey* explores the powerful relationship between mythology and storytelling in a clear, concise style that's made it required reading for movie executives, screenwriters, playwrights, scholars, and fans of pop culture all over the world.

Both fiction and nonfiction writers will discover a set of useful myth-inspired storytelling paradigms (i.e., "The Hero's Journey") and step-by-step guidelines to plot and character development. Based on the work of Joseph Campbell, *The Writer's Journey* is a must for all writers interested in further developing their craft.

The updated and revised third edition provides new insights and observations from Vogler's ongoing work on mythology's influence on stories, movies, and man himself.

"This book is like having the smartest person in the story meeting come home with you and whisper what to do in your ear as you write a screenplay. Insight for insight, step for step, Chris Vogler takes us through the process of connecting theme to story and making a script come alive."
> – Lynda Obst, Producer, *Sleepless in Seattle, How to Lose a Guy in 10 Days;* Author, *Hello, He Lied*

"This is a book about the stories we write, and perhaps more importantly, the stories we live. It is the most influential work I have yet encountered on the art, nature, and the very purpose of storytelling."
> – Bruce Joel Rubin, Screenwriter, *Stuart Little 2, Deep Impact, Ghost, Jacob's Ladder*

CHRISTOPHER VOGLER is a veteran story consultant for major Hollywood film companies and a respected teacher of filmmakers and writers around the globe. He has influenced the stories of movies from *The Lion King* to *Fight Club* to *The Thin Red Line* and most recently wrote the first installment of *Ravenskull*, a Japanese-style manga or graphic novel. He is the executive producer of the feature film *P.S. Your Cat is Dead* and writer of the animated feature *Jester Till*.

$26.95 · 400 PAGES · ORDER NUMBER 76RLS · ISBN: 193290736x

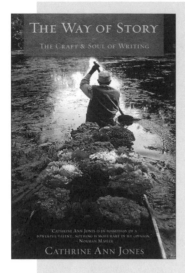

THE POWER OF FILM

HOWARD SUBER

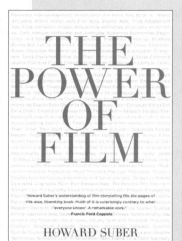

America's most distinguished film professor provides the definitive A to Z course on the intricacies of film. Each entry in this remarkable book, which represents a lifetime of teaching film, has already inspired and educated several generations of Hollywood's greatest filmmakers and writers.

This book examines the patterns and principles that make films popular and memorable, and will be useful both for those who want to create films and for those who just want to understand them better.

"Howard Suber's understanding of film storytelling fills the pages of this wise, liberating book. Much of it is surprisingly contrary to what 'everyone knows.' A remarkable work."
  – Francis Ford Coppola

"Those lucky enough to take Howard Suber's legendary classes in UCLA's Film School made many others want to read his book-in-progress. Now that he has delivered it, filmmakers, scholars, and anyone else with a serious interest in film can rejoice. A fascinating and thought-provoking work."
  – Alexander Payne, Director/Screenwriter, Sideways, About Schmidt, Election

"Howard Suber is admired and valued, not only in the academic world, but by some of the most important creative people in the film industry·. Suber genuinely helps us understand 'the power of film' – why it has been the predominant art form for more than a century, and why it continues to have such power over the lives we all lead."
  – Geoff Gilmore, Director of the Sundance Film Festival

"What Aristotle did for drama, Howard Suber has now done for film. This is a profound and succinct book that is miraculously fun to read."
  – David Koepp, Screenwriter, War of the Worlds (2005), Spider-Man,
    Mission Impossible, Jurassic Park

HOWARD SUBER, has taught more than 65 different courses in 40 years at UCLA's celebrated film school. He was the founder and director of the university's program in film history, theory, and criticism; the UCLA Film Archive; and the UCLA Film and Television Producers Program. The recipient of both a Distinguished Teaching Award and a Life Achievement Award, Suber has been a consultant to every major film studio, and his former students are currently active throughout the world.

$27.95 · 456 PAGES · ORDER NUMBER 61RLS · ISBN: 1932907173

{ THE MYTH OF MWP }

In a dark time, a light bringer came along, leading the curious and the frustrated to clarity and empowerment. It took the well-guarded secrets out of the hands of the few and made them available to all. It spread a spirit of openness and creative freedom, and built a storehouse of knowledge dedicated to the betterment of the arts.

The essence of the Michael Wiese Productions (MWP) is empowering people who have the burning desire to express themselves creatively. We help them realize their dreams by putting the tools in their hands. We demystify the sometimes secretive worlds of screenwriting, directing, acting, producing, film financing, and other media crafts.

By doing so, we hope to bring forth a realization of 'conscious media' which we define as being positively charged, emphasizing hope and affirming positive values like trust, cooperation, self-empowerment, freedom, and love. Grounded in the deep roots of myth, it aims to be healing both for those who make the art and those who encounter it. It hopes to be transformative for people, opening doors to new possibilities and pulling back veils to reveal hidden worlds.

MWP has built a storehouse of knowledge unequaled in the world, for no other publisher has so many titles on the media arts. Please visit www.mwp.com where you will find many free resources and a 25% discount on our books. Sign up and become part of the wider creative community!

Onward and upward,

Michael Wiese
Publisher/Filmmaker

FILM & VIDEO BOOKS

SCREENWRITING | WRITING

And the Best Screenplay Goes to... | Dr. Linda Seger | $26.95
Archetypes for Writers | Jennifer Van Bergen | $22.95
Bali Brothers | Lacy Waltzman, Matthew Bishop, Michael Wiese | $12.95
Cinematic Storytelling | Jennifer Van Sijll | $24.95
Could It Be a Movie? | Christina Hamlett | $26.95
Creating Characters | Marisa D'Vari | $26.95
Crime Writer's Reference Guide, The | Martin Roth | $20.95
Deep Cinema | Mary Trainor-Brigham | $19.95
Elephant Bucks | Sheldon Bull | $24.95
Fast, Cheap & Written That Way | John Gaspard | $26.95
Hollywood Standard – 2nd Edition, The | Christopher Riley | $18.95
Horror Screenwriting | Devin Watson | $24.95
I Could've Written a Better Movie than That! | Derek Rydall | $26.95
Inner Drives | Pamela Jaye Smith | $26.95
Moral Premise, The | Stanley D. Williams, Ph.D. | $24.95
Myth and the Movies | Stuart Voytilla | $26.95
Power of the Dark Side, The | Pamela Jaye Smith | $22.95
Psychology for Screenwriters | William Indick, Ph.D. | $26.95
Reflections of the Shadow | Jeffrey Hirschberg | $26.95
Rewrite | Paul Chitlik | $16.95
Romancing the A-List | Christopher Keane | $18.95
Save the Cat! | Blake Snyder | $19.95
Save the Cat! Goes to the Movies | Blake Snyder | $24.95
Screenwriting 101 | Neill D. Hicks | $16.95
Screenwriting for Teens | Christina Hamlett | $18.95
Script-Selling Game, The | Kathie Fong Yoneda | $16.95
Stealing Fire From the gods, 2nd Edition | James Bonnet | $26.95
Talk the Talk | Penny Penniston | $24.95
Way of Story, The | Catherine Ann Jones | $22.95
What Are You Laughing At? | Brad Schreiber | $19.95
Writer's Journey – 3rd Edition, The | Christopher Vogler | $26.95
Writer's Partner, The | Martin Roth | $24.95
Writing the Action Adventure Film | Neill D. Hicks | $14.95
Writing the Comedy Film | Stuart Voytilla & Scott Petri | $14.95
Writing the Killer Treatment | Michael Halperin | $14.95
Writing the Second Act | Michael Halperin | $19.95
Writing the Thriller Film | Neill D. Hicks | $14.95
Writing the TV Drama Series, 2nd Edition | Pamela Douglas | $26.95
Your Screenplay Sucks! | William M. Akers | $19.95

FILMMAKING

Film School | Richard D. Pepperman | $24.95
Power of Film, The | Howard Suber | $27.95

PITCHING

Perfect Pitch – 2nd Edition, The | Ken Rotcop | $19.95
Selling Your Story in 60 Seconds | Michael Hauge | $12.95

SHORTS

Filmmaking for Teens, 2nd Edition | Troy Lanier & Clay Nichols | $24.95
Making It Big in Shorts | Kim Adelman | $22.95

BUDGET | PRODUCTION MANAGEMENT

Film & Video Budgets, 5th Updated Edition | Deke Simon | $26.95
Film Production Management 101 | Deborah S. Patz | $39.95

DIRECTING | VISUALIZATION

Animation Unleashed | Ellen Besen | $26.95

Cinematography for Directors | Jacqueline Frost | $29.95
Citizen Kane Crash Course in Cinematography | David Worth | $19.95
Directing Actors | Judith Weston | $26.95
Directing Feature Films | Mark Travis | $26.95
Fast, Cheap & Under Control | John Gaspard | $26.95
Film Directing: Cinematic Motion, 2nd Edition | Steven D. Katz | $27.95
Film Directing: Shot by Shot | Steven D. Katz | $27.95
Film Director's Intuition, The | Judith Weston | $26.95
First Time Director | Gil Bettman | $27.95
From Word to Image, 2nd Edition | Marcie Begleiter | $26.95
I'll Be in My Trailer! | John Badham & Craig Modderno | $26.95
Master Shots | Christopher Kenworthy | $24.95
Setting Up Your Scenes | Richard D. Pepperman | $24.95
Setting Up Your Shots, 2nd Edition | Jeremy Vineyard | $22.95
Working Director, The | Charles Wilkinson | $22.95

DIGITAL | DOCUMENTARY | SPECIAL

Digital Filmmaking 101, 2nd Edition | Dale Newton & John Gaspard | $26.95
Digital Moviemaking 3.0 | Scott Billups | $24.95
Digital Video Secrets | Tony Levelle | $26.95
Greenscreen Made Easy | Jeremy Hanke & Michele Yamazaki | $19.95
Producing with Passion | Dorothy Fadiman & Tony Levelle | $22.95
Special Effects | Michael Slone | $31.95

EDITING

Cut by Cut | Gael Chandler | $35.95
Cut to the Chase | Bobbie O'Steen | $24.95
Eye is Quicker, The | Richard D. Pepperman | $27.95
Film Editing | Gael Chandler | $34.95
Invisible Cut, The | Bobbie O'Steen | $28.95

SOUND | DVD | CAREER

Complete DVD Book, The | Chris Gore & Paul J. Salamoff | $26.95
Costume Design 101, 2nd Edition | Richard La Motte | $24.95
Hitting Your Mark, 2nd Edition | Steve Carlson | $22.95
Sound Design | David Sonnenschein | $19.95
Sound Effects Bible, The | Ric Viers | $26.95
Storyboarding 101 | James Fraioli | $19.95
There's No Business Like Soul Business | Derek Rydall | $22.95
You Can Act! | D. W. Brown | $24.95

FINANCE | MARKETING | FUNDING

Art of Film Funding, The | Carole Lee Dean | $26.95
Bankroll | Tom Malloy | $26.95
Complete Independent Movie Marketing Handbook, The | Mark Steven Bosko | $39.95
Getting the Money | Jeremy Jusso | $26.95
Independent Film and Videomakers Guide – 2nd Edition, The | Michael Wiese | $29.95
Independent Film Distribution | Phil Hall | $26.95
Shaking the Money Tree, 3rd Edition | Morrie Warshawski | $26.95

MEDITATION | ART

Mandalas of Bali | Dewa Nyoman Batuan | $39.95

OUR FILMS

Dolphin Adventures: DVD | Michael Wiese and Hardy Jones | $24.95
Hardware Wars: DVD | Written and Directed by Ernie Fosselius | $14.95
On the Edge of a Dream | Michael Wiese | $16.95
Sacred Sites of the Dalai Lamas– DVD, The | Documentary by Michael Wiese | $24.95